Eyelashes of an Elephant

Rescuing rhino, befriending elephant and everything in between

Eyelashes of an Elephant by Megan Richards.

Published by Zuali Publishing.

ISBN 978-1-9163357-1-4

First published as paperback in 2020

This edition published in 2022

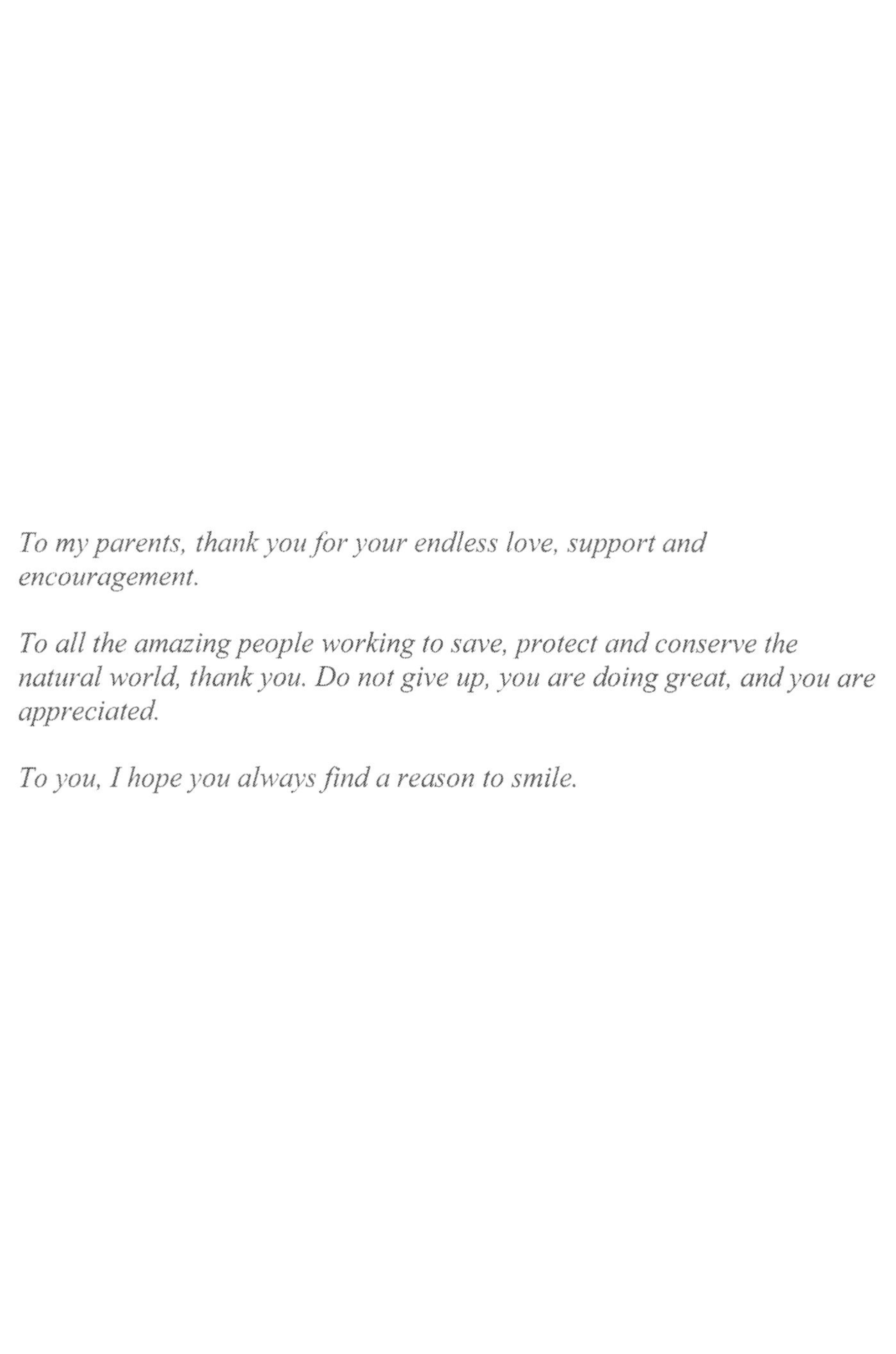

To my parents, thank you for your endless love, support and encouragement.

To all the amazing people working to save, protect and conserve the natural world, thank you. Do not give up, you are doing great, and you are appreciated.

To you, I hope you always find a reason to smile.

Chapters

1: Crossing Continents

Take a moment to picture yourself in the vast wilderness of Africa, befriending the animals and living among them. Imagine the sun on your skin, the clean air filling your lungs with each breath and a rolling, undisturbed landscape… Abundant, diverse and unspoiled by man. As you walk in the wild it feels as though there is endless wonder to behold; from the towering giraffe delicately plucking leaves from the tallest trees to the mighty lion grunting a warning to all who will listen, from the proud kudu watching intently as you pass by to the fascinating chameleon who waits patiently in perfect camouflage. It's something I used to dream of as a child. I would fantasize about being barefoot, muddy and unkempt as I would climb trees and explore the immense landscape without fear or hesitation. I'd be in awe of my surroundings, always on the lookout for a new adventure.

The best part was that I'd never be alone, for I would always be accompanied by animals. Each day would be spent alongside another animal, another species; learning their ways, their secrets, their stories… I'd laze under the trees with lions, play in the mud with the mighty rhinoceros and stride confidently with herds of elephants, dwarfed by their incredible size but completely at home in their midst.

My young spirit seemed to revere the idea of living side by side with Africa's wildest residents. Together we would go about our lives in the untamed wilderness, entirely connected by our similarities and unfazed by our differences. Each day would be a new adventure as we'd walk in areas we had previously undiscovered; spending time playing in dusty sand, rolling in soothing mud and celebrating the life-giving water of the dams.

I'd join the elephants time and time again; fascinated by their strong family bonds, fearless protectiveness and unwavering gentle nature. We'd walk for hours on end without a worry in the world. We'd talk in excited rumbles then race on to reach the shelter of the trees before the looming storm clouds would unleash their downpour. I'd listen to hyena's whooping in the distance, watch vervet monkeys as they'd chase each other through the treetops and all the while I'd be surrounded by a magnificent elephant herd standing tall with their watchful eyes and gentle spirits. The youngsters in the herd would always want to play; pushing, shoving and spurring each other on with their mischievous smiles and chubby cheeks. Settling down for the evening, we'd admire nyala as they walked along silhouetted by the sunset and then, in a heap of tired trunks and tails, we'd fall asleep under the stars. Each morning we'd awaken early enough to watch the sun elegantly rise above the horizon. Every so often I'd feel the light touch of one of the young elephant's trunks against my skin, a gentle gesture of reassurance, love and companionship.

Picture it in your mind; being one with nature, living each and every moment to its full and feeling unconditional love for all that surrounds you. Seeing the love in the eyes of the animals when they look at you and knowing you are home. The thoughts of the warm wind dancing through your hair and the sweet smell of soil underfoot, completely enamoured by the organised chaos of the wild.

Ah, the daydreams of a teenager. I came crashing back down to reality as I half-heartedly pulled an unflattering maroon school jumper over my messy ponytail, hurriedly slipped on a pair of clumpy black shoes and lugged a large, cumbersome bag over my right shoulder. It was time for school on yet another dreary, rainy day on the South coast of England. Back then, when I was a shy, impressionable 13-year-old, these daydreams were inspired more by documentaries and nature encyclopaedias than by the thought that I could one day actually be in Africa. If somebody told me back then that five years down the line I would be raising orphaned rhino calves in the middle of the African bush, I'd have laughed an awkward laugh, blushed a bright beetroot colour and said, "I think you've got the wrong girl".

Although, I would've loved to have lived in the 'African Utopia' that I had envisioned as a teenager it simply wasn't the reality. My story in Africa began in 2013 when I first caught wind of the rhino's struggle for survival. I had no idea that this passion for saving and conserving rhino was going to bring such a vast array of extraordinary experiences, challenges and dangers. I also had no way of knowing that one day an orphaned baby elephant would show up at my door and turn my entire world upside down.

With global rhino populations dwindling, my conservation journey started in the country with the world's largest population of wild rhinos: South Africa. With poaching activity being so frequent (two - three rhinos are being killed in South Africa every day), veterinarians and conservationists have been taking drastic measures to try to protect and preserve the lives of the remaining rhino populations.

One of the ways they have been doing this is by 'de-horning' – a meticulously planned procedure that involves locating a rhino using a helicopter or vehicle, darting it with a carefully measured sedative, taking DNA samples and other particulars, sawing off most of the horn with a chainsaw and filing down the rest. The sawn-off horn is then transported under heavily armed guards to a safe place where it will be securely stored under lock and key in what is often referred to as a 'stockpile'. Once the horns have been carefully removed, the sedative is reversed, and the rhino gets up and stumbles away to continue its battle for survival in the wild.

Ultimately, rhinos are dehorned in this way in an attempt to make them less of a target for poachers. This method can be an effective deterrent but, unfortunately, it does not always work, and poachers have been known to kill de-horned rhino too. Poachers may kill dehorned rhinos to obtain the small piece of horn that remains, but it can also be an action to prevent them wasting their time tracking that dehorned rhino again.

While all of this was going on, there was a small group of rhinos that were at the back of people's minds. Everything possible was being done to protect the remaining rhino populations from the bullet of a semi-automatic rifle and the sharp edge of a machete but it was still happening each and every day. Of those rhinos being shot and killed, how many of them were mums? How many of those rhinos had calves? And, what happened to those dependent calves after the mum had been killed? It is important to note that a rhino is born without horns, at a few months old a small stump may be visible, the horn continuously grows throughout a rhino's life at the rate of approximately two - three inches per year, this means young calves generally have little or no horn, so they are typically not killed by poachers in incidents involving their mums.

In the wild, a rhino calf will stay with its mum for around three years; relying on her for food, warmth and safety. Taking this time to learn the vital skills needed to live independently in the African bush in the overlapping territories of elephant, lions, leopards… It was realized that these young rhinos were essentially slipping through the net, surviving the poaching incidents but passing away due to stress, starvation, dehydration and predators. They could be saved, and they could contribute to the rhino population, but they needed a place to go, people to care for them and protection from poachers. These orphaned rhino calves are where my story began, and it is them that brought me across the world to South Africa back in 2013. In the wild without their mothers, the orphaned calves would not survive. South Africa is a country about five times bigger than the UK, so it is no surprise that one rhino orphanage would not be enough to handle the number of rhino calves orphaned through this ongoing poaching crisis. The creation of one dedicated rhino orphanage was soon followed by a second and in early 2015, I found myself in KwaZulu-Natal about to begin my journey to a newly built rhino orphanage.

Disembarking the plane at King Shaka International on a warm autumnal afternoon, I was eager to get on the road and on my way to the brand-new rhino orphanage. Before I could go anywhere, I needed to pass through immigration and collect my bag. Without a hitch, I was soon waiting at the baggage carousel with my backpack lazily on my shoulder and my phone in hand. I watched as a procession of dull, black bags made their way around the crowds. Suitcases were being plucked away one by one by eagle-eyed travellers who could somehow differentiate between the bags that looked identical to me. As people slowly made their way towards the exit, I wondered if my bag had made the journey. Fortunately, just as I began to question it, my stripy purple and blue hard case emerged on the belt. The "coexist" sticker I'd proudly stuck on the front was now looking a little worse for wear but no matter, I dragged the bag off the slow-moving carousel and made my way to the exit.

I was grateful to have an airport transfer organised and despite Stewart being a complete stranger, it was a relief to know he would be at the airport waiting for my arrival. Although I was a frequent traveller, this was the first time I ever had a transfer organised and I took comfort in knowing I did not need to deal with car rental companies or give myself pep talks for the long drive and the dangerous roads that lay ahead. This time I did not need to worry, I could just load up my bags, climb into the passenger seat and enjoy the views. I didn't need to worry about directions or have concerns about which route to take or experience the anxieties that come with being a lone, young female driving in an African country that is known for its high level of hijacking and 'smash and grab' robberies.

As we drove along the seemingly never-ending highways the sun was already beginning to set, descending beneath the horizon quicker than we could ever chase it. The vivid reds that were splashed along the clouds soon disappeared into darkness and we still had more than 70 kilometres left to drive before we would be entering the gates of the sanctuary. Had I been driving alone; the sun setting would've left me feeling tense, heightening my awareness of my surroundings and leaving me cautious to stop at traffic lights and stop signs, but with Stewart driving us alongside the countless sugar cane fields I could get lost in a daydream about the adventures that awaited.

Just five days before I arrived, a young white rhino calf had been rescued, he was the first rhino through the orphanage's doors - marking its official opening. There was no hesitation when the move to Africa was whispered in the winds of change. I knew I had to book that ticket and board that plane. It took all of five days to book, plan, pack, travel and arrive in South Africa following the message of the newly arrived calf. Astonishingly, it had been almost a year since I'd been surrounded by rhinos, since then I'd been writing full-time and had spent some months on a North Atlantic archipelago protecting Pilot Whales. But now, it felt right, it was time to return.

As with starting any new job, the feelings of anticipation, excitement and nervousness danced around my heart and flipped through my stomach. My mind was dreamy with hopes, the unknown could lead absolutely anywhere, and I had a feeling this was going to lead somewhere magnificent. It was a passion for rhinos and wildlife that brought me here and I was excited to meet the newly arrived calf. As we finally turned into the gates of the reserve I could breathe a sigh of relief, for now, I was home.

I was thrilled to have my feet back on African soil, I had travelled close to 10,000 kilometres and journeyed deep into the South African bush to get here. I hoped the team would like me, after all we were going to be living together in very close quarters in essentially the middle of the wilderness with very few other people passing through. I knew the rhinos would be great, they always were... Despite everything they had been through as soon as you'd show them love and they'd realise you were there to help them, they would return the love tenfold. The rhinos were always gentle, kind and playful.

The journey had been long and arduous, it had been 24 hours since I'd said farewell to my family at the airport in London and boarded the flight that would take me to South Africa. At just 19, although travel sickness continued to plague me, I had become used to the long-distance flights and being away from home for extended periods of time. It was no longer intimidating or overwhelming to pass through security or board a flight that would take me thousands of kilometres away to a place I'd never been, to people I'd never met.

Whenever I was boarding one of these flights, it felt like going to a place I knew was right. It would seem like the blink of an eye had passed before I'd be once again sitting in the window seat of an overnight flight, staring out into the skies, full of new experiences and lessons.

Whenever I go to the U.K. it is to see loved ones and spend quality time with family. Although the weather would invariably be cold; the warmth, enthusiasm and love of my family would make each trip special. Whenever it came time to leave, my parents would know it would be months or more before I'd return to British soil.

Whenever I go to Africa it is to see my wild family. Africa holds my heart and whispers secrets to the wildest aspects of my soul. When I am in the African bush, surrounded by wild, free and majestic wildlife and caring for the most incredible orphaned and vulnerable animals, time ceases to exist. The days transform into weeks, weeks into months and before I'd know it a trip back to England would be long overdue.

In recent years, I've realized that there's no point guessing which way the next adventure will swing and there's little reason trying to plan for it. Simply take each day as the universe presents it, be kind and do what you can with what you have.

Upon arriving at the gates of the reserve, the evening was dark and quiet but the stars twinkled in the most dazzling display of silent beauty. As I climbed out of Stewart's car, I stopped to admire the night sky in all its glory. I'd missed how the darkness of these remote areas allowed the stars to truly shine. The journey had taken longer than anticipated but at least I'd be able to get a good night's rest before starting work the following day.

I was met at the gate of the reserve by Axel, one of the two rhino carers I'd be working with. The young Frenchman was just a couple of years older than me, his hair dark and curly, Axel wore glasses and a constant grin. His enthusiasm was infectious as he tripped over his words talking excitedly about our first rescued rhino calf, Ithuba (meaning Chance in isiZulu). I knew immediately that Axel and I were going to get on well. We loaded up my bags, waved goodbye to Stewart and drove through the maze of the bush to the orphanage. Although short, the journey was full of twists and turns and I was quickly disorientated by the darkness, but Axel seemed to be able to navigate his way around the familiar landscape without hesitation. Any nerves I had were dissipated by the friendliness and passion in his voice as he filled me in on the last five days with Ithuba. As we negotiated the darkness with just the headlights to guide us, Axel turned to me and said in a casual tone

"We just need to be careful of the elephants, we don't want to bump into them at night.". He flashed me a smile and continued along the dirt roads.

After a few kilometres of bumpy, bush-lined tracks we reached the orphanage, thankfully no elephants were encountered during the drive. As we offloaded my bags, Axel told me that Ithuba would be sleeping now but I was more than welcome to go and introduce myself to Alyson - the orphanage manager, trained veterinary nurse and only other member of our team - who was on nightshift. It was going to be the three of us taking care of Ithuba, the other rhino calves who would come through our doors and whatever else was thrown at us. Despite the darkness, Axel gave me a brief tour and after putting my bags in my room he told me where I could find Alyson and Ithuba, as he returned to the house, I went over to introduce myself. I quietly knocked on the door, cautious not to disturb a feed or interrupt a much-needed sleep. In almost no time at all Alyson opened the door and with a huge smile and a welcoming hug exclaimed,

"Meg! We've been so excited to meet you!". This was a moment I will never forget as it made me feel completely at home in a place I had never been. Alyson was also from the U.K.; meeting her was like seeing an old school friend, her whole being overflowed with a gentle kindness. Her dark hair was pulled up into a ponytail and under her unzipped fleece she wore a t-shirt with a picture of two baby rhinos facing each other with their lips together as if they were kissing. Everything about this made me smile. Alyson invited me in and we sat in the preparation room for hours as she talked with a familiar accent about the orphanage and rhinos, all the while Ithuba slept under his heat lamp in the interlinked room next door. These two wonderful people were to become my family for the next while at least and we would be spending more time together than even the closest of siblings.

As I climbed into bed that first night; skin pale and lips cracked from the travel sickness, dehydration and exhaustion of the journey, I could not help but smile as I felt so calm, happy and, most importantly, home. The welcome I had received, despite arriving late in the evening, was magical. Axel and Alyson held their arms wide open for me, they were friendly, passionate and excited. A perfect mix. I had no doubt the three of us would make a fantastic team and have the positive impact we desired. I set my alarm and fell into a deep, blissful sleep.

2: Ithuba's Second Chance

As the golden rays of the rising sun began to peek over the horizon, the alarm on my phone blared into life in an instant assault on the ears. Although the sudden noise startled me, I didn't really need an alarm as I had already been lying awake and contemplating the day ahead for the past 30 minutes. I hastily rifled around the covers searching for the phone that was craftily hiding underneath a pillow and I, slightly forcefully, turned off the alarm. As the room once again descended into a thoughtful silence I squinted at the unnecessarily bright phone screen as I cancelled the two extra alarms I had set to go off in five- and eight-minutes time 'just in case' I had fallen back to sleep after the first one. With the alarms dealt with I jumped out of bed without a second thought, carried by my excitement for working with rhino calves again.

Before falling asleep the night before, I had laid out the clothes I was going to wear, like a child preparing eagerly for the first day of school. Without having to even think, I swiftly pulled on one of my favourite pairs of khaki shorts, threw a zip up grey hoody on over a plain dark t-shirt and forcefully danced my feet into my charcoal grey plimsolls. This was my standard outfit when working with rhinos… Low maintenance, comfortable and dark in colour so that dirt wouldn't be too obvious. Thanks to my prior preparation, I was up and dressed in next to no time. My mind and heart were full of anticipation for my first proper day of work at the rhino orphanage.

After splashing some cold water on my face, putting my contact lenses in and brushing my teeth I went to meet Alyson and Axel outside the rhino rooms. It was seven a.m. on the dot, the sun was already gently shining a soft, warm, orange glow as the world around us began to awaken. The rhino rooms were positioned a mere 30 second walk across the grass from the staff accommodation block where my room was situated and as I began to stride the short distance I realised this was the first time I was seeing the orphanage in daylight.

I noticed that it looked as though we did not have a perimeter fence. We were in the middle of a reserve where elephants, hippos and rhinos roamed freely and it was slightly startling to me that we didn't have anything to separate us from them. Although, in truth, it was not the wild animals that truly bothered me. The lack of fence was a concern, but it was the thought of humans being able to come onto the orphanage without any difficulty or obstacle that truly made me uneasy. We needed an electric fence to deter people (potential poachers) from coming onto the property and to stop them from being able to access the rhino orphans. To not have a fence struck me as very strange so after I reached the rhino rooms I asked Alyson if there was a perimeter fence around the orphanage. Alyson told me that although we did not have a fence yet, we would do in a week. She pointed out certain trees in the distance, using them as marker points to show me where the electric fencing would be going.

Without blinking an eye, Alyson also casually mentioned that the two, approximately 800kg (that's about the same weight as a Robinson R44 Helicopter), sub adult white rhinos on the reserve were going to be disappointed once our fence was up as they rather enjoyed coming and sleeping in the middle of the orphanage on a sandy spot located just outside the care rooms for the orphaned rhinos.

"They've been coming and sleeping just there..." Alyson turned towards the main house and pointed down to the left at a patch of sand a mere 15 feet away from us, "actually, you can still see the indentations in the sand from when they slept there two nights ago." She said with a grin. I laughed in disbelief, trying to imagine two great big rhinos sleeping on the sand in front of us. Upon hearing of this favoured rhino sleeping spot, I was quite relieved the pair had decided to sleep elsewhere last night as otherwise

I could well have bumped into them when I very casually walked through the darkness to my room after I'd introduced myself to Alyson.

Speaking of last night, Alyson was sleeping in the smaller of the two preparation rooms (also referred to as the clinic as it is where we kept the medicines and veterinary equipment) and Ithuba was sleeping in the interlinked High Care Unit. As we stood in the mellow rays of the rising sun and talked about the rhinos on the reserve we were standing outside of the clinic and High Care Unit.

In the daylight, I could see the layout of the orphanage a lot clearer, next door to the Clinic was a bio security shower room and just five paces away was the sheltered food storage area. The other side of the food storage was the larger preparation room which interlinked to the Intensive Care Unit (a room identical to the High Care Unit Ithuba was being housed in). On the other side of the Intensive Care Unit (ICU) was the storeroom and the laundry room (you'd be surprised how many blankets need to be washed when dealing with very young and intensive cases!). The ICU and High Care Unit both had their own outside enclosure connected to them and further back there were also larger outside enclosures that we could move the rhino between as and when it was necessary. Looking onto the orphanage, I would never have imagined the dramatic events that would soon unfold here. It was good to see the centre in the light but I'd have a proper look around later, for now I was going to get stuck in with Ithuba's care.

Many months had passed since the last time I was caring for rhino but it felt like no time at all from the second I saw Ithuba, the five-month-old stood just below hip height and had a gentle, playful demeanour. Axel had painted a clear picture of the young rhino on our drive to the orphanage the previous evening and in a way, I felt like I already knew him. To my relief I was considered part of the team from the get-go, wasting no time in participating with the daily routines of cleaning and milk mixing. I also focussed on building important bonds with Ithuba. I spent most of the first morning sitting outside of Ithuba's room, leaning up against the steel barrier that separated us, talking to him so he could get to know me, my voice and my smell. The young rhino was interested and gentle, coming to the barrier for me to scratch him. His tiny horn was smaller than my clenched fist, his soulful eyes watched my every move and his ears (which were notched by the reserve he was rescued from for future identification purposes) would constantly move back and forth as if they were satellite dishes scanning for sound. Each ear was around the same size as my open hand. Although white rhinos are largely hairless, the outer edge of their ears are lined with dark hair, and the tip of their tails also have long, dark hair – perfect for swatting flies away.

As I sat and spoke softly to Ithuba, he stood mere centimetres away from me, looking deep into my eyes as if to decipher who I was. It was clear Ithuba craved love and attention but he was not yet convinced of me, so I was going to wait before going into the enclosure with him. His body was muscular, his skin thick and tough, but this didn't stop him from enjoying scratches and strokes – particularly on his face in the space just below his eye and on his belly when he'd lay down. When Ithuba was feeling cheeky, mischievous or excited his tail would flick excitedly back and forth, like a puppy wagging their tail. In a day or two, when Ithuba was completely comfortable with me I'd start going into the enclosure with him. Until then, I'd be spending time with him from the safety of the barrier - the last thing I wanted at the beginning of my new role as rhino carer was a broken leg! I may have had a pretty good idea about the nature of rhino by this point and you can often read their intention all over their faces, but I wouldn't dare become blasé with an animal who harbours more strength than the world's strongest man.

At the start of each day we would clean Ithuba's night room; it was a basic 5m x 5m square room with removable floor matting, an infrared heat lamp hanging in the left-hand corner and three large doorways. Each doorway was protected by a sliding steel barrier and a separate sliding opaque black door that would be closed and locked at night. Two of the three barriers were left open during the day to allow Ithuba access to both his room and the outside area while the third remained closed almost all of the time. There were padlocks everywhere, each barrier had its own thick, heavy-duty lock, each sliding door too – the basic rule was if it was closed then it should be locked. The barrier that remained closed separated Ithuba's room from the unfenced staff side of the orphanage and, aside from being used for the initial offloading of the rhino calves upon their arrival at the orphanage, the barrier was used mostly for monitoring and for access to the room by the care team.

Each morning we would let Ithuba out to the outdoor enclosure, which was about as big as an Olympic sized swimming pool. While Ithuba would be busy eating and exploring, we'd close the barriers for a short while, locking him outside (while still being able to monitor him and interact with him), in order to clean his room without him investigating and getting in the way. Sometimes he'd come and push himself up against the poles of the barrier, grumbling about being outside without us, particularly if it wasn't the best weather.

Sometimes one of us would need to go and sit with him while the others cleaned the room. If you were feeling soft and decided to open a barrier for him to come in while you were cleaning you could categorically guarantee one of two things would happen… Either Ithuba would come and push the pile of clean straw bedding all over the place and would urinate where you have just cleaned, or he would come and lay down in the exact spot you are busy cleaning.

One day, precisely that happened when we decided to open the barrier as we were finishing up cleaning and couldn't resist Ithuba's gentle, pleading look as he watched us through the barrier poles. As we opened the barrier, Ithuba did not even hesitate as he waltzed in and laid down in the only spot of the whole room that did not yet have the floor matting in place. Not only did he lay down, but he also fell asleep, so we had to put the work on pause and finish putting the floor matting down once he'd woken up and moved elsewhere! That's what we deserved for falling for his high-pitched cry and story telling eyes I suppose.

I mentioned earlier that the smaller preparation room (where Alyson slept for her nightshift) and Ithuba's room were interlinking, and this was thanks to a wooden half-door similar to what you may find in a stable. This door was also mostly closed as there was no barrier protecting it and if you left it open, ever inquisitive Ithuba would try to barge his way through and into the clinic which was an area that was definitely not suitable, let alone big enough, for a rhino. The stable style half door was used for monitoring at night-time, the top half was always open so we could see and hear everything Ithuba was doing during our nightshifts.

In the afternoon of my first full day, Alyson, Axel and I excitedly discussed ideas, put procedures in place and began drafting out equipment wish lists. As the orphanage was a non-profit, our funds were low and we relied heavily on the kindness of the general public for donations such as milk powder and equipment, a wish list was our way of showing people how they could help us help the rhino.

The journey had begun and nothing was going to dull our shine, not even the regular "load shedding" that would bring total darkness for two hours each evening for the foreseeable future. Load shedding was happening frequently in South Africa, during load shedding all the electrical power is deliberately switched off for a set period of time. I'd never heard of this until arriving in South Africa, but it is supposed to relieve the stress on the system and prevent a total system failure from occurring. This would often happen in two-hour blocks and would mean for that period of time we would have no lights, no oven and no running water (our water system relied on an electric pump). Admittedly, the first few times this happened were a bit of a surprise.

These regular, area-wide power outages were a completely new experience for me and were very unexpected. I'm sure there was a schedule for this load shedding that would've made some kind of sense but for us it felt random. Each week was different, it could've been a few times a week or every evening. I suppose it was dependent on the amount of power people around the country were using and how the system was coping. All I know is that the last thing on our minds when we were busy with rhino care was that the power would suddenly go out because the power company has switched off our area's electricity for a few hours… We'd be in the house or in one of the preparation rooms minding our own business and suddenly there would be a loud click as the power would, all at once, go out. The lights would shut off, Ithuba's heat lamp would stop shining, the whole house would become pitch black, everything would be instantly descended into darkness. Load shedding would happen in the evening, when it was already dark outside and lights were necessary, usually at the optimal time for cooking dinner or showering too. Not only did load shedding impact our routines, but it also cast a dangerous shadow over our security systems.

After the initial shock of being in sudden darkness, we'd use a phone torch or headlamp to gather up some candles or lamps. Then, we'd invariably get to a good vantage point and look around to see if everyone else's power was off too (from our security lookout towers we'd be able to see the lights of a local village and a nearby tourist lodge). After confirming that it was load shedding (again), we'd sit around in the dark clock-watching until the power came back on and we could carry on with whatever we were doing.

Once we knew that load shedding was a regular occurrence that showed no signs of ceasing, we tried our best to make sure there were no rhino feeds and nothing to do that involved using power or water scheduled during those few hours. If it was a cold or wet evening, one of us would sit with Ithuba in the darkness of his room using blankets to help keep him warm until the warm red glow of the heat lamp would flicker back into life. There were multiple times the power would be off for even longer than two hours and we wouldn't be sure when it would be coming back on, whether this was load shedding or another electrical related issue I don't know but one thing I do know is that they occurred frequently. A feeling of relief and appreciation washed over the team when the lights we had taken for granted blinked back on, cutting through the darkness and returning everything to normal.

By day three, Ithuba and I were becoming fast friends, I'd now comfortably go into his enclosure and sit with him for hours on end. He loved the attention but more than that, he needed it. Ithuba was only five months old, and he'd had a very difficult start to life. After his mum was poached during a full moon, Ithuba spent over a week trying to survive on his own. In that time, he tried to join up with another female rhino on the reserve. This adult female had a calf about the same age as Ithuba but unfortunately, she was unhappy with Ithuba's close proximity. Ithuba tried to stay close to them, desperately seeking companionship in order to survive. Unfortunately, this wasn't to be as the adult female was seen by rangers literally throwing Ithuba into the air. In an astonishing demonstration of strength and defence, the adult female rhino (who was clearly concerned about Ithuba hanging around so close) hooked the baby rhino of over 160kg under his belly with her long horn and launched him up into the air, sending him flying. With this all unfolding in front of rangers who were keeping a close eye on the orphan, it became clear Ithuba needed to be rescued and cared for at the orphanage until he was old enough to survive alone. Even though Ithuba looked big to us he was still a baby in rhino terms, something that was startlingly clear when you'd see him crave attention and cry a high-pitched cry which can bizarrely be likened to a whale's call.

Ithuba drank a special milk formula every three hours, day and night and he would never hesitate in letting you know when he was hungry. In between feeds he loved to play, roll around in his mud wallow and sleep in the soft sand. Mud wallows are enjoyed by rhinos of all ages, when wallowing they cover themselves in a layer of mud which acts as a sunscreen and assists with getting rid of external parasites, namely ticks. In fact, you can sometimes see ticks in the clumps of mud left on trees by rhinos rubbing after wallowing!

The one thing Ithuba hated was to be alone, something unsurprising when you consider his age and all he had already experienced in his life so far. He was a victim of the poaching crisis that continues to rampage Southern Africa, he was orphaned after his mother was killed and her horn was taken in a brutal but seemingly common attack. He was brought to us and now he saw us as a source of comfort, a safety blanket and a reassurance of better days to come. It was important that he felt safe with us. We were there no matter what. In the wild a baby rhino will remain with their mum until around three years old, and Ithuba was a mere five months old. If he wanted to have a mud bath, take a nap or play, we were there. If he was hungry, upset or scared, we were there.

Towards the end of his first month with us we noticed that Ithuba would become extremely on edge during full moon, when the nights were bright enough to see without a torch due to the powerful moonlight. In the world of conservation and wildlife protection the full moon has another, more sinister, name. It is referred to as the poacher's moon or blood moon because when the moon is full, poachers frequent game reserves taking advantage of the natural light and the ability to walk with little or no artificial light. It is far more difficult to spot and catch a poacher who walks in the darkness without a light to aid them. During the poacher's moon, Ithuba would become agitated, stressed and more aggravated than we had ever seen him. It was a full moon the night that poachers found them in the bush, Ithuba and his mum. The memories of the night that changed his life appeared to plague him when the moon rose high and spread light on the African plains. The moonlight shone down onto his enclosure, casting shadows beneath the trees and with no clouds in the sky, the moon was highly visible for all to see. We stayed by his side, trying to reassure him and calm him down but, as you may know, there is very little one can do to console a grieving soul. He'd run, charge, throw bowls, blankets and buckets into the air. He wouldn't be able to stay still and we couldn't go into the enclosure to calm him down because he'd charge towards us, controlled by fear. Normally Ithuba would not charge us. He typically never did, not once. No matter what, whether it was early morning and he had not been fed yet, late afternoon or the middle of the night, he would always be gentle and if anything, playful.

When the full moon rose, he became so afraid and traumatised. All we could do was be there to talk to him, we'd clear his enclosure of anything that could be damaged, or cause damage, and wait for it to pass as we'd watch on from the other side of the barrier, trying to comfort him in any way we could. It was like all the progress we'd made was wiped away with the rising of a full moon. Eventually, the young rhino would fall asleep, exhausted. By the time the sun would rise Ithuba would be back to himself, at least until darkness came around once again. During full moon Ithuba would be panicked, anxious and afraid. All we could do was be a presence and do our best to protect him from the shadows of his past. It was only at full moon he would exhibit such behaviour, something that led us to believe he was suffering from Post-Traumatic Stress Disorder. Seeing his anguish reminded us of what we were fighting against. The realities of the situation were bleak, but we had to keep trying, for the sake of the rhino.

The orphanage was brand new and purpose built specifically to house rhino calves. It was created as a direct result of the number of rhino calves being orphaned by poaching. The centre was so new that Ithuba was the first rhino to ever be housed in it. This gave him the perfect opportunity to test every nook and cranny to find the weak points and show us just how "rhino proof" the centre really was. Things may seem strong and "rhino proof" on paper but the reality is often a little different. It did not take Ithuba long to show us that some of the doors required alterations, one flick of his little horn would take the heavy steel gates right off of their rails and tumbling down to the ground with an almighty crash. Some of the items that were heavy and seemed so secure to us were nothing more than pathetic to even a young rhino. He'd move a gate or a barrier in half a second and it would take two of us five minutes to pick it back up and slot it back in the right place. Ithuba would take big heavy doors and throw them to the ground like they were made of paper and then he'd stand on them with his head held high, triumphant and proud. Whenever we'd mix milk Ithuba would hear the whisk hitting the bucket and his favourite words to hear were,

"It's coming 'Thubes!'".

I could hear Ithuba playing around outside while I was busy mixing milk, and I heard a thump just outside the window. I stood up on my tiptoes to peer over the sink and out of the window into his enclosure. I was met with our young rhino's cheeky face stretching up towards the preparation room window. He was proudly standing on top of the large tyre bowl he had just flipped over, in the process emptying all of the food out onto the dusty ground. He was standing tall and trying to peek into the preparation room where he could hear his milk being mixed. His gentle eyes were peeking up at me in mischievous anticipation as I whisked his milk.

"It's coming 'Thubes!" I laughed as I began to pour the milk into bottles ready for the feed. Once all the bottles were filled, I pulled the rubber teats over the bottle necks and went into the enclosure where Ithuba was waiting. We would usually feed him close to a tree or next to the water trough in his enclosure as sometimes little growing rhinos get a bit upset when their milk is finished. Even though they have had enough milk to fill them up, it takes them a bit of time to realize they are full and this means that straight after a feed the baby rhinos may get grumpy and demand more milk. Sometimes they will be very relaxed straight after a feed but at other times they may cry with a large open mouth and give you a hearty nudge, thus the tactical tree or barrier that can be utilized if necessary. I discovered during earlier experiences that giving a young rhino some belly scratches after a feed can help them to relax and avoids any grumpiness.

As everything at the orphanage was new, this meant we also needed to develop the foliage and plant life within the enclosures. To get us started, we had been gifted five young trees that stood at around six feet tall, all with trunks just a few inches thick. We had wasted no time in planting these trees in one of the enclosures that Ithuba was not using, anticipating the trees would grow and one day be able to provide shade and food for rhino that we would rescue in the future.

After a few weeks of regular watering and TLC, we decided to allow Ithuba into the enclosure so he could enjoy more space and new smells while we had these enclosures available. Admittedly, we were a little bit worried the small trees wouldn't stand up to Ithuba's testing methods so we filled the enclosure with lots of other goodies such as logs and tyres so our playful juvenile rhino could be distracted and would stay away from our trees. Of course, our tactics failed miserably and Ithuba made our tenderly cared for, regularly watered trees his next play target. They quickly became his favourite toys as he targeted them one by one.

He would charge them, knock his horn against their skinny trunks and push them down with all his weight. The trees were so young they could bend under the boisterous rhino's pressure, he would push them and rub against them until the tree would be bent under his belly and almost parallel to the ground, he would then spin around and watch excitedly as the tree flung back into the air. As the roots held the tree in place, it would bounce back and stand tall once again, ready for another round of Ithuba's game. He seemed to thoroughly enjoy this game he had created but those small, bendy trees did not last long. Soon, the thin trunks cracked and snapped under Ithuba's weight and they no longer bounced back, leaving them flat to the ground playing the role of logs rather than trees. We were disappointed that the trees had not lasted long but we couldn't help but smile at the utter joy Ithuba experienced when playing with them. His weight and power meant many of the skinny trees in the enclosures did not stand a chance, but any larger tree trunks were utilized for scratching and rubbing against – something all rhinos love to do, especially after a mud bath!

As I mentioned, Ithuba was very playful. We had already stacked some substantial log piles in his enclosure for him to play with and, to keep things fresh, we would regularly re-stack the logs so there would be new angles and grooves for him to hook his horn into. The new log formations were always met with enthusiasm and excitement as the young rhino would charge, lift and defeat them. We would watch as he'd throw logs into the air like they were as light as a feather. Each of the larger logs usually took two of us (and sometimes even the car) to get to his enclosure. No matter how big the logs were, 'Thubes would always make it appear as though they were mere twigs – an incredible example of the strength of even a young rhino. Just the noise of Ithuba's horn hitting a log or a log landing forcefully on the floor sent an unmissable thud through the orphanage.

Axel and I would often go out into the bush to try to find new logs for Ithuba, bigger ones or ones with interesting smells. At the beginning of the search, we would try to get the biggest logs we could find, optimistic of our own abilities yet driven by the confidence of knowing that Ithuba would love them. Axel is taller and stronger than me, but we would struggle to pick up the logs, move them or even roll them. After ten minutes of trying to get the larger logs to the car in the scorching African sun we would end up abandoning them and instead, we'd agree to tackle the more manageable ones that we could lift and move. We wanted to keep Ithuba busy, he was the only calf in our care at first so he did not have any other rhinos to play with or keep him company. It was up to us to keep his life enriched and keep him happy. The logs were a great way to keep Ithuba active and busy; they were a readily available toy we could move, replace and get more of with ease. The logs also brought exciting smells of the bush and wildlife into his enclosure and Ithuba loved them. He would climb on them, fight with them and throw them around without an ounce of hesitation. Although it may sound frivolous, playing is one of the key ways youngsters learn and build up strength.

3: Nightshift with "Friends"

The reality of working at a rhino orphanage is that the moments of cuteness and "cuddles" can be deceiving as not everything is fun and games; the night shifts are continuous, the cleaning is constant and, if we're honest, in the back of your mind is always the risk of poachers. Oh, and not to mention the emotional rollercoaster every wildlife rehabilitator straps themselves in for. A standard day consists of lots of cleaning and milk making with a couple of tender and rewarding moments in between. While caring for Ithuba; Aly, Axel and I would rotate night shifts so two out of three nights we were able to get a good sleep. We were well aware that before long we'd have more rhino orphans in our care and there would no longer be time for a full night's sleep so it was best to make the most of the opportunity while we could.

Thanks to the interlinking preparation rooms and care rooms when a rhino is first rescued and brought to the orphanage we can monitor them around the clock from behind the safety of a barrier. It also means we can sit by the barrier offering comfort and milk without intruding in the rhino's space and risking injury to any of us, rhino or carer.

New arrivals are scared, confused and have no idea who you are or what you are doing so going into an enclosed area with them before they've acclimatised is not a good idea for many reasons. Only the very small rhinos of up to about three months old can be safely worked with within the room from the minute they arrive. Every night one of the care team would sleep in the preparation room to monitor the rhino orphan and carry out the feeds.

Each evening, as the sun was beginning to set, we would go through the night shift check list and make sure everything the person on night duty needed was there in the preparation room for them so they wouldn't have to venture out in the middle of the night to look for equipment or to get more milk powder. Part of the essential night shift equipment was a thin two-inch-thick, uncomfortable (but bearable) camping-style mattress that would be laid down on the clinic floor so the carer on shift could get a couple of hours of sleep in between the milk making, feeding, washing up and any other night-time shenanigans that occurred.

Nightshift for a stable rhino would consist of sleeping on the mattress on the floor in the preparation room adjacent to the care room to monitor the rhino and wake up every three hours, or whenever a feed is required, to mix some fresh milk and feed the orphans. Nightshift for a new arrival or an intensive case would be considerably different in the sense that it would mean closely watching over the rhino allowing for little, or no, sleep. Fortunately, Ithuba was stable and in a routine. If all went well, in between the feeds you could sleep for an hour or two, but not all nightshifts were smooth sailing.

While the majority went by without an issue, there are some I will simply never forget. My own personal nightshifts with Ithuba had been disrupted by many factors varying from bad weather to the full moon and the heart stopping sound of nearby gunshots. Even when everything else was going well and there was no rain, no full moon and no poachers, Ithuba would throw us the occasional curve ball just to keep us on our toes and make sure we didn't get too much sleep.

Settling in for nightshift; I'd typically sit on the thin camping mattress that would fill the shoulder width floor space between the storage shelves we used daily for food and medicine preparations. I'd sit there cross legged, wrapped in a blanket with my laptop or a notebook in my lap, passing the time by reading or writing while waiting for Ithuba to awaken and ask for milk. Ithuba would be sleeping peacefully, the only sound to be heard was that of his deep breaths, regular and relaxed. Everything would be in order for the night ahead; the full container of milk powder would be standing on the countertop waiting to be scooped into the milk bucket, the whisks and funnels would hang on the drying hooks waiting to be used, the teats and the milk bottles would be upside down on the drying rods, now dry and ready for the next feed. The washing up liquid container would be topped up, the worktops disinfected, and the clean record sheets printed ready to be filled with notes and observations. All the nightshift preparations would be complete. However, no matter how much preparation and organisation went into a nightshift there would be times when the plan would simply go out of the window.

This particular nightshift started well, it was still early evening and everything was ready for the night ahead. Ithuba was sleeping peacefully in his room, laying comfortably on his side with his legs stretched out lazily, his head resting on the floor and the sound of his soft snoring filling the room, like a dog sleeping deeply on their favourite bed after a long walk. With a sudden jerk, Ithuba let out a cry, high-pitched and urgent, and was immediately on his feet. The noise of his cry and the thumping of his feet as he ran out of the room was startling and by the time I'd clambered up and looked over the half door that separated our rooms, Ithuba was already disappearing outside.

"Hey 'Thubes, it's ok boy..." I called from the door as I fumbled in the dark to switch on the lights. With a quick glance across the room, I could not see anything out of the ordinary so I unlatched the door, grabbed my head torch from the countertop and went outside to see Ithuba. Something had given him a fright, but he was sleeping so soundly. The orphans sometimes had nightmares but this would cause them to stir and cry in their sleep, so I don't think it was a nightmare that had awoken him. By the door of his room, Ithuba stood hesitantly, looking up at me,

"What happened boy? It's okay." I assured him. Ithuba was clearly anxious and needed reassurance, he took a couple of steps towards me, lifting his head for scratches and kisses.

"It's ok 'Thubes, let's go back inside and have a look." I said with false confidence as I was still completely baffled about what had happened. We walked back into his room together, he was so close to me that his left side was brashly brushing against my right leg with every step, and I draped my right hand over him to rest on his shoulder.

"You're ok my boy, it's ok." I reassured in a soothing voice. In the light of his room, I saw a small, raised bump on the right side of Ithuba's neck hump. A closer look at the swelling revealed it had just one tiny entry hole, meaning the wound was likely caused by a scorpion. It would've made sense, he jolted up and ran out of the room which could've been because he felt a sudden surge of pain… Ithuba was laying on a pile of straw bedding on top of the floor matting when he was rudely awoken, and it was not unusual for us to see scorpions around when cleaning the night rooms first thing in the morning.

In all the fuss, I'd radioed Alyson and Axel and asked them to come down to give me a hand. They were fantastic in helping to establish the cause of the wound and decide on a plan of action. The three of us worked together to pull up some of the floor mats in the area Ithuba usually sleeps to see if we could find the culprit, but it was no use. After getting over the initial shock of being stung, and with the sudden attention of the whole team in his room at 8:30 p.m. Ithuba decided he wasn't overly fussed about the scorpion sting after all, and he was more than happy to lie down lazily to receive belly scratches from us. The lump on his neck was not swelling any further and I was going to keep an eye on it overnight. After another check of the room and bedding, there wasn't a whole lot more we could do about the suspected scorpion situation. So, after giving Ithuba some TLC, Axel and Alyson went back up to the house to enjoy the rest of the evening, Ithuba soon took himself back off to bed and our nightshift was back on track.

The scorpion encounter reminds me of another early evening incident. It was around five p.m.; the afternoon was warm and there was not a breath of wind. The sun was slowly approaching the horizon, the birds were singing and Alyson, Axel and I were with Ithuba playing games of tag in the outside enclosure. As we ran around, laughing and using the last of our energy before the sun set, we saw something slowly moving along the floor next to the outside wall of the preparation room. We stopped in our tracks and watched as an olive-brown snake measuring about half a meter slithered alongside the wall, passing under the preparation room window and continuing towards the door leading into Ithuba's night room. Not knowing what kind of snake it was, we were terrified this could lead to disaster. We decided to block off the snake's route in an attempt to deter it and we kept a close eye on it until we'd verified the species. Knowing the calibre of snakes that occur in these areas, we were cautious to get anywhere near it. Instead, we finally made use of something we had long thought of as useless - Alyson's selfie stick. We attached Aly's phone to the stick and used it to take a couple of good photos of the snake to send to an experienced ranger.

The snake had incredible black detailing under each of its scales, a blunt head and black bars on its front. While all of this was happening, we were also trying to keep Ithuba distracted by playing with his favourite tyre bowl in another area of the enclosure. Ithuba was just as curious about things as we were and this snake was something we did not want him to be anywhere near, especially considering the strength of the venom of some of the African snake species. Within moments of sending the photograph we received a response, 'Mozambique Spitting Cobra, VENOMOUS! VERY DANGEROUS!'. Great, that's all we needed.

Fortunately for us, our barrier seemed to be working and the cobra, or Mfezi in isiZulu, had headed in another direction. We did not take our eyes off the snake from the second we first saw it and now we watched intently as the Mozambique Spitting Cobra slithered across the dirt and away from the rhino rooms. Finally, it made its way towards the bush and away from us.

Aly, Axel and I were happy with this outcome and were pleased with our decision not to attempt to handle the snake, it would have been extremely dangerous to do so without the correct equipment or experience, the venom from a Mozambique spitting cobra can spray two-three metres and is potently cytotoxic (cell destroying). Knowing the snake was definitely not inside the rhino care or preparation rooms and with dusk approaching, we began our night shift preparations, got Ithuba inside and locked the doors. We locked up, thankful the spitting cobra had chosen to go a different way and thankful nobody was hurt in the process.

Many of my nightshifts were silently tormented by the creepy crawlies of Africa. There was a small jumping spider that lived in the clinic so I'd frequently see him. I'd often lay on the mattress and gaze up at the ceiling, feeling relaxed and getting lost in thought, then I'd be pulled back to reality as my eyes would focus on the spider above me. He'd first appear at the corner of the light strip, the light strip I presumed he lived inside of, then I'd watch (nervously) as the spider would begin to abseil down from the ceiling. "Don't land near me, don't land near me" I would repeat in my mind, as if chanting a mantra. I didn't mind the spider and I being roommates too much, he was small and inoffensive… I just wanted there to be a certain level of respect. Just a silent law or mutual agreement between us that he does not land on me or crawl on me and I do not intrude on his living area. This rule looked as though it was about to be broken as the spider abseiled towards me with speed and confidence. Suddenly, the spider stopped and hung - 15 inches above my face - in the space between us. After a while of hanging there, he climbed back up his silk line, returning to the light and disappearing once again into the unknown.

Happy with this, I'd eventually fall asleep, satisfied that the small spider hadn't chosen to abseil down any further. However, when it came to doing the next rhino feed, I couldn't help but be cautious of standing up in the area I'd seen the spider dangling in. As I began mixing milk in a half-asleep daze, almost forgetting about the spider altogether, I looked up and there he was, sitting on the window ledge. The spider was looking suspicious (well, he always looked suspicious to me) and I was pretty sure he was watching me. I paused for a moment to look at him properly, I'd only seen him during the night when I'd be lying on the floor and he'd be up on the ceiling. As I looked, I was full of concentration.

Although he was only about the size of my thumb tip, the brown spider had some amazing detailing. He had a lighter strip across his back and red tips on his fuzzy legs. He had two large, dark, forward-facing eyes which were each flanked by another smaller eye. I was taking in the incredible details of him, all his eyes, his colours and the slight hair on his legs, then in a flash he was gone. The movement was so fast that I gasped and jumped backwards. The spider had leaped away and had disappeared. Knowing my luck, he'd probably leapt straight onto me, I had been leaning in staring at him after all.

I suppose I should've been thankful this spider was small and harmless, especially considering the huge spider with a big red abdomen that had been making some kind of web mansion of the other side of the clinic window. I definitely didn't want to be sharing the clinic with that creature! It took me a while to decide that the jumping spider was on his own mission and wasn't going to get in my space, not that I really believed that. In truth, the jumping spider was just the tip of the iceberg and simply reminded me, as I slept on the floor, of all the other creatures that were lurking in the shadows; the scorpions, snakes, strange looking insects, ticks and more.

The jumping spider was a resident of the preparation room, but someone who most certainly was not was the large spider who'd hitched a ride on one of the folding camping chairs we had been using outside during the day. The chairs had been brought in for the night and were leaning against the counter in the clinic. As I went to pick the chairs up to move them to the corner, a hairy spider the size of my palm ran into view. I recoiled, leaping backwards. "Here we go." I thought to myself. In my mind, I quickly listed the possible ways of dealing with this; 1) move the chairs outside as quickly as possible, 2) spend the nightshift wide awake at the opposite side of the room or 3) call someone else to deal with the giant while I stand in the distance with a broom in my hand. Let's face it, my nightshift had already been ruined by the presence of the unwelcome spider. As if I wasn't going to spend the whole night laying on the floor thinking about that mammoth of a spider coming back in, only this time it would be angry at me and wanting to get its revenge because I relocated it. After some serious thought and a pep talk with Ithuba we decided that I needed to graciously throw the chairs outside, close the door and not go outside again until the morning. So, that's what I did. I chose speed over technique; I opened the door and launched the chair outside as quickly as possible. As soon as the chair left my hand, I pulled the door closed and I even blocked the bottom of the closed, locked door with a blanket to avoid the spider coming back in to take its revenge on me. Problem solved, well aside from the mental torment at least.

It wasn't just creepy crawlies that disrupted nightshifts, the weather conditions did too. We found out that the noise of rain on the roof of the high care unit was something Ithuba, understandably, did not know and did not like. It made him worry and he would cry until someone would sit with him. As soon as you'd sit with him under the heat lamp, he'd rest his head on you and drift off to sleep. The first part of a rainy nightshift would be spent sitting upright, leaning against the wall with your legs straight out in front of you and a sleepy baby rhino resting his head on your thighs. If the wind blew just right, you'd feel the tingle of water droplets as they would blow through the ventilation holes of the wall and into the room. If it was still raining by the next feed, I'd come back into the high care unit with a blanket and pillow in hand, preparing for the night of sleeping side by side under the heat lamp. Ithuba wanted to have contact with you in some way when he felt uneasy so it would usually be with his head resting on you or with his back pushed up against you. I wonder if there's a more bizarre, or enjoyable, way to fall asleep than in a pile of straw under a heat lamp with a pillow under head and a baby rhino resting on you peacefully as you listen to the rain on the roof and the hushed tones of nocturnal wildlife in the distance. Although not all nights were like this…

4: The Bullet of a Semi-Automatic Rifle

While there were some nightshifts that made our hearts full and some that we could laugh about, there were some we never wanted to experience again. A moment that stops everything is hearing a gunshot. To hear a gunshot makes your stomach drop and your heart fly to your mouth.

One night at around 9:30 p.m., I was sitting in the clinic with my laptop on my lap typing away as I waited for Ithuba to wake up for his next feed. The evening so far had gone by without a hitch but suddenly I heard the unmistakable noise of a gunshot rip through the darkness, the gunshot reverberated through the bush; so out of place, so unexpected and, worst of all, so close by. You can never be sure how far away a gunshot is, it's so disorientating but I was convinced the shot was fired just a couple of hundred metres away, way too close for comfort. Before I even had time to react, another shot rang out. I jumped to my feet to see Ithuba still sleeping under his heat lamp, the doors leading to his enclosure were open as he liked to explore outside during the night as he got older. I was immediately thankful that tonight he had chosen to sleep inside. As I stared at Ithuba over the door, a hurricane of thoughts raced through my mind while time stood at a standstill. As I grabbed my keys for the high care unit padlocks from the worktop, my phone began to vibrate. It was a phone call from Axel, I picked up the call as I took the keys, unhooked the door and snuck past Ithuba. As much as I didn't want to go outside, I needed to close and lock the doors that led to Ithuba's night room as a precaution.

"Hey." I mumbled into the phone as I stepped outside.

"Meg, was that a gunshot? Did you hear it? Is everything alright?" Axel asked with urgency - the concern was clear, as was the confusion.

"Yes, I heard it. We are okay, there were two shots, but it wasn't down here. It sounded really close, like it was coming from the direction of the gate. I'm outside now… I need to lock Ithuba in just in case. Just stay on the phone with me…" I said in a hushed tone as I fumbled with the keys in my hand.

"Ok, be careful. I'm trying to get hold of the anti-poaching unit to find out what's going on..." Axel responded without missing a beat, "stay on the phone." He added.

As I stood outside Ithuba's room I was surrounded by darkness, I listened for a moment as I quickly scanned the scene, but I didn't see anything out of place. With all my strength, I pulled the first of the two large, heavy doors, these doors would frequently get jammed and stuck because of mud in the rails but I did not have time for this to happen now. With a second pull, I lugged the door the last ten inches. The catches aligned and I thread the padlock through, pushing it closed with a click. The doors to Ithuba's room could only be locked from the outside meaning I had to lock myself out in order to lock Ithuba in. Once I'd locked the doors I'd have to walk across the outside enclosure, through another locked gate and then from there I could get back to the door of the clinic. I had no idea if poachers had come for Ithuba or what was happening and the last thing I wanted was to bump into someone in the dark. After pulling the second door closed and locking it, I turned to look out into the enclosure.

I stood dead still, looking for any signs of movement and listening for the sound of breaking twigs or crunching leaves. I heard nothing, so after a deep breath I slowly began to creep across the enclosure towards the gate, my eyes were adjusting to the darkness but I could barely see in front of me. As I moved as stealthily as I could, a third gun shot rang out. I stopped in my tracks to listen. The silence that followed was palpable. I was conscious of the sound of my breathing and I could feel my heart beating in my chest, in fact it was so intense I could hear the thudding of my own heartbeat. I had absolutely no idea what was going on but whatever was happening, it was close. I was standing in the open, exposed in the enclosure, I knew I needed to get out of there and back to the clinic as quickly as I could. I was convinced that the gunshots were coming from our gate. The third shot didn't seem to be any closer than the second, but it was also no further away. With Ithuba now locked inside, I silently told myself to take a breath and to keep going.

I remembered I was still on the phone.

"Axel, are you there? That was another shot, have you managed to get hold of anyone?" I whispered desperately, trying not to let my fear overtake me.

"Not yet, no one is answering … I'm coming to the clinic." He said in a low, firm tone.

Too worried to shine a torch and holding the phone awkwardly between my ear and shoulder, I slowly tiptoed across the enclosure towards the gate, the noise of each step seemed amplified like a beacon that would attract whoever was out there shooting directly to me. Although it was only ten more steps until I reached the gate, it felt a hell of a lot longer as I navigated through the darkness, terrified I may be shot or grabbed. As I reached the gate, I paused to listen and take a breath. I was surrounded by silence, and I didn't know if that was a good thing or a bad thing. The gate to the enclosure is always locked, I fumbled for a moment trying to unlock the padlock so I could get out of the enclosure and back to the clinic. My phone began to beep, another call was coming in. I let go of the still-locked padlock to glance at the screen.

"I'm going to put you on hold for a minute, ok? Alyson is calling me." I told Axel.

"Ok, I'll be at the clinic in a minute anyway. See you now." I answered the call, hoping Alyson had some information on the situation.

"Hey, what's going on?" I asked hastily as I picked the padlock back up.

"I don't know, I wanted to make sure you and Ithuba are okay. I haven't been able to get hold of anyone, I heard the gunshots…" Alyson replied.

"Ok, we are okay, I've just locked Ithuba in and I'm at the gate of the enclosure on my way back to the clinic. I can't see or hear anyone around here; can you see anything towards the gate? It sounded like the shots were coming from that direction…" I explained in a lowered voice as I stood on the inside of the gate of the enclosure, locked padlock in one hand, set of keys in the other and the phone pressed against my shoulder.

"I can't see anything. I'm coming down to the clinic now. Lock yourself in. Remember the code word." Alyson said without missing a beat. We had created code words so that whenever one of us would knock on a locked door the other could easily identify the person and know it was safe to unlock the door for them. It was something that took away the sickening unease of a silent knock at the door during the night.

"Ok. Axel is on his way too. See you in a minute." I responded, hanging up. As the call cut I regretted hanging up because now I was truly alone but I shoved the phone into my pocket so I could focus on unlocking the padlock.

Trying not to jingle the keys, the lock finally popped open, I pulled the gate just enough for me to slip through and quickly and quietly pulled it closed behind me, pushing the padlock closed. I wanted to run back to the clinic but remaining composed, I skulked as close to the enclosure fence as I could, moving with silent urgency. Unlocking the clinic door was easy, it was the longest key in the set.

Once I was inside, I hastily locked the door behind me and with a sigh of relief, looked over to see Ithuba still happily sleeping. No more than

30 seconds later, a knock at the door along with the code word signalled Alyson and Axel's presence outside. We locked ourselves in and stood in Ithuba's room not wanting to be in view of the clinic window, just in case. We tried desperately to get hold of the anti-poaching team to find out what was happening. Through all of this Ithuba remained blissfully unaware as he gently snored beneath the heat lamp. He was not due a feed for another 30 minutes, so I wasn't expecting him to wake up anytime soon. Getting no response from our phone calls and not willing to take another step outside of this locked room until we knew what was happening, it was clear there was nothing more we could do aside from continue in trying to contact the anti-poaching unit or someone on the reserve to either shed light on the situation or send us back up.

An agonising ten minutes of deafening silence went by, we heard nothing else, no more gunshots and not a peep from the outside world. We didn't dare move from Ithuba's side until we knew exactly what was happening. Finally, the silence was broken as we managed to contact the head of the anti-poaching unit. He calmly informed us that it was his team firing warning shots. I felt a wave of relief wash over me, like the floodgates had been opened on my emotions. He continued, telling us that bush meat poachers had been spotted from the orphanage watch tower and the rangers fired warning shots in their direction. The poachers were using torches to guide them, and it was this that had given their location away. After the shots were fired, the rangers watched as the lights quickly dispersed and moved, hastily, back towards the boundaries of the reserve. The gunshots sounded close because they were being fired from our fence line, 150 metres away from Ithuba and I.

When I heard those gunshots, I was filled with an indescribable dread as I thought the worst was happening. When we heard that everything was okay I felt the tension ease, I exhaled the breath I had been holding onto as it finally felt we could breathe again. We were incredibly grateful for the anti-poaching unit who were protecting us and the wildlife on the reserve and we were extremely thankful Ithuba was not being targeted. On that evening, some prior warning could've saved us some stress, but we were safe and that's what mattered.

The helpless feeling of being nothing more than an unarmed animal lover up against poachers with guns is dreadful. To feel so powerless and unable to protect the animals you've raised is nothing short of heart-breaking. Rhinos carry a bounty on their heads in the form of their horns and it is something that is worth more than gold to some. There are people in this world who are desperate to get their hands on rhino horn and this is something you risk overlooking when you work with rhino day in, day out. When I'm with the orphans I see the horn of a rhino as something you need to dodge or avoid being knocked by more than anything else.

The thought that others of our species would be willing to kill or maim one of these animals in order to get the horn (which is just keratin, the same as our hair and nails) is beyond reason. However, there are times when the reality of the situation cannot be ignored. It can be difficult to put the realities to the back of your mind, particularly when you're dealing with a newly rescued orphaned calf, when there is poaching activity nearby or when the poachers moon (full moon) shines high in the sky.

The worry of poachers is very real. A month later we received a phone call to say there had been a tip off that rhino poachers were planning on targeting both the reserve and the orphanage that night. It was late afternoon and Alyson, Axel and I were giving the storeroom a thorough clean when Alyson took a phone call. As she walked away with her hand hovering over her mouth and a look of fear in her eyes, Axel and I knew there was something very wrong. We carried on cleaning, waiting for the phone call to end and just under ten minutes later Alyson came back to the storeroom. Now pale and no longer smiling. It was clear there was a problem, there was a thick and worried atmosphere in the air. As Alyson approached us, her unease was clear. Something was terribly wrong, and we all knew it.

"Just tell us." Axel said, knowing Alyson was trying to protect our feelings and avoid worrying us. After a little persuasion and a deep breath, Alyson responded,

"There's been a tip off that we are being targeted. That poachers are coming for our rhino." Aly's eyes were fixed on the ground as she played nervously with her hands. Worried glances were exchanged over the tense silence that followed.

"What should we do?" I asked in an almost inaudible voice. Another silence, all knowing we were powerless and it was in the hands of the anti-poaching unit. The question felt redundant, but I didn't know what else to say.

"We need to carry on as normal, make sure everything is locked at all times. Everyone carries a radio, and we move around as little as possible." Alyson responded, repeating what she had been advised on the phone. Aly nodded as she spoke, but her eyes did not convey the same level of confidence.

I looked at the floor as my whole body filled with anxiety and dread. How could we carry on as normal? Then again, what else could we do? As the sun began to set everything felt different. I was nervous as I got ready for my night shift, once I was in the clinic I would be locking the door and not leaving for any reason. I hardly felt brave enough to grab the mattress from the storeroom let alone venture to the house or the bathroom in the dead of the night. It was my night shift and I was terrified. I was so frightened Ithuba and I wouldn't make it to see the sunrise. I knew there were guards patrolling and the anti-poaching unit were on high alert, but I also knew poachers were targeting us and as I sat next to Ithuba I couldn't help but think of all the possible outcomes of the night. The minutes passed by slower than I had ever experienced, Ithuba slept soundly as I sat wide-eyed listening out for noises and wondering how I could stop anyone who came here with a gun. My conclusions were bleak.

Slowly but surely, the night continued without a sound from the outside world. I remained on high alert, receiving no updates on the situation as Ithuba and I waited it out, pleading for the sun to rise. Each click, crack or creek would cause me to freeze, listening carefully to determine the source. I was on edge and helpless. Admittedly, I had freaked myself out so much that I was refusing to turn the light on or mix milk near the window.

As the hours ticked by, there was a knock at the door followed by Alyson's code word. The knocking startled me at first, but the code word put my anxieties at ease. It was nearing on eleven p.m., in the early evening when I was getting sorted for my nightshift with Ithuba, Alyson had gone to the reserve to help ensure the safety of the two hand-reared, wild rhinos. She had not long returned to the orphanage and came to the clinic to see how Ithuba and I were doing.

I opened the door to let her in and, for the first time all evening, I smiled as I saw her standing there with a blanket in hand ready to join me on the night that felt like it would never end. Having Alyson there made a difference, we both sat wrapped in blankets not talking much but just being there, together. Supporting each other through the dark night. This demonstration of team spirit and support in an event that so many others would've run from gives you a glimmer into the special soul that Alyson is. At the next feed, I mixed the milk (still keeping the lights off and staying away from the window) and while I fed Ithuba, Aly washed up. This teamwork meant that in no time at all we were back in our blankets leaning against the shelves with tired eyes and exhausted minds. My thoughts had continued to torment me since the very first hour of my nightshift. My mind had speculated every possibility in detail and replayed each of them over and over. As the early hours of the morning began to creep in, I was struggling to keep my eyes open.

It was coming up to four a.m. and my heavy eyelids refused to stay open, without realizing it, I fell asleep sitting upright against the shelves of the clinic with my knees pulled to my chest. Waking up startled, I checked the time. I hadn't been asleep for long, no more than an hour had passed, but I could see the beginnings of the sunrise through the window. I couldn't believe it. I was so thankful, so grateful nothing had happened through the night.

As Ithuba awoke for his next feed, Aly and I hugged in celebration of the sunrise. We were beyond thankful that Ithuba was okay and nothing had happened. We had made it through the night, but I wondered if we could ever truly relax or feel safe. I wanted to be able to fall asleep without worry, without fear, without dread but I knew that when the sun would once again descend below the horizon it would bring a certain kind of darkness, the kind where dawn is not promised.

In the city, there are safes and fancy security systems in place to protect gold, money, jewellery… Whatever precious commodity it is, it's heavily protected. In the bush, a handful of trained, passionate guys with a firearm and hundreds of kilometres of reserve to cover and protect doesn't seem to quite cut it, particularly when you're dealing with an animal carrying something worth more than gold on its face. But what other options are there? When security costs so much and the people trying to protect wildlife are often non-profit organizations or private individuals. What is the answer?

These harsh realities brought home the most startling truths of the rhino poaching crisis. It was always something that was at the back of our minds. On one hand, we have a cheeky baby rhino who drinks milk formula and needs reassurance during rainy nights, on the other we have poachers and semi-automatic rifles.

5: Food, Drought and Independence

No matter what threats we faced, our priority remained caring for the orphaned rhino calves. Although we were always on standby for new arrivals, we experienced a quiet couple of months after Ithuba was rescued. We knew this could change at any moment but for the time being, Ithuba kept busy playing, drinking milk and taking naps while Aly, Axel and I kept a close eye on him, visually health checking him every day.

We would also occasionally record his vitals too so that if we were ever concerned that something was wrong we could use our previous notes as a comparison. With a clipboard and stethoscope in hand, I quietly went out into the enclosure and sat next to Ithuba as he slept in the sand. I stroked his side while watching the rise and fall of his body with each breath he took. I wanted to take down his respiratory rate and heart rate while he was relaxed. First, I started the stopwatch as I counted his breaths per minute and noted this down. Then, I took the stethoscope from around my neck, placed the earpieces into my ears and gently held the flat, circular chest piece against Ithuba's thick skin as he slept undisturbed. The rest of the world fell silent as I focused in on the gentle beat of the heart of one of the most prehistoric mammals on Earth. I counted the beats as Ithuba continued to sleep, completely unconcerned by the stethoscope that was gently resting against his grey, wrinkled skin. His steady heartbeat echoed through me, so soothing and rhythmic. Even after noting down the observations, I held the stethoscope in place, letting this moment etch itself into my heart. Are we really that different?

We kept a note of Ithuba's vitals and recorded his growth and condition as a way of monitoring his progress. Despite the initial colic Ithuba experienced when he first arrived, he was in excellent health. He happily drank all his milk every single feed and was even eating dry food, although he could be a little fussy with that at times. Every day we would mix some dried grass (teff) and a cultivated flowering hay (lucerne, also known as alfalfa) together, spread the mix out into the large tyre bowls that we used for feeding and put the bowls into Ithuba's outside enclosure for him to enjoy at his leisure. Between teff and lucerne, rhinos tend to prefer the lucerne. It's greener in appearance and more nutritionally dense, it has higher protein levels and all the rhinos I've met seem to find lucerne considerably more appealing than teff. As we would want the rhino to eat a mix of the two, with a higher ratio of teff than lucerne, we would always mix the two grasses together. That way the rhino would be able to get the benefits of both and we could reduce the risk of them overindulging on lucerne, something they would definitely do if we didn't mix the two together.

Ithuba developed a system to beat ours. We'd mix the dried teff and lucerne together as thoroughly as we could before placing the mix into the feeding bowls for him. Almost immediately, Ithuba would happily overturn the food bowl, push the tyre out of the way and begin sorting through the grass mix. Using his big square lips, he'd pull a small pile of the dried grass to an empty patch of ground and meticulously separate the pile so he could pick out and enjoy the lucerne. He'd do this until it was mostly teff left in the batch in front of him then he'd push the teff to one side and pull a new pile of mixed food to the open area of ground. Of course, this was a time-consuming activity and, in the end, he'd eat the teff anyway but I found it fascinating to watch him. He took such time and was so delicate while being completely gripped by the task at hand, as if he was a young child picking chocolate chips from a cookie.

We were amidst the worst drought to hit South Africa in 30 years. The drought was the worst seen since 1982 and the lack of rainfall had meant there was very little grass around for the rhinos to graze on. As Ithuba was being housed in an enclosed area, it did not take long until there was no grass left for him to graze. To combat this, we had started driving to grass rich areas of the reserve to collect bags of the fresh grass that was growing close to the shrinking rivers. We would give this to Ithuba but we worried this was not enough to sustain him so we also began to give him what we would simply call "cubes". Cubes are a concentrated food source of grasses and plants; they are dry pellets often given to horses but have been used as a supplementary food source for rhino orphans too, so we started to give Ithuba a small handful of cubes each day.

As with introducing any new food, we needed to start with feeding small amounts and build up to the amount necessary for Ithuba's weight. To avoid any confusion, we created a feeding chart to show how many grams of cubes we needed to feed each day and the amount would marginally increase every few days until the target was reached. Ithuba loved the cubes, if you held a handful of them out he'd open his mouth as wide as he could and try to grab them with his big, square lips. The cubes were only about the size of a fingertip so were not the easiest thing for a rhino to pick up or grab. Ithuba would try to pick them all up at once and some would end up balancing on the outer edge of his lips, he'd try to avoid dropping them by holding his head up while chewing and moving his lips. Despite his best efforts, a few cubes from every mouthful would end up on the floor for later. White rhino lips are large, square and flat; they are perfectly adapted for eating grass, even very small shoots of grass that are close to the ground. As white and black rhinos do not have teeth at the front of their mouths (both species lack incisor teeth), they rely heavily on their lips to bring the food into their mouth. The white rhinos are grazers meaning they eat grass while the black rhinos are browsers and have a hooked, or pointed, upper lip that is prehensile and allows them to pluck leaves and branches from trees.

Getting Ithuba to eat all the right things wasn't the only challenge as during the initial stages of Ithuba's rehabilitation we were concerned that he did not seem to go to the water troughs to drink water on his own. If he was close by when we were cleaning and refilling the trough then he would come to drink and check whether or not we were doing a good job but aside from those moments he rarely showed any interest in water. We began to encourage him to the troughs; we would have to literally put our faces over the trough and make slurping noises to show the cautious youngster that it was safe and the water was good to drink. Only then, would he come and stand next to the trough and drink too. It would always make us laugh because we looked so silly; with rhino in tow, one of us would get down on our hands and knees, put our face over the water bowl and pretend to drink. Encouraged and confident, Ithuba would come and stand next to the trough and take long, thirsty slurps of the fresh, clean water. This would happen again and again; we'd pretend to drink from his water trough so he would too.

Just as a young rhino would learn from their mother in the wild, Ithuba was learning from us. Before long, we could encourage him to drink at the troughs just by swishing a finger across the surface of the water and, as time went on, he began to drink from the water sources on his own. We were thrilled. It may sound trivial, but this was a big and important step for his future life in the wild.

Ithuba loved the comfort of laying with you and resting on you, but he equally loved making you run as fast as you possibly could around the enclosures. This young rhino was very playful, and he saw Axel as a well-matched play mate. The pair had a brotherly relationship, Ithuba would always make Axel run the fastest and was that little bit more boisterous when the two of them would play together.

Ithuba would still insist on playing with all of us and once the games start, the playful rhino calf would be throwing his weight around and jumping with excitement. His eyes would watch us playfully, waiting for us to decide which direction to run in. As soon as we'd make the first move Ithuba would be hot on our heels. A white rhino can run at speeds of up to fifty km per hour. The average human runs at less than half this speed.

We could run with all the energy we had and Ithuba would still be a fraction of a second behind us. As we ran and tried to keep the pace up, we could feel Ithuba running dangerously close to the backs of our legs. The game would always be in his full control, and it was up to him whether he'd wipe us out, overtake us or keep ever so slightly behind. When we'd run with him, he'd usually choose to stay behind us. Sometimes he'd overtake us on a corner and if we tried to get the upper hand during the games by turning and running through the bushes, Ithuba would carry on knowing that he could cut us off on the other side of the trees. As we'd be ducking under the acacia's thorny branches and sprinting to the opening thinking we were now ahead of the game, Ithuba would already be on his way there ready to catch us as we'd emerge. It was so much fun.

Ithuba loved to run and chase us around, but he would never wipe us out, although he could at any point as he was always faster and stronger, even at his youngest. He always kept that hairsbreadth behind. While we were running and playing during a quiet afternoon, my hair got caught up in a branch of one of the acacia trees, pulling me back forcefully as I ran. This stopped me dead in my tracks as I yelled,

"Ahhh! Wait 'Thubes… Stop, stop, stop!" and threw my hands up to my hair to try to untangle myself. Even though Ithuba was running behind me enthusiastically, he halted when he saw me stop. He stood next to me and patiently waited while I disentangled my hair and clothes from the thorns. He just stood there, looking up at me with his soft, kind eyes… Waiting patiently until I was ready to run again. Ithuba was innately gentle, and it showed.

In another near-miss, Ithuba and I were enthusiastically sprinting around the enclosure, enjoying a rare storm on a warm July afternoon. As I turned the corner, I decided to stop to catch my breath and wait for Ithuba to emerge from the trees. With my hands on my hips and a big exhale, I looked up to see Ithuba come flying around the corner a lot faster than I was anticipating. As he turned towards me, he saw I was not running anymore. While I watched on at this fast-unfolding disaster, Ithuba's eyes widened as he tried to stop to avoid hitting into me. He dug his feet heavily into the dirt but because of the rainstorm, the ground was too muddy, causing him to continue sliding towards me. As the gap between us closed, Ithuba left deep channels in his wake as he desperately dug his feet into the ground. With everything happening so fast I didn't react to the now 250kg rhino hurtling uncontrollably towards me. We both watched helplessly as Ithuba skidded in my direction. As he was just 30cms away from me I closed my eyes to brace for the impact. As I waited with my eyes tightly closed, all went quiet.

I slowly opened my eyes to see Ithuba standing just millimetres away from my legs. Against the odds, Ithuba had managed to stop himself just a whisker away from me. For a second, the two of us just stood there, tense and bewildered. I looked down at myself, then at Ithuba - who was looking up at me with the same edgy expression - and we both relaxed realising neither of us were hurt. I laughed out loud and gave Ithuba scratches. No longer tense, we enjoyed a few quiet moments then decided we would stop running but would play with the tyre bowl instead.

The tyre bowl was one of Ithuba's favourite toys. The large tyre bowl - which when on its side was the same height as Ithuba - was a perfect, hardy toy for an energetic young rhino. Ithuba would hook his horn onto the edge of the inner lip of the bowl and lift it up onto his face. Now, with his head inside the bowl, he would hold his head up as high as he could so that the bottom of the bowl would lift off the ground. He'd only be able to lift the bowl a couple of centimetres from the floor but it was enough, now he would begin to walk forwards carrying the bowl on his face. He'd begin to trot with the tyre balancing on his small horn, stopping every now and then to try to throw the bowl up into the air. He had to hold his head high and lift his feet very carefully when running to avoid knocking the bowl off balance and, the best bit, when doing this the bowl completely covered his eyes. It took practice to get it right and then he'd usually knock the edge of the tyre on a branch or against a wall and it would fall from his horn to the ground.

Ithuba thought this game was brilliant, he'd trot around with the tyre bowl balanced on his face time and time again. Sometimes we would balance the tyre over the logs as another game for Ithuba. He would use his horn to hit and knock the tyre bowl until it fell to the ground. Then he'd pick it up and the amusements would begin all over again. Watching 'Thubes run around with the tyre bowl was hilarious. Sometimes he'd let us pick the tyre up and roll it away or drag it behind us as we ran – this would really fire him up to play. Ithuba would be right behind the tyre as we'd pull it, chasing it and trying to knock it with his horn. The best thing about the tyre bowl was that it was tough and incredibly robust. Ithuba could throw it, stand on it, launch it into the wallow and it was good to be played with at any time. The tyre bowl, which was originally used to hold dry food, could have easily been one of Ithuba's favourite toys to play with.

Although Ithuba enjoyed our company, as the months rolled on we knew he needed to spend less time with humans and ideally, he needed to be with other rhinos. We began to reduce the time we spent with him so he could get used to not being with us around the clock. Our aim was to slowly cut down our time together so we would be there for his feeds, at night and for a small portion of the day. We decided that we would play as usual and keep him entertained but when he slept, wallowed and ate his dry food we wanted him to have the confidence of doing it on his own. When the rhino orphans are young, they need someone with them all the time but as they get older, this human contact is reduced so the rhinos can be successfully reintroduced back into the wild.

As Ithuba took the changes in his stride, it wasn't long before Aly, Axel and I found ourselves with a lot of spare time. At first, we spent time close to his enclosure, monitoring him and listening out in case he cried. At this point Ithuba had full roam of three interlinking enclosures and loved to explore them. Each day we'd clean the high care unit, preparation room and storeroom while keeping an eye on Ithuba. We also regularly cleaned and organised the "rhino café" (where the teff, lucerne and straw bedding bales were kept). This storage area allowed us to stow our vital teff and lucerne supplies and keep them sheltered from the elements, effectively preventing mould and damp from creeping in. The drought was a continuing problem that meant it was extremely important we kept our supplies topped up to ensure we had enough to keep our rhinos fed despite the country's dwindling supplies. While keeping the orphanage maintained, we kept an eye on Ithuba. If he needed us for anything, we were there in a flash but as he got used to us not being around all the time he largely kept himself entertained. Alyson, Axel and I were very proud parents as we watched Ithuba thriving and becoming increasingly independent.

As Alyson prepared to leave for a short trip to the UK, we decided Axel and I would each have a day off to rest. I took my day off first and as soon as I finished my night shift I climbed into bed and slept in until midday! I'm not usually one for sleeping in but this was my first day off since we started this project and I clearly needed it. Once awake and feeling refreshed I washed my clothes and relaxed, taking the time to call my parents and my brother to catch up with them. The following day was Axel's day off, he also slept a lot. We didn't see him until the afternoon when he emerged from his room, found a comfy spot on the sofa in the main house and slept there until the evening. I guess we hadn't realised how much we needed these days off. The next day, Aly and I scrubbed Ithuba's room from top to bottom before she left to go to the UK for two weeks. With Ithuba getting more and more independent, Axel and I spent a lot of time sitting at the house listening out for Ithuba in case he called or cried. We would've benefitted from CCTV as it would've allowed us to monitor Ithuba from anywhere. Instead, we sat in tactical places around the orphanage, areas where Ithuba couldn't see us but we could hear him if he cried. We were also trying to get Ithuba to go four or five hours in between feeds instead of three, he was now drinking ten litres of milk per feed as well as eating dry food and cubes. Just a couple of days into the new routine Axel and I were ecstatic when Ithuba went over five hours between two of his feeds.

Ithuba was spending more and more time alone, his confidence was growing and he was enjoying what the bush had to offer. He was now waking up earlier than ever and we were leaving the high care unit doors that led to the outside enclosure open, so he had free roam during both the day and the night.

In the early hours of a crisp, cold July morning, Ithuba and I sat outside and watched as the moon set through the trees. The almost-full moon was a truly spectacular shade of orange as it slowly disappeared beyond the horizon. While I watched the setting moon with a baby rhino by my side it struck me that this was something very few people get to experience and enjoy. What an honour it is to enjoy the company of another species so comfortably. The time spent with Ithuba was time spent with nature. Together we witnessed many sunrises, sunsets, moonrises, moonsets, starry skies and storms.

One of my most precious memories was during a nightshift with Ithuba. It was just past midnight, and it was coming up to feeding time but there was no sign of the young rhino inside so I went out into the darkness of the enclosure to check on him and make sure he was okay. I found him lying next to the trees, sleeping peacefully under the star-lit sky. I had wrapped myself in a blanket to combat the bitter night air and decided to sit by Ithuba for a few minutes. He was growing up and I knew it wouldn't be long until he'd just come to us for milk every now and then and nothing else, so I wanted to take this opportunity to sit with him under the stars and simply, feel the magic.

As I sat next to Ithuba, he looked up at me with gentle eyes and exhaled softly as he lifted his head and placed it tenderly into my lap. I stroked his face as he drifted back to sleep, now resting on me. I could feel each soft breath through my jumper and the warmth of his skin on my legs. He slept so peacefully as I admired the stars above us, it was a perfectly clear night and the moon was only in its first quarter so its light did not overpower the stars in any way. I listened as the nocturnal birds called, the hyenas whooped in the distance and Ithuba breathed peacefully. As I leant back against the tree and admired the sky, a shooting star soared across the darkness in a swoosh of light and wonder, I was in complete awe of this moment. This was Africa. It's moments like these that keep my heart beating to the rhythm of rhino. All the sleepless nights, all the worry, the heartache, it all dissipates when you can have just one of these precious moments.

I looked down at Ithuba, he had grown so much. 'Thubes was now waist-high and still growing but he remained so gentle. Like a proud parent, I looked at him with love, feeling such gratitude that he had found his confidence in spending time within the enclosures alone and deciding to do all the things wild rhinos do such as wallow and graze. He even had a midden forming; a midden is an area rhinos frequently pass faeces, creating a dung heap, something that in the wild is used to mark territory and share information with other rhinos who are passing through. A rhino midden is kind of like a social network that rhinos use to find out the latest gossip about other rhinos in the area.

With Ithuba now largely independent and Alyson on her way back to the orphanage we readied ourselves for new arrivals. We made sure we had all the equipment we needed on hand, we read up and studied in our free time and we kept everything clean and sterilized. We were balancing on a very thin line between being thankful that there had been no call outs in the hope that this meant there had been no poaching victims and being realistically uneasy as we knew that the situation on the ground and the stats indicate poaching is rife so, maybe the orphaned calves weren't being located in time...

Rehabilitation can be a little bit like that, you never know if you are doing enough but all you can do is try. Especially at the beginning of a project, you can find yourself in a lull with free time to organise, study, plan and dare I say it, even get a full night's sleep… A lull, however, is not the norm. It's a false sense of security, suddenly you blink and there's no longer a second of the day left to spare. With that in mind, as the sun would rise and set each day we waited knowing such blissful routine was not going to last forever.

6: The New Arrival Has a Trunk

We were always ready to accept new arrivals, but we never thought the next animal to be brought to our rhino orphanage would not be a rhino... Just one day after Alyson returned from the UK and almost five months after Ithuba was rescued, on Thursday the 13th of August, we received news of a very young, extremely weak elephant calf who had been spotted wandering through the veld on his own. We were called by the owners of a game reserve located several hours away from the orphanage and they told us that the young elephant was in great distress, visibly weak, underweight and dehydrated. At the time of contacting us the rangers had managed to capture the calf and place him in a secure outside enclosure. While the elephant was being temporarily held in a makeshift enclosure, the rangers frantically tried to find the elephant herd and, ultimately, the mother of the baby elephant. It was decided that, as an elephant's best chance of survival is to be with their herd, a reintroduction would be attempted to get the tiny calf back with his family. Should the reintroduction fail, or the herd not be located we would step in and bring the elephant to our facility for intensive care and rehabilitation.

The news of the elephant sent a buzz of excitement through my body - it was, however, mixed with extreme trepidation. My rehabilitation experience had been primarily with rhinos, I did not have experience caring for baby elephants but the very thought of it melted my heart. It was the ultimate African adventure, the very essence of childhood dreams. Our lives could be turned completely upside down in less than 24 hours so we spent our time studying and preparing. We accessed all the online resources available, spoke to all the contacts we had and read up everything we could find on elephant calves, feeding elephant calves and raising elephant calves. We wanted to be as prepared as we could in case this little elephant needed rescuing.

The articles, journals and first-hand accounts we read gave us a better idea of what to expect but the conclusions were far from promising. It seems that elephant calves are beyond complicated, they are emotional to the point of dying as a result of the stress of being left alone, they are fussy eaters, they have sensitive stomachs and without other elephants around it is, at the very least, an uphill struggle. Should this elephant need rehabilitation our biggest task would be keeping his spirits high and his will to live strong. We pondered over the thought of Ithuba taking the role of an elephant stand-in for the time being so the elephant calf wouldn't feel alone but we weren't so sure. Ithuba was already big and strong, a small elephant might not appreciate the brashness of a young rhino. Aly, Axel and I sat together in the office in between Ithuba's feeds; discussing and reading as much as we could but deep down we were all silently hoping the elephant herd would accept the calf back and it would be a "…and they lived happily ever after" story. We were a capable team but we were realistic and we knew that the young elephant's best chance of survival was with his mother. After a long day of researching, planning and organising I fell asleep with a tingle in my body and a knowing that no matter what happened, I was ready. Part of me knew everything was about to change forever.

The following morning, I sprung out of bed at the crack of dawn eager for an update on the situation. With no news since the previous afternoon, Aly and I gave Ithuba's room a clean while we waited to hear about the elephant calf. After the rhino care routine was complete, we left Ithuba to his own devices and headed up to the kitchen to make tea. Axel was already in the kitchen and the kettle had just boiled, perfect timing. We had got into a habit of sitting on the kitchen floor and talking for hours on end, it had become something of a casual team meeting area. As we poured the steaming water into our mugs, we leant against the worktops and talked at length about the baby elephant. The room was filled with our thoughts, predictions and concerns.

As we discussed how we thought Ithuba would react to a baby elephant moving in Alyson's phone began to buzz, the vibration rippled its way through the kitchen counter, filling the room with intermittent noise. Our conversation stopped, eyes all darting to the phone on the worktop. The phone screen was lighting up and Axel and I watched in anticipation as Aly answered the call we had all been waiting for.

The last update we had received on the elephant was the previous day when the herd had been successfully located. In the late afternoon, the rangers loaded the elephant calf into a trailer and took him as close to the herd as possible. When they had driven as close to the wild herd as they were able, two of the rangers took the tiny elephant in their arms and carried him as near to the wild elephants as they could without risking their safety. As the rangers quickly made their way back to the safety of the vehicle, the elephant herd approached the calf. We had not heard any more on the situation since then.

Our fingers had been firmly crossed that the calf was accepted into the herd, but we knew there would be more to the story. If the baby elephant was initially abandoned rather than becoming accidentally separated, there would be a reason for it and the herd wouldn't accept the calf back if he was sick. We stood silently waiting for the information to be passed on to us. Standing in the kitchen that Friday morning, with our cups of tea in hand and nervous smiles on our faces, our lives were about to totally transform. As Alyson thanked the caller and hung up the phone, she told us the news…

"It looks like we have a baby elephant. We need to go and rescue him now as he is going to be even weaker today, it sounds like he spent some of the night alone as he was with the herd when the rangers left him last night but was found on his own again this morning. The rangers said he is very stressed, so I think we need to load up and get on the road now."

"Alright, let's do this. I'll load up the ambulance, you two get ready and I'll meet you outside." I exhaled and placed my cup of tea on the side.

"You're sure you'll be okay here if Axel and I go to get the elephant?" Alyson asked.

"Of course! I'll keep an eye on Ithuba and get everything sorted here for when you guys get back" I said as we all nodded to one another and left in different directions to get organised.

I went down to the storeroom and quickly packed everything that the rescue team needed to take with them while they got themselves ready for the long drive ahead. It would be a 300km round trip to pick the elephant up and bring him back to the orphanage. We'd already sorted the important rescue kits and cleaned the ambulance the day before, just in case this was the outcome of the attempted reintroduction. It pays to be prepared. I loaded the emergency and medical kits into the back of the ambulance alongside blankets and drip bags so the team would have everything they may need on hand. The ambulance was kitted out and ready for the journey. Aly and Axel would be gone all day and they would be returning in the afternoon with a vulnerable baby elephant.

With the patchy information we had been given, it seemed as though the calf had been abandoned as opposed to initially becoming separated due to getting stuck or lost. There was no doubt that no matter what the backstory was, the calf would be anguished by the situation. Family is everything to an elephant and to be left alone is very distressing, not only for the calf but also for the mother.

The only reason elephants would abandon one of their own is if they sensed that individual was sick beyond reasonable hope of survival. The mother would have stayed with the calf for as long as she could without jeopardising her own survival. Our team now had the colossal task of raising the elephant. In the past couple of years, I'd been involved in the rehabilitation process of lots of rhino but never an elephant… We knew it was not going to be easy, we knew it was not going to be like caring for Ithuba or any of the rhinos we had cared for in the past but there was no way of knowing just how difficult it was going to be. We would soon be discovering how stark the contrast between raising rhinos and raising elephants truly is.

Aly approached the ambulance with a nervous smile,

"Okay, Axel is bringing the car around so we can hook up the trailer then I think we are ready to go."

"Perfect. The emergency kits are in the front of the ambulance with the drips, blankets, flasks and there's a box there with electrolytes and sterilized feeding equipment too." I pointed.

"Brilliant, thanks Meg. Okay, I think that is everything. It's going to take us a few hours to get to the reserve, but I'll keep you updated." Aly said as she closed and bolted the ambulance door. We guided Axel as he reversed the pickup truck towards the ambulance,

"Okay, okay, stop. That's perfect." I shouted to Axel. With a deep breath, we hooked the trailer to the truck and connected the cables.

"I'll close the orphanage gate once you've gone, do you have the key for the access gate?" I asked, the key was essential for getting off the property and onto the main road without having to spend an extra 20 minutes driving across the uneasy ground of the dirt roads within the reserve. There'd been more than one occasion we'd driven to the access gate only to realise we'd forgotten to bring the key.

"Okay thanks, yeah Axel's got the key. Alright Meg, I think we are ready to go… We'll see you this afternoon!" Aly smiled as she climbed into the passenger seat of the car.

"Drive safely, call me if you need anything. I hope everything goes smoothly! See you later." I responded, talking through the driver's side window.

A mere five minutes after we were standing in the kitchen drinking tea, I was waving off Aly and Axel as they went to rescue the desperate baby elephant. I watched as they disappeared into the distance, listening as the noise of the car engine faded into nothing. I walked down to the orphanage gate, pulling it along its rails until the steel of the gate clanged against the frame. I hooked the gate closed and walked back up to the house, surrounded by a silent orphanage. I returned to the kitchen, made a fresh cup of tea and took a moment to collect my thoughts. I had my notebook in front of me, a pen in my hand and, for the first time in months, I was alone. It's funny how close the three of us had become, when you work and live together you really do end up living in each other's pockets. We had become family. I was so used to Aly and Axel's chirps and chimes, our laughter as we'd plan the days and the endless conversations that would flow effortlessly between us. Now I was surrounded by silence. It was quiet, completely quiet.

After a call out, we aim to get on the road as quickly as possible so after the rush of getting everything ready for the rescue all was now still. I took a radio from the charging point in the office and hooked it onto my belt in case there was an emergency, security breach or someone needed to contact me and then I got to work prioritizing the tasks for the day.

There was not a lot to do for Ithuba as we'd already cleaned his room first thing in the morning. I just had to keep an eye on him and prepare his regular feeds, I set alarms on my phone for his upcoming feeds so I wouldn't lose track of time while I was cleaning and organizing. This was more for peace of mind than anything, I knew Ithuba wouldn't let me forget his feeds anyway.

While things were quiet for the rhino care, there was a lot to do in preparation for the arrival of the elephant calf so I pulled on my overalls, boots and a pair of disposable gloves and set to work disinfecting the intensive care unit. The ICU is situated next to the main preparation room ensuring it is quick and easy to make feeds or prepare medication for intensive cases. The larger preparation room was about four times the size of the clinic next to Ithuba's room, this extra space was going to be very useful as the elephant calf would be an 'all hands on deck' situation. After over an hour of scrubbing the floors, walls and protective floor matting of the ICU with disinfectant I hosed it all down and swept the excess water into the drains. The room was well and truly disinfected, but I needed to leave it to dry before putting the floor matting back in place so while the sun sped up that process I moved on to the next job on the to-do list. I had, very vaguely, written in capital letters "EQUIPMENT".

Sorting out the equipment meant making sure that everything the baby elephant and team would need was on hand, ready to be used. We didn't want to have to dig through the storeroom for equipment, so I needed to make sure it was in the preparation room already. I asked myself,

"What could this baby elephant need upon arrival?". The list was almost endless so I began to move the most important items such as drip bags, bandages, antiseptic solution, gloves, feeding equipment... and so on... from the storeroom to the shelves of the preparation room. I steam sterilized all the feeding equipment, boiled and cooled over ten litres of water ready for feeding the compromised calf and fitted a new bulb into the heat lamp of the ICU. As I looked around, I was satisfied I had covered all eventualities. I checked the clock and saw it was almost Ithuba's feeding time. Closing the preparation room door behind me, I walked the ten paces to the clinic.

"Hey 'Thubes! How's it going boy?" I called to him over the half door as I entered the clinic. Ithuba, who responded with a high-pitched squeal, had been snoozing in the sunshine and was now in his room waiting patiently for his milk. I took the bucket from the drying hook and filled it with warm water.

"It's coming boy!" I called as I measured the milk powder using the scoop, added in a pinch of probiotic and began to whisk the mixture. All the while, Ithuba softly cried on the other side of the door. He was listening to the whisk hitting the bucket and knew milk was on the way.

"Almost ready 'Thubes!!" I responded as I quickly poured the mixture into his feeding bottles. I pulled the teats over the bottle tops and went to the interlinking door that separated Ithuba and I. By this point, making milk was second nature and took mere minutes to prepare.

"Move back boy, let's go outside." I said as I nudged him back away from the door to give me enough space to get through. Unconvinced, he took the smallest step back, thinking about one thing and one thing only – milk. Once I squeezed myself through the tiny gap Ithuba had given me at the door, he opened his mouth and stepped towards me.

"Ha! You think I'm crazy enough to feed you in a corner?! Not a chance 'Thubes. Come on silly, let's go outside." I laughed as I walked ahead of him and he eagerly followed me outside.

Now by the trees, I stopped and turned to face Ithuba, who was right behind me with his mouth wide open. He glugged the milk enthusiastically as I gave him an update on the day so far. After a minute, all the milk was gone! It took no time at all for these hungry little rhinos to drink litres of milk. Satisfied, Ithuba lightly leant against me as I scratched his belly.

The feeds were always over in an instant, but I still loved them. They were a highlight; they broke up the day and gave you the chance to check in with the animals. I hadn't seen much of Ithuba that day, so I stayed for an extra five minutes giving him scratches before I left him to his own devices and went to wash up. With Ithuba fed and happy I could continue with the elephant preparations.

The ICU was now more or less dry, so I began to put the floor matting back in place. Putting the floor matting down was time consuming, the heavy squares needed to be hammered (or stomped) together as each block interlinked with the next until the room was covered. Dealing with the floor matting is usually a job for two of us and even then, we find it tedious. Once the floor matting was in place, I covered the room with a thick layer of straw bedding and with that, the ICU was ready for the elephant.

Feeling satisfied with the progress of the day I took a break to go up to the house and check in with Aly. After a few rings, the phone was answered,

"Hey Meg. How's it going?"

"All good here. Ithuba is great, he's being very independent today! The orphanage is so quiet without you guys here. All's good and the ICU is ready. How's the journey going?"

"It's long. We are probably about…", there was a brief pause as I heard Axel say '30 minutes' in the background, "30 minutes away from the reserve so it has taken a little longer than we thought to get there but we should be on our way back in about 45 minutes. I'm going to go in the back of the ambulance with the elephant on the way home and Axel will be driving."

"Okay, that's great. You're doing great you two! Is there anything else that needs to be done?" I asked.

"Oh! Actually! Can you take a look in the storeroom and see if we have any of this brand of milk powder…? I'll send you a picture of it. If not, we'll need to get someone to pick some up for us."

"Okay, send the picture and I'll look now. I'll see you later."

"Thanks Meg, see you soon!" Aly said as Axel yelled "See you later Meg!" in the background before the call went dead.

The picture came through immediately, but I was confident that we didn't have that particular milk in the storeroom. I went down to have a dig through our stock anyway just to double check. We couldn't feed the elephant the same milk formula that we feed the rhinos and while we kept a few different types of milk powder on hand just in case we were brought another species in an emergency, we didn't have the one we had been advised to feed the elephant. As we didn't have the milk powder in stock, we quickly arranged for some to be picked up by the experienced elephant carer who was arriving at the orphanage that afternoon to help us get the elephant settled.

Aly and Axel would only be arriving back in the late afternoon, by two p.m. I had finished my to-do list, so I went to the office to sort all the relevant paperwork for the elephant's arrival. Record keeping is an essential part of wildlife rehabilitation; records are kept for every individual animal and are used to note down everything from arrival information and body condition to details of food and medication given, behavioural observations and so much more. I put together a new record folder with daily feeding and observation sheets and, with the record folder in hand, I went back to the preparation room. After placing the folder onto the side with a couple of pens ready for later there was no more to do for the new arrival, so I went to see how Ithuba was doing.

With the sun still blazing, I pulled the hosepipe through the fence of Ithuba's enclosure and used it to top up his wallow. While Ithuba rolled around in the wallow, I sat under the trees in the enclosure watching the young rhino and reading the elephant care resources. I watched with a smile as Ithuba covered himself with mud, every now and then he would flick his tail or his ears and send splodges of mud flying everywhere. He managed to get me with a few blobs of mud too. As I watched him, I wondered how he was going to react to the newest addition to the orphanage. After reading over the materials a couple of times, I decided to do the night shift preparation. It was four hours earlier than usual, but I wanted everything to be ready for the rhino care that night. Once that was done, I couldn't think of anything else I could do so Ithuba and I sat in the sun together while I read about the challenges others had experienced when caring for orphaned elephants.

Knowing three of us would not be enough to juggle the increased workload about to be experienced, we had arranged for an additional team member to join us at the orphanage. By mid-afternoon, with bags of the special milk formula in hand, our new volunteer arrived on site (astonishingly beating the arrival of the elephant calf by a few hours!). It was quite something that not only were we lucky enough to have a South African contact who had previous experience with elephant calves but that they could also spend some time with us while we stabilised the elephant calf. With the milk powder now in the preparation room ready for feeding, everything was ready. Now all we could do was wait.

The ICU was ready, we were ready, and we were very eager to get the elephant to the warmth and safety of the orphanage. I regularly checked on Ithuba, he was now keeping himself busy with his log pile and the thuds of the logs tumbling to the ground could be heard all the way from the house. We watched from the veranda of the house as the sky transformed with streaks of red and the burning orange sun disappeared beyond the horizon. With the daylight disappearing I checked in with the team, Axel said they were coming off the tarred road and onto the dirt road which meant they were in for a slightly slower, bumpier ride for the final 30-45 minutes of the long, tiring journey.

Finally, in the dark of the late evening, the vehicle and trailer made its way through the gate. The deep growl of the generator used to power the heating within the ambulance could be heard before the glow of the headlights of the truck could be seen. The car slowly pulled up outside the intensive care unit as Axel positioned the trailer to offload the elephant. I stood back, trying to keep an eye on Ithuba as I knew the rumble of the generator was going to make him uneasy. With the doors of the ICU open and the trailer in place, we could offload the elephant. We honestly hadn't noticed the lack of an outside light until that exact moment, fortunately the light from the intensive care unit and preparation room spilled out onto the trailer so the area was just about well-lit enough for us to work safely.

Axel nodded to me as he unhooked the ambulance ramp and lowered it to the ground. We didn't need to discuss the plan because we all knew exactly what we were doing. I was standing close enough to help offload the elephant if needed but also in a position to comfort Ithuba through the unusual noise and activity that was around the ordinarily quiet orphanage. As I stood by I watched, unblinking, as Alyson walked the tiny, hip-high elephant (smaller than I had ever imagined an elephant could be) out of the trailer. He was unsteady on his feet and looked so frail.

The light was just bright enough to allow me to see the broader details of the elephant. Alyson and Axel were calmly guiding the baby elephant, directing him using their bodies as barriers. I stared as he shuffled down the ramp of the trailer and into the ICU. The elephant did not argue, he walked exactly where they guided him. The light encased him and despite the surrounding darkness I could see the fuzziness of his hair, his jiggling trunk, his ears pressed flat against his body… I watched in disbelief. It was as if I was daydreaming or watching a film, it didn't feel real. It was difficult to comprehend that this was happening, that this was our lives and how different they were about to become.

It was clear that this little elephant was no more than a couple of weeks old and was extremely weak and undernourished. To see an elephant of such a small size so close, so vulnerable, it was surreal. To see his every tired and heavy step and his wobbly trunk as he was led into the intensive care unit. I had to pinch myself. As I looked back at Ithuba - who was happily eating the green grass I had collected for him as a special treat - I knew that we had just reached the top of a rollercoaster that would take us on the craziest of rides.

7: I Am Me Because Of Us

The young elephant was securely in the Intensive Care Unit and Ithuba was now happily snoozing under his heat lamp so I locked the clinic, slipped the key into my pocket and went to the preparation room. As I quietly opened the door, Alyson was in the ICU carrying out a thorough health check of the elephant while Axel stood in the preparation room filling out the arrival forms with the details of the rescue and initial observations.

"How's he looking?" I asked as I approached Axel.

With a sigh, Axel replied,

"Not good, it looks like he has a bad infection in his umbilical area… He is really underweight and dehydrated but Aly managed to get him to drink some electrolytes so that's good."

It was troublesome news. The initial prognosis was bad, really bad. The health check notified us to a terrible umbilical infection and abscess. The open wound seeped with thick yellow pus and needed immediate attention. This infection was undoubtedly the reason the herd had left him. The fact that the infection was in the umbilical was even worse as it meant it was being carried throughout the elephants' whole body via the bloodstream. The odds were stacked against the elephant, his chances of survival were so slim they barely existed, but they did exist, so we had to try.

I peeked over the bottom half of the split stable-door between the preparation room and the ICU and saw a very desperate baby elephant. I could see it written all over his face, what he craved was not there in that room. He did not know what to do, he did not know where he was, he did not know if he was safe. He was terrified and it wouldn't have mattered how many people were in that room trying to comfort him, he was alone. His first night with us was going to be a long one. I made the young elephant a silent promise that we would be his family from now on and that we would love him unconditionally every single moment he was with us. The elephant, who was less than two weeks old, was named 'Ubuntu'.

Ubuntu is an African word that means humanity towards others, it describes a quality that includes the essential human virtues; compassion and humanity. To me the word Ubuntu means connectedness, family, everyone coming together and being their best selves for a cause.

"I am me because of us".

As much as we loved the name and the meaning behind it, we couldn't help but call the young elephant Ellie. It felt like he would need to grow into the name Ubuntu. The nickname stuck and to me, he will always be Ellie (or El for short).

As we worked to get Ellie stabilised, hydrated and warm, the hours passed by as if they were minutes. In order to help settle Ellie's stomach, we began offering him small amounts of electrolytes every 30 – 60 minutes. The electrolytes were to get the elephant hydrated and replace the fluids he was losing through diarrhoea. Unfortunately for us, the young elephant didn't seem to like the electrolytes. Although extremely beneficial, electrolytes tend to taste salty and Ellie wasn't keen on the flavour. We knew we had some other electrolytes stored away so Axel and I dug around in the storeroom to see what we could find while Aly kept Ellie company in the ICU. After a few minutes of searching, we came across a cardboard box filled with a variety of electrolyte flavours and brands and in anticipation of Ellie's fussiness, we took the whole box to the preparation room.

Now at each feed we offered Ellie a different flavour or brand of electrolytes until we found one he liked (or at least one that he hated less). Every hour we would mix the electrolytes with warm water and offer it to Ellie. Before we knew it, it was the dead of night and the stars were glistening high in the sky. With everyone so busy with Ellie and it almost being time for Ithuba's next feed, I went to the clinic for the rest of the nightshift with Ithuba. I spent the whole night thinking about little Ellie, I could feel his desperation and I wished I could take that feeling away for him. As I settled in to spend the remainder of the night with Ithuba, I looked over the door at the young rhino, he was sleeping blissfully under the red glow of the heat lamp. I hoped one day El would be doing the same, with the same level of contentment. The nightshift with Ithuba went by without issue and before I knew it, dawn was breaking.

As the sunrise filled the sky with mellow shades of pink, Ithuba was eager to go out to play and explore the fresh morning smells and I was eager to see Ellie. With Ithuba outside and not due another feed for several hours, I cleaned the clinic, put away the night shift equipment and refilled the milk powder jug for the day's feeds. I knew we had a demanding day ahead of us, so I wanted to make sure we had everything we needed clean and ready for Ithuba's care.

Our weekends at the orphanage were usually very quiet and relaxed. Despite there being no real difference between the weekends and weekdays in terms of workload, there was still a different feeling to the weekends. I can't quite explain it, when the weekends came around it just felt as if everything was slowed down. Maybe it was because we would rarely hear from the outside world at weekends so there were no external pressures on our team. This Saturday was going to be very different. It was going to be far from quiet, of that I had no doubt. With everything clean and organised in the clinic and Ithuba outside enjoying his dry food, I went to my room to change my clothes. As soon as I was in clean clothes, I went to see Ellie.

"Morning guys." I said as I entered the preparation room where the team stood, quietly conversing,

"How's it going?". I asked as I looked over the door to see Ellie pacing the room with heavy, wobbly steps.

"Urgh. No changes. He didn't sleep, he drank only a small amount of electrolytes but not much. He doesn't want to drink, he is fighting with us." Axel sighed deeply, standing next to me and looking over the door at the baby elephant.

"He's been really unsettled but if we can carry on getting him to drink small amounts regularly then we are on the right track at least." Aly added.

"Why don't you go in and say hello to him Meg." Aly said encouragingly, smiling despite the difficult night they had experienced. Each time I had popped in during the early hours of the morning, everyone was wide awake. Whether they were mixing more electrolytes, cleaning diarrhoea or trying to convince Ellie to drink, they were busy. It was a demanding first night and it showed in the dark rings around the team's eyes. I'd been desperate to properly introduce myself to the tiny elephant from the moment he'd toddled out of the ambulance the previous evening, but I kept back as I hadn't wanted to overwhelm him when there was already so much going on. Now, it was time, I unhooked the door and slowly swung it open,

"Hey boy, it's ok, I'm just coming to say hello.". I spoke softly so he wouldn't panic or get a fright. His big brown eyes were watching me from behind those long eyelashes. The eyelashes of an elephant. The light shade of pink that encircled his eyes and bordered his ears were an indication of his young age. He did not move, he simply watched me intensely as I approached him. I stepped forward, the straw bedding crunching underfoot with each step I took. I walked slowly, cautiously. I couldn't wrap my head around what was happening, I was introducing myself to a baby elephant. Better yet, he was introducing himself to me.

As I closed the distance between us, Ellie began to walk towards me. The elephant shuffled through the bedding, smelling the air as he went. Due to his young age, he did not have much control over his trunk yet but he was trying his best. As Ellie walked towards me his steps were short, shallow but almost excited. Like me, the elephant was inquisitive and wanted to say hello. Within seconds he was standing in front of me, an

African Elephant - the world's largest land mammal - except this one still had a lot of growing to do… The top of his head barely reached the height of my hips.

"Hello, little one…" I said, looking down at the tiny, underweight elephant who was now mere centimetres away from me. I admired him, I had never been so close to an elephant before and I felt utterly transfixed in the moment.

I could see now that the delicate, light shade of pink was not only around his eyes and ears but also around his mouth, the underside of his trunk and between his front legs, I had never seen anything like it. This alone showed how young he was, he was born no more than two weeks ago. The rest of him was a dark shade of brown and he was covered in a light brown fuzz. Who'd have thought baby elephants were fuzzy? His deep brown eyes had a baby blue ring around them and each eyelash was at least four times longer than the length of a human eyelash with the odd one even thicker and longer. The elephant's skin was dry and his ears were wrinkled, a sign of dehydration. His cheekbones, spine and hips were prominent – showing that he had not been well for some time. A healthy elephant calf has chubby, round cheeks but this little elephant had likely been sick since shortly after birth. I gently placed my hand on him as he lifted his trunk, inhaling my scent and deciding what to make of me. I slowly moved my hand along his side, stroking him softly and talking to him in a gentle tone.

My fingers passed over his skin, to my surprise it felt completely different to a rhino's skin. The young elephant was covered from head to toe with about one inch of fuzzy hair and it gave him an almost woolly appearance when you looked at him in the right light. This hair made him feel wiry in places… I was fascinated. My eyes studied him, there was so much I had not realised about newborn baby elephants. His large ears were pressed firmly against his body. His ears at their widest point went over his shoulder blades, and in total they covered around a third of his body. As I traced his ears with my hand, I felt the underside of them and was surprised by the smooth skin under my fingertips, the underside of his ears felt almost like cling film that has been pulled tight.

"Hey Ellie…", I said with a smile. He lifted his trunk up to me, pausing for a moment to rest on my hip bone before continuing, pressing the triangular tip of his trunk against my stomach. I could feel the warmth of his breath through my t-shirt as he was smelling me. He was trying to figure me out and I couldn't help but laugh. The gentleness of the touch tickled through the t-shirt and for a second, I could think of nothing else but how ludicrous the situation was. I laughed and I don't think anything could've wiped the smile from my face.

"Hello little elephant", I smiled to him as I touched his fuzzy forehead and ran my fingers across his cheek. I felt completely relaxed as I crouched down in front of him, coming down to his level. He rested his trunk on my shoulder and his eyes locked with mine. The elephant's expressive eyes spoke a thousand words; they were so communicative that the thoughts translated across species. In that moment, I knew this was the beginning of a beautiful friendship. No matter how hard it was going to be to take care of Ellie, I was always going to remember how full my heart felt as we met for the very first time.

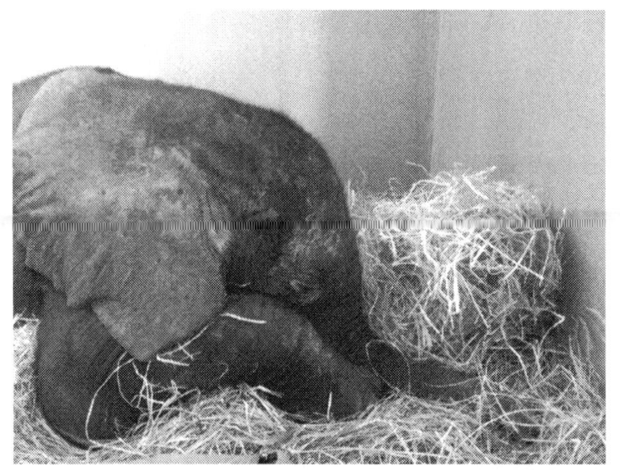

8: The New Normal

It turns out caring for a baby elephant is a colossal challenge and a complete contrast to caring for a rhino. After Ellie's arrival, we worked around the clock trying to stabilize him and get him through the nights. It was stressful beyond belief. We had a few extra pairs of hands helping with the milk mixing and care while we tried to get Ellie stable but even with the additional help, our team hardly slept. Ellie was so fragile, so sick, so desperate and we were doing everything possible to help him, but we feared it would not be enough. There was immense pressure and strain on our shoulders as we desperately tried to get this tiny baby elephant through this vulnerable period. With Ellie unable to communicate to us what the problems were, we had to do the best we could from our assessments and health checks but it felt like there were so many contributing factors, so many unknowns and so few answers. No day was guaranteed, and we knew this all too well.

We were battling against Ellie's infection, diarrhoea and his unwillingness to drink. When it came to feeding time, we never knew what to expect. For some feeds, Ellie would take a few sips before spitting the teat out of his mouth, while for others, he would turn away the moment we offered it to him. We tried to have two of us there for each feed because every attempt was a challenge. Even though he was small, Ellie was very strong and he struggled to find a position he liked drinking from so each feed we would have to stand in different ways, feed him from different angles and ultimately, try to find a way of feeding that was comfortable for Ellie. We would also try changing the mixtures, the bottles, the teats, whatever we could do to find something that worked better. Each feed would consist of a lot of spillages and a huge amount of being pushed around the room - it was surprising and quite unexpected how strong the young elephant was for such a small, emaciated calf.

The experience of feeding Ellie was completely different to feeding Ithuba, or any rhino for that matter. A baby elephant will stand almost underneath the mother and will often have their trunk resting up against their mother's side while they suckle from her, every now and then they'll nudge the mum to try to get more milk. The sturdiness of the mum allows the baby elephant to push and lean on them however they feel comfortable. To an elephant mum (being so big and strong) the pushes of a baby such as young Ellie are next to nothing, but to us, it's a different story. Being pushed by a baby elephant is like having a very burly person forcefully shoving you repeatedly. At times, Ellie would even lean his head heavily into us and push himself up onto his hind legs so he could use all his might to push into us. It was physically exhausting to try to brace ourselves against the pushes of the young elephant and our bodies were quickly becoming battered and bruised.

Feeding a rhino would never involve any pushing like this, once a baby rhino begins to suckle on the teat, they drink in big slurps until all the milk is gone. The rhino calves would stand more or less on the same spot for the whole feed, even if you had more than one bottle to feed them they'd wait for you to switch bottles and then carry on drinking. You wouldn't have to fight with a rhino or stand your ground while they push up against you to drink, so when Ellie was pushing and shoving during feeding time it came as a great surprise to us. Each hourly feed became a test of strength and resilience for our team, that's why we tried to have two of us on hand so we could share the task.

Throughout the first night, the team had managed to get Ellie to drink small amounts regularly. We had decided to continue offering electrolytes throughout the morning. In a much-needed breakthrough, we found out that our little elephant preferred the orange flavoured electrolytes. This revelation made our lives slightly easier as El would be more willing to drink the orange flavoured electrolytes and this meant he'd drink it with less pushing and less fuss. We were astounded when during a feed on Saturday morning, Ellie finished a full 500ml of orange flavoured electrolytes in just a few hearty slurps. Aly and I grinned at each other and praised Ellie for the feed, hoping this was the first of many successful feeds.

This small but significant breakthrough brought a new lease of life to our worn-out team, we had found something our agitated little elephant liked. Not only this, for the time being, we had found a way that El was willing to drink full feeds. With the bottle of orange electrolytes in hand, whoever was feeding had to crouch down facing away from Ellie and offer him the bottle over their shoulder so he could lean against them while he drank… It sounds strange, it felt strange too but, bizarrely, it worked! At this point, we would do whatever the little elephant wanted if it would get him to drink. We were entirely at his mercy. With this new unorthodox feeding position combined with the orange flavoured electrolytes, our elephant had started to drink full feeds with a lot less pushing. It was such a huge relief to have Ellie drinking his electrolytes and now we could begin to focus on the other issues.

Ellie's first 24 hours with us were dedicated to getting him hydrated and comfortable. We wanted to get him used to drinking from a bottle as quickly as we could as he needed the hydration, energy and nutrition the feeds would give him. Ellie was very wobbly and unstable on his feet; he didn't have much strength and he was very unsettled. We had managed to get Ellie drinking the orange electrolytes and by late Saturday morning, we started to offer him a diluted milk mixture.

A few times a day we would clean the tiny elephant's umbilical wound. The infection was likely the reason Ellie was abandoned by his herd. Ellie's umbilical area was very sensitive so while me or Axel would try to distract him, Aly would flush and clean the wound then apply an antiseptic solution to help it heal. Ellie hated when we would do this, he would scream at us and try to move away but we needed to clean the wound to help him fight the infection and, ultimately, help him get better. He would scream because he didn't know how to trumpet yet. Although the little elephant was resistant to us cleaning the area, after a few days of treatment I think he began to realise why we were doing it. With regular cleaning, the umbilical wound, abscess and infection was beginning to show signs of healing.

As the days rolled into one another we remained strong for the tiny elephant. Our bodies were bruised, and we were usually covered in milk as we pushed through each day. El was drinking the feeds we made for him, but it was a battle. He no longer liked to drink over our shoulders (the magic of that wore off after half a day) and we were back to trying new feeding positions. We were living on next to no sleep; the three of us and a handful of volunteers worked all day, every day. Aly, Axel and I rotated on a three-day night shift cycle. Two of the nights would be taken up with Ellie shifts where we'd get a maximum of three hours of sleep and the third night would be caring for Ithuba. The nightshift with Ithuba was a welcome break that would give us a much more generous broken sleep of between six and eight hours. Looking after Ithuba gave us some much-needed respite, it was a shift we all looked forward to.

It wasn't just physical exhaustion our team were dealing with; we were also mentally exhausted. We were desperately trying to think of new ways to get this young elephant through some of the worst days of his life. If Ellie did not have a will to live then he wouldn't survive and we knew it. We needed to keep him happy, keep him busy, keep him from feeling lonely. We needed him to know he was part of a herd while also not letting him become too attached to just one of us because then he could become distressed if that person was not around. It was a balancing act, as if we were spinning plates trying to keep any one of them from hurtling to the ground and smashing.

Each day we would find new things to keep the young elephant occupied; with Ellie now drinking his feeds and getting to know us better we began taking him for walks and letting him explore different areas. We'd play together and he'd practice using his trunk. Being so young, Ellie couldn't grab or pinch things with his trunk yet. It took a lot of thought and effort for him to reach out and touch something with the tip of his trunk. He still had so much to learn, at only a couple of weeks old he was still a newborn finding his feet in this world.

The first week went by in a blur; we continued to clean Ellie's wounds, persuade him to drink milk and build a bond with him. As we passed the one-week mark, we allowed ourselves a rare moment to breathe and celebrate the successes. We had been so busy, so focused on getting the young elephant through each day, searching desperately for answers and now we were starting to see glimmers of hope. As Aly and Axel leant against the worktop in the preparation room and I stood in the ICU leaning on the half door, we had a team catch up and exchanged words of encouragement. Although we saw each other all day, every day, things had been so busy we didn't really have a chance to talk properly. Our eyes were bloodshot, our hair messy and our half-smiles weary.

"He's drinking better now and at least the infection is clearing up. I looked at it this morning and it's looking loads better." Aly said encouragingly.

"That's fantastic!! Do we need to clean it again at the next feed? He is definitely getting a lot more comfortable with us too!" I replied, stifling a yawn.

"Yeah, let's clean it again and then that'll be good until this evening. You can see its healing and feeling better as he is a lot less stressed about us treating it now." Aly paused for a moment, "He is more settled but it's not stopping him from pushing us around at feeding time… Do you guys have bruises from him too?" She said as she lightly touched her legs.

"Oh my goodness, YES!! My thighs and stomach are so sore and sensitive. I'm more bruise than anything else right now…" I laughed.

"Oooo!" Axel suddenly exploded into life, "Let's get an exercise ball out for him!! Maybe he'll play with that then he can stop pushing us around so much!" Axel grinned and nothing else needed to be said. We all beamed as Axel went to get one of the exercise balls from the storeroom. As Axel and Aly pulled the big grey ball from its packaging and used the hand pump to inflate it. I opened the barrier of the ICU and walked Ellie onto the grass outside. In that moment, we had forgotten how our muscles ached, how heavy our eyes were and the stress on our shoulders. For that brief moment in time, we were celebrating the wins and playing with the elephant we were working tirelessly to save.

"Look Ellie!! We have a new toy for you!!" Axel said energetically, rolling the ball towards him. The large exercise ball was something that you'd more likely see at a gym or yoga studio than at a wildlife rehabilitation centre but Ellie couldn't resist it. It was about the same size as him and as it rolled towards him, he charged at the ball, pushing against it with his forehead. As the exercise ball began to roll away, you could almost see Ellie's mind working as he saw the potential of the new toy. He pushed the bouncy ball along with his forehead, and then as it began to gather momentum and roll away from him. Ellie would trip over himself trying to catch up with it and stop it with his trunk. As he didn't have much control of his trunk this was very amusing to watch. Once he managed to stop it, he tried to throw his front legs up to climb on top of the ball. We were all laughing watching Ellie enjoy the new toy. We pushed the ball around and watched Ellie run after it. We ran, rolling the exercise ball and laughing heartily as Ellie played enthusiastically, so full of life.

Our little elephant was very goofy, he remained unsure on his feet so when he would run it looked like he was running downhill and he couldn't quite keep up with himself, similar to how a young child looks when they tackle a hill that's far too steep for them. Ellie's trunk would be flying all over the place, his ears flapping in the wind and he'd be almost falling over his own feet while the ball rolled away a few inches in front of him. It was such fun, a reminder of why the orphanage existed and why we were working so hard. Ellie was running around and having fun with his whole human herd around him. Our smiles were genuine and we were loving every minute of the games. Although we knew there was still so much stacked against this little elephant and against our team, we hoped this light-hearted afternoon under the clear blue sky was a sign of things to come.

9: Finding A Formula

Ellie was coming on in leaps and bounds, he was feeling more comfortable and would always be found at one of our sides. When walking together, he'd often reach out and touch the back of my legs for reassurance. Sometimes, I would walk with one hand behind my back and every so often I'd crouch down so he could reach my hand with his trunk. Elephants are very tactile and these seemingly insignificant touches meant a lot to Ellie.

Although things were going well, we urgently needed to find a milk formula that suited Ellie. The formula we had been recommended was not helping with the little elephant's stomach issues and it needed to be changed for us to have long-term success raising Ellie. Unfortunately, finding a suitable milk formula was not going to be as easy to solve as the electrolytes situation.

First of all, we did not have a storeroom full of different brands and flavours of elephant-appropriate milk formulas to take advantage of. We started off with a recommended formula that other elephant orphanages use but not only did it not work for our little elephant, it worsened his diarrhoea. Needless to say, this was extremely problematic for our already complicated situation. Once we gave the formula a chance to work and saw no improvements, we tried another formula and then another. With every new mix we tried, we were hopeful for promising results but nothing seemed to work. With such a compromised immune system and with his weight so low we didn't have much time to find a formula that suited our elephant. We were trying our best to save him, but he was teetering on the edge. It was one thing getting the milk formula into him but getting it to stay in his system long enough for him to get the nutrients he needed was another issue in itself. We had a milk formula shipped to us from another African elephant orphanage, but this too caused worse diarrhoea, we once again found ourselves back at the drawing board. The situation was extremely troubling as nothing was working. It wasn't making any sense, all the formulas that should have worked for him were making him worse. After again consulting with our wildlife vet and talking to experienced elephant rehabilitators, the only explanation we could come up with was that our little elephant was allergic to something in the formulas.

While we continued to search through our dwindling options to find something to feed our potentially allergic elephant, we decided to begin making him a vegetable stew in the meantime. The new vegetable stew diet meant one of us had to drive the 45 minutes to our closest town to buy some fresh food. This was a good thing as our fridge was looking very empty so this was an opportunity to restock our supplies too. After feeding Ithuba his 10am feed, Aly took the pickup truck and went into town to do the shopping. This drive into town was one of the few opportunities for us to have a break from the intensity of the orphanage.

While Aly was on the town run, Axel and I played games with Ellie on the open grass of the orphanage garden. Ellie loved spending time in the garden and he loved to run. Axel and I pushed the grey exercise ball between each other while El chased it around. When we held it still, Ellie would push into the ball with his forehead and then throw his legs up to clamber over it. If anyone ever crouched down near El, he would immediately try to climb onto them. While playing, Ellie would flare his ears out, hold his tail rigid and hold his head up. We were already starting to see the little elephant's personality and it was easy to forget how young he was. Something that would remind us that Ellie was only a few weeks old would be when he would hold his trunk in his mouth and gently suck it, something that gave him comfort like a child sucking their thumb.

El's umbilical infection had cleared, and we were applying ointment each day to ensure it remained clean and free from infection while it healed. We were also regularly cleaning his ears and we were applying an aqueous cream mixture to his skin to stop it from getting dry. This was all helping

Ellie to feel better. Despite the diarrhoea and everything he had been through; this little elephant was a fighter. Ellie had a clear desire for life and a will to live that was unfaltering. He was not going to give up, and we would not give up on him.

At around one p.m., Aly returned with bags of groceries,

"Town was packed!!" Aly said while grabbing bags out of the truck, "I got everything on the list, and I went to the chemist to get more orange electrolytes and a few other bits for Ellie so we should be stocked up for at least the next week…"

"Perfect! Look at all these vegetables!! Ellie better appreciate this new mixture." I smiled while carrying bags filled with fresh vegetables into the kitchen. I placed the bags onto the countertop and turned to go back outside. On my way back to the truck I was met at the front door by a very determined little elephant.

"Oh! Hey boy." I said, but without greeting me Ellie nudged into my legs as if to say, "excuse me, you're in my way!".

"Woah. Where do you think you're going?!" I asked as he tried to push past me.

"You want to go inside? Not a chance! You are an outside elephant. Turn your butt around." I stood my ground as I pulled the front door closed behind me. Now Ellie stood there trying to push his way into the house.

"Come on El, let's go see what Ithuba is up to." I said as I nudged him away from the door and began to walk away from the house. As I looked over my shoulder Ellie was just a couple of steps behind me. We walked down to the poles of Ithuba's outside enclosure and watched as 'Thubes lazed in his mud wallow. Despite all the recent changes, Ithuba was doing very well and was happy to be independent most the day. As long as he had his milk feeds, his dry food and a muddy wallow to roll in, Ithuba was happy. Ellie pressed his face up against the enclosure poles as he watched Ithuba inquisitively. I think the little elephant wanted Ithuba to come over and say hello but once he realised that wasn't going to happen we left 'Thubes to it and went to explore elsewhere. The pair were yet to meet but were aware of each other's presence.

By mid-afternoon the new mix was ready: this mix was a selection of fresh vegetables that we chopped, boiled and blended with a few extra vitamins, minerals and probiotics. Ellie's stew took far longer to prepare than any milk mixture but when it was finally ready, it smelt divine. I could've happily dug into the stew myself. We poured some into a bottle, pulled a teat over the bottle neck and offered it to our hungry little elephant.

"Look Ellie, a delicious new mix!! Are you going to try some?" Aly held the bottle in her hand letting El smell it with his trunk. Then he nudged forwards, lifting his trunk up and opening his mouth.

"What a good boy! Here, have a few sips… We made this specially for you…" Aly put the bottle into Ellie's mouth, and he began to slurp. To our delight, he glugged down the first few hundred millilitres with minimal pushing.

"Aly, that was amazing!! He actually likes it!!" I grinned before turning my attention to Ellie, "Was that delicious El? We'll have that for the next little while, shall we? It'll help you grow big and strong!" I said while giving him lots of fuss after the successful feed. At the next feed, he drank even more. Despite each feeding time being a test of strength and patience, the hard work was paying off. Ellie was drinking the electrolytes and he was drinking the formula we were offering. We knew this formula would require adaptations but for now it was enough. It was enough to buy us the time we needed.

With El drinking the vegetable stew, we'd been able to have a few days of focussing on bonding more closely with him and we could see things were moving in the right direction. The vegetable stew formula was perfect for giving us short-term respite, but we still needed to find a long-term solution. We finally hit the breakthrough we needed when we tried a simple rice mix. The base of the mix was cooked rice and we added coconut and a mixture of other goodness into it, blended it up into a "milk" and offered it to Ellie. He seemed to like the new concoction and best of all, it seemed to work for him. After a few days on this new formula and a couple of tweaks we knew this was the mixture the little elephant would thrive on. Although it was not a conventional mixture, it worked, and it provided Ellie with the nutrients and energy he needed. The rice mix helped with settling his sensitive stomach and thankfully the watery diarrhoea he had been suffering with since his arrival finally began to dissipate. Although we still had a long way to go, we took great comfort in the progress our baby elephant was making.

We were getting to know Ellie's personality as he became increasingly playful and cheeky. He loved to be social, he always wanted to be where the "herd" was. Ellie had no problem walking away from the person looking after him to join others as he saw them walking across the grass to feed Ithuba or do something not related to Ellie's care. Ellie just wanted to be involved, like a little kid who's always asking questions,

"Whatcha doing??? Where are you going??? Can I come???". Every time I'd go to see him after being away doing something else, he'd toddle over at speed, rumbling receptively and waving his trunk in the air like he hadn't seen me in days when it had really only been about an hour. Ellie was quickly becoming quite the character.

Walks around the orphanage grounds were a big highlight for Ellie, he loved to walk along the dirt, smelling the path and touching plants with his trunk. Once he was stronger, we would start taking him out into the reserve to explore, but for now the orphanage provided enough to keep him occupied. He enjoyed pushing and chasing the large grey exercise ball around the garden and he loved to climb over us when we'd be sitting or crouching on the ground. Ellie's cheekiness was becoming more and more vibrant as he began to feel better. If we stood still for any length of time,

Ellie would find a nearby stick and practice grasping and lifting, curling his trunk around the stick and raising it up to his mouth. He still had much to learn, he was getting much better with lifting and touching things with his trunk and that would continue to develop as he grew. Ellie was gaining confidence and was endlessly inquisitive. Whenever he ran it seemed as though his legs were going faster than he'd anticipated although this did not stifle the young elephant's enthusiasm and he took great pleasure in running around, playing games and learning how to be an elephant.

As Ellie was underweight we would cover him with a blanket during the colder hours of the day. Ellie had a large stack of blankets ready to keep him warm and we would always be washing used blankets to ensure he'd never run out. My favourite of all El's blankets was a knitted patchwork one, it was full of colour and kept El toasty warm. We'd lay the blanket across his back and place his ears over the top so he wouldn't overheat. There was no denying that our little elephant looked unbelievably cute as he shuffled around the orphanage with his legs poking out from the bottom of a patchwork blanket, his tail poking out from the back and his big ears resting over the top.

10: Snuggles, Sleep and Snoring

With Ellie becoming stronger, this meant his body felt as though he was now able to deal with issues that had been previously suppressed. Up until this point Ellie had been in "survival mode", his body had been focussed purely on survival rather than healing. Now, the true impact of the infection in his body was beginning to show, small black dots were appearing on the underside of his large ears and he developed white blisters under his tongue. The infection had travelled throughout his whole body and it was taking its toll. With the infection making itself clear to us, our local wildlife vet arrived to assess Ellie's progress and help us treat the infection. The wound care on his umbilical area had been effective, the abscess had now gone and the open wound was almost completely closed. Ellie had completed a course of antibiotics, but it was clear the internal infection was still raging through his compromised body. After assessing Ellie and reviewing his symptoms, the wildlife vet injected a dose of antibiotics. As the needle punctured Ellie's rump he let out a scream, very unimpressed by the unexpected actions of the vet.

"It's ok boy. Just a little sting, don't worry… It'll help you feel better." I said, rubbing Ellie's side while he tried to hide behind me. Although he hated the injection, it was over in a second and the dose of antibiotics should help rid El of the infection. Ellie's increased energy levels and his obvious will to live was very reassuring, it gave our team hope.

With the vet visit done and dusted, it was now early afternoon and Ellie watched as his blankets were hung out on the washing line to dry. He ran over eagerly, wanting to play. The inquisitive elephant instantly put his trunk into the washing basket and began pushing it across the grass. He enjoyed playing with the blankets that were suspended in the air above him too, trying to hold his trunk up to grab them and running beneath them as they lightly skimmed his back. El played even more vigorously as he tried to run away with a blanket and a tug of war broke out between us. Ellie loved these games, he managed to make a game out of everything and playing was helping him to gain strength and get used to using his trunk. Once he became bored of playing with the washing and had finished smudging mud onto the clean sheets that had been put out to dry, Ellie decided to walk around the garden and enjoy all the different smells of the plants. With playtime over, I swapped with one of the volunteers who were helping so Alyson, Axel and I could get to work with the mammoth task of cleaning Ellie's room.

We got into overalls and wellington boots, put on face masks and pulled the floor matting up so we could pressure hose and disinfect the whole room. The mixture of spilled milk and other fluids under the floor matting was disgusting. As Ellie was spending time outside, had just drank a full feed and was showing no signs of wanting to come back in we jumped at the opportunity to give the room a clean. The combination of smells emanating from the floor was becoming nauseating and there was no way we could do another night in that room without disinfecting it. This task was one of the only times we made use of the white dust face masks that covered our noses and mouths, and even they did not do much to help the situation. Once we'd pulled the floor mats out, Axel got to work disinfecting and pressure hosing the matting outside while Aly and I tackled cleaning the floor inside. Although we were used to cleaning up after animals, Ellie's room was in a league of its own. Seeing the white bubbles of the disinfectant as we enthusiastically scrubbed gave me a strange level of satisfaction and once the whole room – walls and all – were thoroughly cleaned, we left the solution to work its magic for ten minutes before washing it away. Stepping outside and taking off our face masks we breathed in the fresh, cool air, it was satisfying after an hour of stuffy, sweaty and muffled breath. Axel had just about finished pressure washing the floor matting so we all took a break, sitting on the grass for a few minutes. We did not want to sit down for too long because there was a risk we'd not want to get back up or worse, fall asleep!

"That room was in such a state. It actually made me feel a bit sick at first." I commented, immediately regretting bringing it up as I felt my stomach turn again.

"Who'd have thought a little elephant, so small like that, could cause such mess!!!" Axel remarked, putting his hand to his forehead before saying

"Oooh la la, Ellie, what a mess." in his strong French accent. This made Aly and I start laughing, catching the joy in each other's eyes caused the three of us to laugh even more.

After a few minutes of chatting on the grass, we prepared ourselves to finish cleaning the room. As Aly hosed the room down and I brushed the water into the drains, we heard a volunteer shouting in the distance,

"Ellie's coming! Ellie's coming!!!".

We were a little confused about this distant shouting but upon poking our heads out of the door, we saw little Ellie sprinting towards us as fast as his legs would take him. He was running down the hill with his ears flapping and his trunk wobbling. Through our laughter, we quickly closed the barrier to the room so he couldn't come in until we had finished cleaning. When Ellie reached the barrier and saw he couldn't come into the room, he decided to trot over to Axel and start playing with him instead. While Axel kept Ellie distracted, Aly and I put the floor matting back into the intensive care unit. Once the mattresses (we had started using mattresses instead of straw bedding for Ellie) and a bowl of clean water were back in place we opened the barrier to let the inquisitive elephant back in. It was so satisfying for his room to be spotless but we knew it would be only a few days before we had to pressure clean it all over again.

Ellie wasn't hungry or wanting to go to bed when he ran down to us, he was simply being cheeky and wanted to see what we were doing in his room without him. Now his room was clean and he'd spent 30 minutes playing around with Axel, Ellie was becoming sleepy so I offered him some milk and then took him into his beautifully clean room. I closed the barrier and sat leaning against the wall as El walked around, touching everything with his trunk as he went. Every now and then he would walk past me so I held my hand out and let his body brush against it as he passed. Eventually, Ellie stopped and stood still, his eyes were getting too heavy for him to keep open and the end of his trunk now rested on the floor.

Generally, Ellie would not want to lay down to sleep, instead he would doze off while standing. His legs would lock, his trunk would rest on the ground and his eyes would slowly close. As he'd fall into a deeper sleep his head would nod causing him to wake up again. This happened time and time again, but the little elephant did not want to lay down to sleep. If El was a rhino I'd have just given him belly scratches until he couldn't resist laying down, but he wasn't a rhino and as we were learning, dealing with an elephant is a completely different ball game. I sighed as I sat leaning against the wall of the ICU and watched Ellie once again drift off to sleep while standing up.

"Hey El, you think it's maybe time for a snooze?" I asked, patting the mattress beside me in encouragement.

"If you go to sleep now then we won't worry about your next feed and you can just have a good rest? Come on, I know you're not really a fan of feeding time yet." I negotiated.

"We've had a busy day El, I'll nap with you."

He was becoming overtired but he didn't want to lay down and sleep. As Ellie continued to stand and doze, I got up and stood next to him, talking to him and stroking his weary body. Slowly, he leaned into my legs, gradually pushing all his weight into me as he drifted to sleep only to wake again a minute later. El did this a few times, continuing to lean against me as he slept. As I couldn't hold Ellie's weight up with my legs, when he woke up again I moved the mattresses and made him a comfy spot next to me in the hope it would encourage him to lay down and have a proper sleep.

I sat down close to where we were standing and encouraged Ellie the few steps over to me. To my surprise, he dragged his tired body towards me, each step dragging a little more than the last and when he reached the newly positioned mattresses, he plonked himself down almost on top of me! I couldn't believe it. We had watched him stand and snooze again and again but now he finally felt comfortable enough to relax, lay down and sleep properly. It was such a relief. Now, Ellie was laying almost on top of me and he fell asleep instantly. I was so shocked that I held my breath for a few moments, terrified of disturbing him as he drifted to sleep. It was amazing to sit with El and admire him as he slept. I put my arm over the tiny elephant and lent back against the wall. Ten minutes later, Aly came to check on us and couldn't believe it when she saw Ellie was laying down in a deep sleep.

"Yay!!" Aly mouthed to me with a big grin, "call me if you need anything." She whispered before sneaking away as quietly as possible. As Ellie slept peacefully, I looked down at him and observed his features. His crinkly ears, the lines and little bumps on the underside of his trunk, the pink colour around his eyes and mouth… I looked at his feet, they were slightly smaller than my hands and were completely flat with four large toenails on his front feet and three on his back feet. He didn't have toes like us or like the rhinos, an elephant's feet are completely round with toenails sitting along the edge like little shields that look as though they are protecting areas of the foot more than individual toes. This means the tracks of an elephant are simple and round with no obvious toes visible. They are truly amazing animals and I couldn't believe I was sitting with my arm around a baby elephant.

From that day on, Ellie and I had reached a new level in our relationship. He now saw me as a source of comfort. He'd decided that he felt comfortable with me and that he trusted me. He'd now lay down and fall asleep resting on me when he felt tired. He could be agitated, fighting with everyone and showing no signs of going to sleep (despite his obvious tiredness), then I'd go and sit in his room to talk to him and comfort him. Without hesitation, he would come over to me, put his trunk on me and he'd calm down. Something had clicked and it was amazing, as though he was now using me as a comfort blanket or a night light… As though he now saw me as family. Whenever he was really tired or really agitated, I was able to be there and help him. While sleeping by my side, every ten minutes or so Ellie's eyes would slowly open as his trunk would reach up and gently touch my face.

"I'm still here boy, don't worry. Go back to sleep." I'd reassure him as he'd look up at me with sleepy eyes and lightly touch my cheek with his trunk. His trunk would then gently fall back to the floor and his soft snoring would start again.

One night Ellie rolled up his trunk while he was asleep and the rhythmic sound of breathing turned into colossal snoring. It was two in the morning and quite frankly I was worried the whole orphanage was going to wake up. After watching in amazement for a few seconds, bewildered at how this little, pink, fuzzy elephant could produce such an astonishingly loud noise I unravelled his trunk so he could breathe easily and sleep quietly again. It happened a handful of times when he was in the deepest of sleeps, such a deep sleep that he wouldn't even wake up when I was lifting and repositioning his trunk! I remember just looking down at Ellie and laughing, his forehead pressed against my thigh, his trunk curled into a perfect swirl under his chin and with every exhale a noise similar to an idling tractor boomed through the room.

11: Falling Apart

Every day with Ellie was a challenge but every day was a joy too. Our orphanage was positioned in the middle of a game reserve, the reserve had wild rhinos and elephants roaming its land and, if we are being perfectly honest, the fence that was erected a week after my arrival would've been ineffective had a rhino or elephant truly wanted to come in. The elephant herd were around, I'd seen them almost every day for the past couple of weeks. I had been living at the orphanage for months and I'd seen the elephants from our grounds just a handful of times. Since the day after Ellie arrived, they were always within viewing distance, never too close but I'd see them. I was sure they knew there was something going on and they wanted to keep an eye on us, keep an eye on Ellie. I have no doubt El would've loved for them to come and get him, but he would've died out there with his health the way it was, hell, if he was in good health I would've probably tried to get the wild herd to adopt him myself.

With the minimal sleep and physically demanding workload it was undeniable that we needed more people to help balance the jobs and prevent us from burning out. We were completely drained and after the initial assistance it was now back to just Axel, Aly and I with the volunteers returning to their normal jobs and lives. One of the volunteers would be coming back in a few days to give us long term help but, for now, it was just the three of us. We split the nights with Ellie into three-hourly shifts as we did not want Ellie to become too attached to just one of us and the nightshifts with him were extremely stressful and demanding so we did not want to leave a nightshift to be handled by just one of us… I think a whole night alone with Ellie would've been enough to push us over the edge. Dividing the nightshift up may have been hard on our already sleep deprived bodies but it was the best way for us to handle Ellie. We had moved one of the spare beds - a cheaply made wooden frame and a single mattress - into the ICU to try to allow each of us at least some sleep while on shift but it wasn't going to be enough.

After a couple of days, a local wildlife rehabilitation centre heard of our situation and very kindly provided us with two of their own volunteers to help tide us over during this period of intensive nursing. We were so grateful for the help but to throw yet another spanner in the works, Ellie quickly made his feelings about volunteers known to us. You guessed it; he didn't like them.

Ellie didn't know the volunteers and, apparently, he wasn't too keen on getting to know them either. The problem was that the volunteers were not able to stay with us for longer than a week as they had other commitments which meant there was not enough time for Ellie to get to know them before they left again. After a volunteer tried to feed Ellie and struggled with how pushy and strong he was we decided maybe the volunteers were better off helping Ithuba who, thankfully, was much more welcoming. The care for Ithuba was less hands on and he only needed a few feeds a day so that was a much more manageable task.

We showed the new volunteers how to mix Ithuba's milk and they were excited to help keep Ithuba fed, his wallow topped up and his room clean. The wooden bed we had placed in Ellie's room was unfortunately broken beyond repair when a volunteer had tried to feed Ellie and sought the bed as refuge from his relentless pushing. As I saw the feed was not going to plan and the volunteer was unable to hold their ground against the pushes of our hungry elephant, I went to take over but Ellie didn't see the bottle of milk being handed to me. This meant that when the volunteer climbed onto the bed, Ellie tried to follow her and as soon as he put his front feet onto the bed and pushed his weight down, the cheap wood cracked noisily beneath him. Under the elephant's weight, the whole bed crumbled with almighty snaps and a final thud as it came crashing down to the ground.

With the bed now in pieces, I showed El the milk bottle and encouraged him towards me, but my usual feeding technique of leaning against one of the foam mattresses failed miserably. It was a technique I'd started using when we moved the bed into the room as the mattress would stand up against the foot of the bed and would provide stability against Ellie's pushes. During the chaos of this feed, I offered our hungry and demanding elephant the bottle but not thinking, I positioned myself in front of the mattress, as I always did, ready to let it absorb any pushing or shoving during the feed. The second Ellie took the bottle and nudged into me we were both on the floor, surprised at the lightning-fast effects of gravity. The mattress had nothing to support it as the bed frame was now just scraps of wood and as a result, we were now in a heap on the floor too. I thought it was quite comical but Ellie did not see the funny side of it. I quickly got back to my feet, put the foam mattress up against the wall and fed the unimpressed young elephant. After the feed, I sat next to El and sighed.

"Guess that didn't work out, hey buddy?" I nudged him as he stood playing with my shoes with his trunk, "they are here to help us boy. Give them a chance, please." I gave the stubborn baby elephant a kiss on the head, pulled myself up and went to wash up the milk bottle and mixing jug.

After the washing up was done, Axel and I took the broken bits of the bed out of Ellie's room. The broken bed was reduced to a sad symbol of our broken nights of sleep. With the volunteers unable to help with the nursing of little Ellie, we went back to the drawing board. It felt like everything was going wrong so we tried to put it all into perspective. The darkness around our eyes and heaviness in our steps showed how fatigued we were. The three of us were emotional, we tried to support each other but we were all in the same boat. It was frustrating because we had people on hand who wanted to help but the reality of the situation was that they couldn't do much to help. We so badly wished they could help with the intense care of the young elephant but it wasn't that simple and when we tried, it wasn't working out.

We needed people who could commit to a longer period of time to help us and for now, that wasn't available. Aly, Axel and I decided that each of us would go and sleep for two hours during the day so we could try to regain our strength. As I'd been up and working since three a.m. Aly encouraged me to go and try to sleep. We opened the opaque door between the intensive care unit and the outside enclosure just a touch so that we could keep an eye on Ithuba while still sitting with Ellie. Axel and Alyson were working together in the Intensive Care Unit, Ithuba was playing with the logs outside and I went to my room.

I climbed into bed, my whole body aching a dull and constant ache, my eyes were heavy but my brain was whirling. I drifted to sleep but I startled awake as there was a sudden, urgent knock at the door.

"Meg. We need you." Axel said sombrely from the other side of the closed door. I jumped out of bed and opened the door as I pulled on my jumper and forced on my shoes. For the first time since we had met, the young grinning Frenchman who had become like a brother to me was tearful. Although I had only been in my room for around 40 minutes, something had happened.

"What's wrong? What's happened?" I asked Axel as I pulled my bedroom door closed behind me.

"We were with Ellie in the ICU then we heard this crying noise and Ithuba had been playing with the tyres. He must have been climbing up the stack of tyres that's in his enclosure but he slipped and his foot got stuck inside the tyres and he couldn't free himself, so he was struggling and squealing to be free. Me and Aly went to help Ithuba and had to leave Ellie in the ICU. We rushed because Ithuba was panicking. We thought maybe he would hurt his leg, we had to pull him free. Ellie was shouting because we left him alone in the ICU. We got Ithuba out but Aly has hurt her wrist and now Ellie won't relax because he is upset that we left him on his own." Axel was visibly stressed and upset about what had happened. He was trying to explain in all to me as quickly as he could as we walked to the ICU.

"Okay, it's okay Axel. Is Ithuba hurt?" I asked.

"He seems like he is not hurt but I don't know. I don't know how this even happened." Axel said as we walked through the preparation room into the ICU where Ellie stood, glued to Aly's side.

"Hey my boy." I said to Ellie as we entered, he grumbled and greeted me, "Don't be upset El, everything's fine. Just relax." I said as I kissed his forehead and draped my arms across his shoulders in an embrace. As I straightened up, I looked at Aly.

"I'll go and see Ithuba in a second but are you okay?" I asked as we both looked out of the ICU into Ithuba's enclosure.

"I think I just caught my wrist funny when we were pulling Ithuba out. I think his weight pushed into me and I was just in an awkward position." Aly looked down, as she placed her fingers down on her wrist she sharply inhaled as it was clearly sore and sensitive to touch.

"Oh man. Okay. Jeez… it's amazing you guys were able to get Ithuba free. Do you think you need to go get it checked and get some painkillers or something?" I looked down at Aly's wrist. Out of the corner of my eye I saw Ithuba enter my field of vision. My eyes flicked up to him and I watched as he walked across the enclosure. To my relief, he looked unharmed by the incident.

"It should be okay, I'll put some ice on it in a minute and see how it feels after that."

"Okay, sorry I wasn't here to help you guys. You honestly did so well." I looked up to see Ithuba walking towards the barrier,

"Axel, shall we go to Ithuba quickly? Then I'll take over with El." Axel joined me outside to see Ithuba, and explained which foot was caught and what had happened. Ithuba nudged into me as I stroked his face and said hello.

He did not appear to be hurt and was more than happy to receive some attention from me and Axel. After looking at him closely and making sure he didn't have any injuries, we walked around the enclosure with him to confirm he wasn't limping or anything. To our relief, Ithuba was unscathed by the incident. Happy with this, Ithuba began to play with the logs in his enclosure while Axel and I got to work removing the tyres that were stacked around a pole. Not wanting this to happen again we removed the tyres one by one and took them out of the enclosure. Although Ithuba loved to charge and knock into the tyres, after this had happened it simply wasn't worth the risk. As a special treat, we dragged all of his logs into a pile and stacked them up. This would keep 'Thubes entertained for the rest of the day so we left him to play and returned to the ICU.

With everything back in order, Axel, Aly and I sat for a few minutes in Ellie's room and just talked. It was a bit like having a therapy session and I think we all needed it. It was the dynamics of this team that was keeping us going through the hard times we were experiencing.

At times, it felt like everything was going wrong; the night shift bed breaking into pieces, Ithuba getting his leg stuck in a tyre stack that he had played with for months without any issue, the volunteers not being able to help with caring for El. I knew that we weren't taking it as well as we usually would because of the exhaustion. When we stepped back and looked at the situation, we really weren't doing so badly. Despite all the odds, Ellie was alive and he was beginning to thrive with us. Ithuba was flourishing into a happy, healthy, independent rhino. Everything else was just day to day stuff that we could work through. We took a deep breath and with the encouragement and reassurance of the team we brushed ourselves off and continued on. I sat with Ellie while Aly and Axel went up to the house to ice

Aly's wrist and take a break. Axel agreed to come back for Ellie's next feed and I said I'd call them if I needed anything.

Later that day, we let Ithuba and Ellie meet and interact through the barrier. Ithuba had been interested in what was going on since the day Ellie arrived so he jumped at the opportunity to take a closer look. We pushed open the large, opaque door that had separated them since day one, Ithuba's ears were up and alert as soon as we opened the door. Ellie pushed himself against the steel poles of the barrier to try to see and smell what was going on. The little elephant thought he was going to be let out as he had been in the enclosure behind his room before. We had let Ellie wander around a few times when Ithuba was in the other enclosures, giving El a chance to explore and smell the areas Ithuba had spent so much time playing in. Ellie grumbled at us impatiently when we did not open the barrier but soon his interest shifted to the rhino that was approaching him. Ithuba cautiously moved towards the door with his alert ears pointing in our direction. Once Ithuba was close enough to see the small elephant staring at him from the other side of the barrier, Ellie reached his trunk out. Ithuba was not expecting this, frightened by the elephant's trunk the young rhino turned on a dime and bolted the other way. 'Thubes obviously hadn't expected the little animal on the other side of the barrier to have a trunk! Axel tried to reassure Ithuba,

"It's okay Ithuba, it's just a little elephant. Nothing to worry about." He said with a smirk. After a few minutes of composing himself, Ithuba returned for another approach. A rhino does not have good eyesight so Ithuba was relying on his hearing until he could get close enough to see what was on the other side of the barrier reaching out to him. Ithuba's ears and eyes were fixed on Ellie, who remained with his trunk stretched through the bars of the barrier. Despite Axel's reassurance, Ithuba was very skittish. Ithuba was trying to be brave but, to be honest, he was failing. As Ellie reached his trunk out once again, Ithuba ran away.

"Ithuba, why are you running away? Ellie is so small. You are much older than him! It should be Ellie that is scared of you not the other way around. Come on boy, it's fine." Axel said to 'Thubes. He was right, Ithuba was not far off being a year old and Ellie was only just coming up to four weeks old, yet it was young Ellie who was steadfast in the meeting of species.

It was third time lucky for the two of them as Ithuba finally realised Ellie was not going to hurt him and he came close enough for Ellie to smell him. Ellie held his trunk so close to Ithuba that they were almost touching, the pair were equally interested in each other but I think they were both thankful for the barrier that separated them. They spent several minutes interacting at the barrier, both were now as close to the bars as they could be, inhaling the smells, taking in the sights and listening to the other so carefully. Ellie was gently touching Ithuba's face and horn and Ithuba was not at all scared anymore. They continued to be in awe of each other, taking the time to slowly interact. Their eyes were fixed on each other, and although I was worried that Ellie's trunk would end up being squashed between Ithuba's horn and the barrier they were both gentle. Interestingly, the interaction was completely silent. They were making eye contact and were making very slow, slight movements but they were not making any noise. After the pair had become acquainted, they wandered their separate ways. It was lovely to see them meet each other but we knew we needed a more fitting solution for them, Ithuba was just too big for little Ellie.

By the end of August, Ellie was finally keeping food in and getting the nourishment he so desperately needed from it. This was incredibly exciting for us and it meant we were on the right track with the rice mixture. It felt as though the tide was turning, each day we battled through made the next seem increasingly likely to occur. Only a few weeks prior we did not think Ellie would survive the night, but we were seeing massive progress and we couldn't help but get excited. Ellie was slowly learning to use his trunk more and he would spend most of his time outside exploring. Our little elephant had become quite a busy body, he would have his trunk everywhere; from feeling down the gap in the side of your wellies to playing with your hair or clothes. He had developed a bit of an obsession with door handles where he would stand at doors and reach up licking and chewing the door handle, but we were working on that. I think the coolness of the metal handle was a refreshing feeling inside Ellie's mouth and the height and steadiness of the door was probably quite comforting. Ellie was never in a rush; he took everything in his stride and he did everything his way. The only time you'd see him running was down the hill to the door of the preparation room or towards a very noisy land rover that he had developed a personal vendetta against.

It was wonderful to spend each day wandering around outside with a bouncy and energetic elephant, in just a few weeks he had grown so much and his personality was exploding into life. The umbilical infection and abscess had healed, it was a miracle.

12: New Arrival

On the 1st of September, only 18 days after Ellie arrived, we received a call that a two-month-old white rhino calf was on his way to us. This rhino calf had lost his mother to poaching and had been by the side of her lifeless body for almost a week. The younger calves tend to stay with their mothers, even long after she has died, as they are so heavily bonded to her and rely on her for life. Without her, they will die and no matter how hungry, thirsty or desperate they become they remain by her side hoping, wishing and pleading for her to stand back up. This rhino calf was in a bad way and was severely traumatised.

We had a quick team meeting (of course, because Ellie could not be left alone our team meeting was held in the garden where he was busy exploring) and discussed the course of action for the day. As we had made such amazing progress with Ellie, we decided to move him into another room and give the intensive care unit to the new arrival. This meant we had a few hours to thoroughly disinfect both rooms and get them ready before the rhino orphans' arrival. The clean-up and rearranging of the rooms were using the last of our energy, something as routine as a room disinfection felt like it was happening in slow motion but we were getting it done. Once Aly and I had disinfected the intensive care unit, I cleaned and disinfected a former volunteer room for Ellie to stay in while Aly focussed on organising and sterilizing equipment for the new rhino calf. With the teamwork, we had everything sorted in a couple of hours.

Ellie's new room was ready just in time for him to take an afternoon nap. I showed him to the new room but he took a lot of convincing to even go inside and then once he was in, he immediately wanted to leave. I knew the room smelt like him because I'd taken his bedding from the intensive care unit and his used blankets to make sure he would feel at home. The new room was perfect for El, he just didn't know it yet. After a bit of arguing I came up with a new plan.

"Ok El, I'm going to sleep in this lovely new room! Goodnight!!" I walked into the room, laid down on the mattresses and closed my eyes, if he wasn't going to sleep in there then I was. I was beginning to know Ellie quite well and just as I had anticipated, 20 seconds later I felt Ellie's trunk softly touching my arm - testing to see if I was really sleeping. I didn't move and he did it again, this time a little bit harder and accompanied by a deep grumble as if to say, "if you are asleep, I'll wake you up". I opened my eyes slowly as if I'd been sleeping for hours and grumbled at the young elephant whose face was 20cm away from mine,

"El, are you going to just stand there or are you going to sleep too? This is your room and I know you're tired. You'll get bored of standing there because I'm going to sleep." I said as I half opened my eyes and looked up at him. Ellie's deep brown eyes were smiling at me as I got myself comfy and closed my eyes again. Within a few seconds, Ellie found himself a comfy spot next to me and lay down by my side. I put my arm over him as he rested his head on me and I watched as he drifted to sleep. I smiled as that was far easier than I thought it was going to be. It didn't take him long to get used to the new room after all.

Ellie could never be left alone, if I tried to sneak out of the room to help with the rhino arrival preparations he would be up before I'd even walked the seven steps to the door and if I carried on walking he would scream at me. I know because I've tried to sneak away before to go to the bathroom or to grab some food, I've never made it out of the door. So, for the next little while at least, we slept. I could fall asleep in an instant and I could wake up and work at the snap of a finger so a little snooze with El wouldn't hurt.

Laying on a mattress with an elephant was very comfortable until he'd decide to lay on top your arm or your legs, then you'd be faced with a decision that every pet owner has experienced at one time or another… To move at the expense of the comfort of the animal who's resting on you or to stay still so as not to wake them. Of course, I'd stay still for as long as possible, usually until my limbs no longer had any feeling and I had begun to worry about the future of my toes or my fingers. By that stage I'd try to wriggle free slowly, without jolting or waking the young elephant. Bit by bit I'd shimmy away trying to use pillows to support his body instead. Once free, I'd sit dead still to see if I'd managed to free myself without El waking up. My limbs would tingle as the blood flow was restored, this would soon be followed by intense pins and needles as I regained feeling and movement. On good days, if El did wake up after I'd managed to wiggle my way free but wasn't quite finished napping he'd just half open his eyes, stretch his trunk out to touch my face then fall back to sleep. As we lay there, I fell asleep feeling very comfortable and content with my head rested on one arm and the other arm laid lazily across El.

After our nap, we went to make some milk and see what the update on the rhino calf was. The new arrival was being brought in by road and was about an hour away, so I was going to stay with Ellie until the evening and then I was going to do the night shift with the new arrival. After a feed, Ellie and I went for a walk in the reserve to burn off some energy. We'd started to venture further afield, with Ellie being so inquisitive and full of energy it was a great way of keeping him busy. As I walked, Ellie plodded behind me, stopping to smell the paths of wild animals and rub his trunk in the dirt. He walked with a strut in his steps and his trunk swayed to-and-fro picking up scents as we'd go. Every so often, he'd reach out and touch my leg and I was always right there to comfort and encourage him when he needed it.

Once the hour was almost up, we went back to Ellie's new room for another feed. At the door, he hesitated, still not entirely convinced by the new décor but it was growing on him. It's funny how particular elephants can be. I closed the door to Ellie's room as I heard the rumble of car engines approaching the orphanage. While the new arrival was offloaded into the intensive care unit, Ellie and I played games in his room to pass the time. His room was filled with enrichment, there were branches hanging from the cupboard door, a small football, a tyre... Ellie loved to use his trunk to explore the objects and would often push them around and charge at them. Most of all he liked to play pushing games with us, just as baby elephants would play together. Young Ellie was extremely inquisitive so I knew if he was out in the garden while the rescued rhino was offloaded he would be very keen to investigate the vehicles, people and rhino. He'd have his trunk all over the place, exploring the smells. There was no doubt he'd get in the way and he'd push his way past people to see what was going on so it was better for us to stay inside until everything was calm again. You'd be surprised how much disruption a baby elephant can cause if they feel like it.

Once the rhino calf had been offloaded and the wildlife capture team had left, Ellie and I ventured back outside. We spent the last of the daylight in the garden and then it was time for me to switch shifts. As I always did when my shift was over, I gave Ellie a big kiss and told him I'd be back to see him soon. He lifted his trunk, which was covered in mud from our outdoor adventures, and pushed it against my face with his eyes brightly looking up at me in delight. The mud that was now smeared across my cheek was the mark of a goodnight kiss from a baby elephant. I laughed and thanked him before I turned and went to my room to collect my stuff for the night shift.

13: Impy's First Night

As I opened the door into the preparation room I was hit by the smell of death. It was potent and held within it the grim realities of poaching. I was taken aback by the smell but continued into the room. I quickly put my bag and nightshift gear down on the floor and placed the pillow and blanket into one of the gaps on the preparation room shelves. I silently looked over the half door and into the intensive care unit. On the other side paced a two-month-old male white rhino calf who was covered in the dried blood and carcass fluid of his long-deceased mother. The strong smell emanated from the room, from the blood that covered him. I sighed a heavy sigh as I was given the lowdown on the story of this newly arrived orphaned calf and the handover information for the night.

"Oh, Aly. My heart already hurts. How's he doing?" I asked. Aly exhaled as she picked up the record folder,

"Okay… He's been at his mum's carcass for around a week so he is very dehydrated and has a lot of dried blood from his mum on him." She paused, looking over at the young rhino with sadness in her eyes,

"He's got a lot of ticks, and I mean A LOT. We've removed a few of them but there's still loads, you'll see when you go in there. So far he's had one milk feed and two electrolyte feeds so in about 30 minutes he should have milk again, he's actually been really good with taking the bottle and you can go in with him without a problem. He's about two months old so he's quite easy to work with in that respect but he is visibly traumatised, he's been pacing and calling like this since he arrived…" Aly looked up at me as she sighed, "Tonight, the best thing to do is just be in there with him and alternate between milk feeds and electrolytes then we will review the feeding schedule in the morning. I think that's about it. The feeding stuff is all here ready. If you need anything, give me a shout. I'll be on the first half of the night with Ellie then Axel and I are switching so I'll be with Ithuba from around 1ish." Aly handed me the folder and I looked through the notes.

"Poor boy… Alright..." I said as I sighed, I could feel the emotion welling up within me as I thought of all this little thigh-high rhino had experienced.

"Thanks so much Aly. We'll see you in the morning, I hope El behaves himself!" I said before turning my attention to the orphaned calf,

"Alright, let's do this little one." I placed the folder down, unhooked the door and stepped into the ICU.

This was one of the most hard-hitting cases I have experienced first-hand. The rhino and I were now alone, and I had a feeling we were both in for a very long night. Rhino calves tend to be inconsolable on their first few nights; they are afraid, unsure of what is going on and, above all else, they are traumatised. The young calf paced back and forth, calling out for his mum as I watched on, speechless. The blood had dried to his skin and was causing sores, irritation and itching. He had blood on his face from where he had been nudging his mum, trying to wake her and suckle from her.

We named this rhino calf 'Impy'. The isiZulu word 'Impy' when roughly translated means warrior. It is a word often associated with war. We named him Impy because he had been through a war and he was a warrior.

Impy was very small, he only stood at thigh height which made him easier to work with. To our great relief, he took to the bottles quickly. He was very dehydrated and in a bad way but thankfully he was drinking all the milk and electrolytes we offered to him with no problem at all. Usually, it takes a few days for a calf to take to the bottle but we were grateful this was not the case with Impy, who had already gone so long without food or water. As the night air cooled, I turned on the infrared heat lamp to provide some light and warmth for the night ahead. At least with the infrared lamps the shadows were less intense, it was not unusual for the shadows on the walls to cause great unease for new arrivals.

"Are you getting hungry little one? I'm going to make you some milk, okay? It will only take a moment, I'll be right here on the other side of the door." I slowly went into the preparation room and mixed the milk. As I entered the room and approached Impy with the bottle he opened his mouth willingly and began to drink. In no time at all he had finished the milk I had made.

"Wow, what a good little rhino you are! Was that delicious?" I said as I stroked his cheek gently. Once I'd washed up the bottle, teat, whisk and jug from the feed, I slowly went back into the intensive care unit and sat on a bale of teff near the heat lamp. Impy continued to pace and call without even acknowledging me. The only moment of quiet we had was during the feeds, other than that the small, concerned squeal of a baby rhino rang through the room. Each call came just a few seconds after the last, this went on for hours as I sat there, powerless.

I tried to talk to Impy but he did not appear to even register the sound of my voice, I kept trying because I did not want him to feel alone. He was lost, desperate and distraught. I could do nothing but be there for him, but I wish I could do more. The baby rhino walked in circles, calling and calling in short, high-pitched squeaks. After hours of watching Impy pace the room, I was feeling drained. I gave up talking and decided to hum to Impy instead. It must've been just after midnight by now and I knew the rhino orphan was exhausted and distressed by the events of the past week. I had a song I would always sing to calves when they were stressed or anxious, but I decided singing was not a good idea for Impy so instead I hummed to him. As I began humming the tune of Phil Collins – You'll Be in My Heart Impy stopped pacing. He raised his head slightly and turned in my direction. Slowly, he walked over to the hay bale where I was sitting and looked at me in the eye. I held out my hand and looked back at him, continuing to hum. Impy let me touch his side with my hand and after a few seconds, he let his body succumb to the tiredness he had been fighting for so long. He lay down against the hay bale, his body pushed up against my legs and my hand resting on his side. Impy was exhausted, he needed sleep and did not want to be alone. The humming had given him some level of comfort, enough that he finally stopped crying and slept. It was like he suddenly realized I was there for him. He fell into a deep and much needed sleep as he rested against my legs, and I didn't dare move in case it woke him.

Now that Impy was lying next to me instead of pacing around the room I could get a better look at him. The infrared lamp didn't give too much light but it was enough to see the dryness of his skin, the wounds on his back legs and the infestation of ticks all over his ears, nose, legs and tail. Some of the ticks were so grossly engorged that when they came off they could not even move as their legs could no longer reach the ground. I couldn't help but think of the horrors the rhino calf sleeping at my feet had experienced, this was probably the first time he'd been able to properly sleep since the poaching happened the previous week. For hours, I sat and watched as Impy slept. For hours, I didn't dare move a muscle for fear of waking him and I didn't sleep in case Impy awoke or had a nightmare. The orphaned baby rhinos sometimes fidget and cry in their sleep, they sound worried or afraid, so we gently wake them up, telling them that everything is okay and pulling them out of the dream that's making them cry out. When Impy awoke, he pulled himself up and stood looking at me. He nudged into my legs, opening his mouth to ask for milk. This was a great sign.

"Well good morning sleepy head, feeling a bit hungry are you? Let me get you some milk." I said as I stroked his side.

"I'll just be on the other side of this door, okay? I'll be right here." I went out of the half door as I continued to talk so Impy wouldn't feel like he was alone.

"Let's have a look shall we, shall we make you some nice, warm milk? It'll only take a minute boy." I continued talking as I picked up the measuring jug, filled it with warm water, added the milk powder and whisked the mixture. Impy was waiting on the other side of the half door, every now and then he'd make a small squeak. It was a "I'm hungry" squeak, the sleep had obviously done him some good.

"Oh I hear you boy, you're hungry. It's okay, the milk is ready." I said in response to his high-pitched squeak, I pulled the teat onto the bottle and went back to the door. Impy shuffled backwards allowing me just enough space to squeeze through the door before he opened his mouth ready for food. He gulped the warm milk down in less than a minute. I quickly washed up and then went back into the room. The last few hours sitting on the hay bale were not the most comfortable so this time, I sat on the floor against the wall under the infrared lamp. Impy wandered over to me and began to settle back down too. He lay next to me as I spoke to him,

"Hey beautiful boy, when the sun rises I'll get some warm water and give you a clean. It'll help your skin… Everything's okay Impy, get some rest, I'll be here when you wake up." As much as I wanted to, I couldn't clean the blood from Impy's skin during the night as he would get cold and sick but as soon as the day had warmed up, I would wash him. There was no doubt the blood that covered him was making his skin itchy and sore. Gently washing him would help to make his skin feel a lot nicer and to not walk around with that odour attached to him would surely help him start to heal in some way.

As the sun rose on a new day, Impy and I had experienced a very successful night. He drank his feeds with no problem and from midnight onwards he slept well. When it was time for shift change I was sitting on the floor, resting my back against the wall, and lying next to me was little Impy. He did not want to be alone and he knew I was trying to help.

The sun was up and the day was already warming so I went into the preparation room and mixed some warm water and aqueous cream, took some cotton wool and a sponge and sat back down next to Impy. I scratched his legs so he would not get a fright and then I slowly began to wipe away the dried blood. Gently, I cleaned the past week of hell from his body. He seemed to enjoy the attention and stretched his legs out as if to ask for more scratches. With his body clean, I then moved onto his face. I scratched under his neck and began to wipe around his mouth and nose. He wasn't as keen on this as he was with the belly cleaning but he tolerated it as long as I was scratching his chin. After 20 minutes of slow, gentle washing, Impy's skin was clean and I was hopeful it would be less itchy and a lot more comfortable for him. At the very least, the smell had been washed away. This young rhino had such a softness to him, he was innocence personified and it was clear to see he would never hurt a fly. Axel arrived to switch shifts, I handed over to him so I could go for a shower and put on some clean clothes. I felt drained but I had a clearer mind knowing Impy was hydrated, warm and clean. Now all I wanted to do was wash away the smells of the night shift and see my favourite little elephant.

14: Persevere

I stood under the warm running water and let it wash away the worries, the sound of the water splashing over my ears overpowered the thoughts in my mind. I washed away the smell of death that clung to me and I removed all the ticks I found gripping to my skin. I was beat, my eyelids heavy and my soul battered. Sometimes I wished the water could wash away memories. With a sigh, I turned the taps off, wrapped a towel around me and paused in the stillness of the bathroom. I had an hour or so to rest and then I'd be back to work. Sleeping during the day was never real rest, if you managed to fall asleep it was a kind of half sleep where you'd hear everyone going about the day and you'd be ready to jump out of bed at any moment to help with something. Usually, it wasn't even worth trying to fall asleep while the sun shone through the curtains and there was hustle and bustle around the orphanage.

I went to my room with my towel lazily wrapped around me, and my dirty clothes bundled up in my arms. As I walked into my room, I threw the clothes into the already overflowing washing basket before closing the bedroom door. As the latch clicked closed I paused for a moment, sighing as I leant my head against the door. Feeling a wave of emotion bubbling up inside me, I leant my back against the door as I felt all the pressures and strains pressing down against me. Sliding down the door until I reached the floor, I pulled my knees up against my body and the tears began to flow. I sat there against the door and silently sobbed, feeling so deeply the exhaustion, the stress and the realities of the poaching situation. Feeling the pain of these animals in our care and the fading light of the future. Everything was amplified through my heavy eyes and desperate heart.

I'm sure the rest of the team felt the same strain that had led me to this moment, but we couldn't show it, we couldn't express these emotions when we were around the animals, we had to be strong for them. With so much going on, we had no time to sleep or deal with the emotional undercurrent that came with seeing the first-hand impacts of poaching. I wiped my eyes and lent the back of my head against the door, looking up at the ceiling. I knew we couldn't carry on like this, we were burning out.

A few days before this moment I had spoken to the team about the growing pressure and increasing workload and everyone agreed when I suggested inviting a potential long-term volunteer to join us. Almost immediately after the conversation, I went outside, sat under the trees by the house and I called my mum, Menna, about helping us. She was the first person who came to mind when we were beginning to struggle and for good reason, my mum and I had worked side by side during intensive wildlife cases before, and I knew how well we worked together. The orphanage needed someone who could slot in and be part of the team for a couple of months rather than a week or two. I knew Menna would jump at the opportunity to join us and would be more than happy to get stuck in with helping us care for Ellie. It was a couple of years prior to this that she had come out to South Africa with me and helped raise rhino calves. In fact, mum had spent almost the entire three months she was volunteering at the orphanage side by side with a premature white rhino calf, and I knew if I called her she'd definitely help us.

When I made that phone call to my mum, I voiced our desperate need for help and the physical and emotional strain we were all under. My voice wobbled as I spoke of our struggles, we were having a hard time and that was the reality of it. Caring for a baby elephant was hugely demanding and we didn't have enough people on hand to share the load, to make matters worse we did not know if Ellie would survive from one day to the next which caused huge emotional strain. I paused for a moment to compose myself and, smiling through tears, I began to tell her that she could come and volunteer with us if she wanted to.

Mum had always told me she wanted to work with baby elephants, and I knew this opportunity was a dream come true for her. At first, she couldn't believe it and then she said,

"Of course! Of course I will come Meg! Yes. Oh my goodness. Yes…Of course! When? When do you need me? Tell Ellie I'm on the way to meet him!". I have no doubt that mum began to pack her suitcase the second she hung up the phone. To be honest, there's a good chance she already had a suitcase packed 'just in case'. We agreed that she would arrive as soon as possible, and I hung up the phone feeling a sense of relief and excitement. Things were becoming increasingly intense at the orphanage, and it wasn't just the animals that needed to come out at the other side of this, we did too.

As I sat on the floor of my room after my nightshift with new arrival Impy, there was no doubt in my mind that calling Menna was the right move. Particularly considering the undeniable fact that there would be more orphans coming to us in the near future. Menna would be landing in South Africa in three days and I knew that she'd be a huge asset to the team. It had been a challenging few weeks and there were no signs of things slowing but we were getting through it. I leant my head into my hands and closed my eyes, trying to silence my mind. I took a few deep breaths as I reminded myself that the animals needed us and that however hard it was, we were making a difference. I sighed as I pulled myself up and readied myself for the day ahead. I got dressed, pulling on the cleanest of my worn t-shirts and a pair of slightly muddy shorts (thanks Ellie). There was no ignoring the overflow of dirty clothes in my wash basket so I made a mental note to deal with it at some point in the day then I made my way outside.

My first stop was Ellie, he was in the garden exploring so I went to say hello. As he saw me approaching, he ran towards me deeply grumbling with bright eyes and a spring in his step, I gave him a big hug. If I ever needed a reason to smile, this was it. This little life that was so overflowing with love. I had a chat with Aly who was watching over his garden adventures, she said his night was pretty good, but he didn't sleep much which wasn't a surprise. I was due to switch shifts and take over watching him in 30 minutes, so I told Aly and Ellie that I was going to put my washing in the machine, have a bite to eat and then I'd be back.

I went back to my room to grab my washing basket and take it to the laundry room. As I was about to put the dirty clothes into the machine, I suddenly remembered I hadn't checked the water level yet, so I went outside to check the tank. As I knocked against the side of the water tank, I heard the unmistakeable echo…

"Surely not." I thought as I moved my hand further down before knocking again. The knock echoed inside the tank, moving my hand slightly further down I finally knocked against the water. There was not enough water to wash my clothes, in fact there was barely enough to get us through the day. The sad reality was that this was an all-too-common situation. Getting water was a challenge, our water was pumped from the same source as two tourist lodges and rather than a strict pumping schedule, the lodges would take priority over us and we'd frequently be left with dangerously low water levels. We were due to have water pumped to our tank the following day and with such low levels we needed to conserve water where we could. Experiencing low water levels had been a regular occurrence for weeks now; our showers were becoming increasingly infrequent, our clothes remained dirty and despite our very best efforts to conserve water where we could, it took a lot of water to properly care for our wildlife orphans. To make matters worse, the drought meant our water source was not being replenished and should the drought continue, we would have to find a new water source altogether. I took my washing back to my room and gave everyone an update on the water level. We had a whiteboard that hung next to the front door of the main house, we used to use it to write down shopping lists and items we needed but now we used it to note how much water we had left in the tank.

The top priorities were the orphans milk feeds and washing up the feeding equipment. Even with careful conservation of water there were still times when we ran out entirely. It was usually a result of not having water pumped to our tank on the agreed upon day but this wasn't always the cause, on one occasion, we ran out of water because of the wild elephant herd. The herd broke the water pipe that ran, underground, across the reserve to the orphanage. The elephants could smell the water that was traveling through the pipes, and they dug them out from underground. Breaking the pipes to access the water, the elephants were overjoyed – trumpeting, drinking and cooling themselves at their newly created water point. When there was no water coming into our water tank, we called to confirm that it was being pumped to us and the people were adamant that they had been pumping water to us for the past 40 minutes.

Knowing that this was more than enough time for the water to travel through the pipes, we knew there was a problem so Axel and I decided to follow the pipeline through the bush to find out if there was a break. We eventually came across the site of broken pipes and dampened ground. The elephants had since moved off but had clearly enjoyed the fresh water. With the ongoing drought, it was becoming harder and harder to find sources of water in the bush so I was not surprised the elephants had taken this initiative. Although, it was a great inconvenience to us at the orphanage I was glad the wild herd had found some hydration. Once we reported the broken pipes to the team of maintenance workers, they managed to get the pipes fixed and back in working order that same day meaning the following day we could have water pumped to our tank.

In situations where we had run out of water, we would load the car up with as many ten litre and fifteen litre water bottles we could find and drive to one of the lodges on the other side of the reserve. We'd then fill the water bottles up at one of the outside taps. It wasn't much but it would at least be enough water to get us through. We'd count the amount of milk feeds we needed to cover, how much water we'd need for washing up and anything else we would desperately need to use water for and, based on this, we'd distribute the necessary water bottles out to cover the care of each of the orphans.

Once everyone knew that our water levels were low, I made some toast and went back out to see Ellie. When I took over the shift, there was still a chill in the air so El was wearing a soft, grey blanket and he had become determined to master picking up sticks with his trunk. He was in a cheeky mood; you could see it written all over his face and by the look in his eyes. He hovered his trunk over the grass looking for a stick and then he'd pinch the stick using the tip of his trunk and try to lift it to his mouth. He was getting far more precise at closing his trunk around the sticks but he seemed to have a hard time lifting them in the way he wanted to. He was practicing and practicing and had made a huge amount of progress in just a few short weeks. The technique was there but he needed to build strength and confidence to be able to lift the sticks up and manoeuvre them as he desired. He enjoyed learning and he liked to test himself, he didn't seem to mind having to try at something again and again before eventually getting it – it was all part of the fun.

After he was finished playing with the sticks, El and I went for a walk to get some fresh air and use up some of this energy he had. We walked through the trees and came face to face with some giraffe who stared down at us intensely. Ellie wasn't fussed about the giraffe and carried on walking, deciding the direction of the days adventure. The giraffe soon turned around and walked away from us. The only thing I didn't want to do during these walks was bump into the wild elephant herd. There was no telling how they would've reacted to me and Ellie, so it was a situation best avoided. Fortunately, we'd yet to cross their path and I hadn't seen any tracks or broken branches to indicate they were around.

As we started making our way back to the orphanage Ellie was getting tired. I could see it in his eyes, they now appeared far heavier as El struggled to hold them open and his steps were slower and less enthusiastic. He walked a couple of steps behind me as we made our way home. It was obvious he was already thinking about taking a nap, sometimes we'd find a quiet spot on the softer, sandier dirt in the bush to lay down. El would lay on top of me with his front legs and head across my lap. He'd feel safe and comfortable – just like the younger rhino orphans craved physical contact to feel safe, so did Ellie. He'd look as though he was smiling as he'd drift off to sleep. We'd stay there for a while, cozied up under the trees, enjoying the gentle breeze and the sound of nearby weavers courting and building nests.

When El was laying with me like this I could see how much he had grown since the day he had arrived. I smiled as I looked at his increasingly chubby cheeks and couldn't help but laugh as I saw he remained as much of a fuzz-ball as he ever was. He still hadn't quite figured out how his ears could help keep him cool, so I'd check the temperature behind his ears every now and then to make sure he wasn't getting too hot.

The skin on the underside of his large ears was free from hair, completely smooth and relatively thin. The skin behind the ear is something of a contrast to the rest of an elephant but it makes sense as an elephant uses their large characteristic ears to help keep them cool on hot days. The lack of hair helps to make this process faster as the blood vessels are close to the skins surface and when the elephant flaps their ears the breeze cools down the blood which goes on to cool down the whole body. If I could feel Ellie was beginning to get hot I'd try to encourage him to flap his ears so he could learn how to naturally cool himself down and if we were near water I'd encourage him to play and splash around too.

The day went by fast, with shifts that were split between Ellie, Ithuba and Impy there was always something to do. I was on the Ellie one a.m. shift that night so in the early evening once I had finished my day shift,

I went to do the rounds and see how everyone was doing. Impy's first full day with us was great, he drank well and remained at the side of whoever was on shift, gaining comfort from their presence. It was going to take a bit of time for him to settle in completely but we were relieved at his positive response to us. Saying goodnight to Impy, I went to spend some time with Ithuba so he knew he wasn't being left out, I'm not sure which one of us benefitted from the cuddles more. Being with Ithuba was good for the soul, he would just love every drop of attention you'd give him and you could feel it reflecting back at you. After a heart to heart with 'Thubes, I gave him his milk feed and went up to the house to make us all some dinner.

The first half of the night I was caring for Ithuba but with his increasing independence this meant I had a few hours free. After I took a plate of food to Aly, who was on shift with Impy, and to Axel, who was on the first part of the night with Ellie, I dragged myself back down to the clinic. I wrapped myself in a blanket and lay on the camping mattress. Knowing I would be very quickly falling into a deep sleep, I set an alarm on my phone for Ithuba's next feed.

15: The Ellie Team

As the days disappeared into one another in what I can only describe as a "busy blur", we received another phone call. It had been four days since Impy arrived and now there was another orphaned rhino in need. This male white rhino calf was just a couple of months older than Impy and came from the same reserve as Ithuba. While we waited for his arrival we shuffled the room arrangements so that this new arrival could go into the High Care Unit and receive monitoring around the clock. Fortunately, Ithuba was now spending almost all his time outside so he didn't need the room anymore. We moved some of Ithuba's bedding to one of the outside shelters then closed and locked the barriers and doors so Ithuba couldn't come back into the HCU. We got to work disinfecting the room ready for the new arrival. The room was ready just in time, the rhino calf was offloaded into the high care unit and Axel stayed with him to try to get him settled.

We named the young, four-month-old, white rhino Thando, meaning love. With two new intensive cases, a cheeky, demanding elephant and Ithuba keeping us busy we were being fuelled by coffee and toast. The saving grace was that Ellie was now stable and in a routine. El still required hourly feeds and always needed someone with him but he was no longer battling with the infection and was flourishing. We decided that the best way to move forward was to separate ourselves into two teams so we could ensure all the orphans were getting the 24/7 care they needed. With three intensive cases and Ithuba also needing care, we knew we couldn't keep constantly rotating shifts. Instead, we split ourselves into "The Ellie Team" and "The Rhino Team".

The Rhino team was Aly, Axel and any volunteers who were on hand while the Ellie team was me, Menna (who would be arriving later that day) and our long-term volunteers who would lend a hand by taking a portion of the night shift with Ellie too. With the new teams in place, we were able to more effectively rota our time and we knew all the animals were always fed and cared for. Otherwise, it felt like constant handovers and always playing catch up, with so many shift changes there was too much juggling going on and by now, we were way too tired to juggle. Team Ellie was exactly where I needed to be, our little elephant had stolen my heart and we had built a very strong rapport over the last three weeks together. We had come a long way, now I could see in his eyes what he was thinking and how he was feeling.

To my elation, Menna was due to arrive the afternoon Thando was brought in to us. It was perfect timing; things had snowballed in just a few weeks and this was the boost our team needed. In the past three weeks alone, a completely unexpected, demanding and critically ill baby elephant, a two-month-old white rhino poaching orphan and a four-month-old white rhino orphan were brought to us, all requiring 24/7 intensive, around the clock care. Our team of three was growing and we had a handful of frequently changing volunteers.

There was no question that Menna was going to be on the Ellie team with me, I'd introduce them and show her the ropes and I was sure she would be eager to get stuck in. Even though El didn't seem to be particularly fond of new people I knew this was going to work out. After spending the morning checking my phone for messages, I finally climbed into the pick-up truck and made my way through the wilderness of the reserve. I drove with the window rolled down, revelling in the fresh air and freedom. As I picked my way through the bumpy bush roads I realised I had not left the boundaries of the orphanage in over a month. I admired the giraffe and impala who crossed my path as I drove along the winding dirt roads. Finally, I reached the main gate where Menna was waiting. I pulled up at the same spot Axel had picked me up all those moons ago when I had first arrived.

"You made it!!!!" I grinned as I climbed out of the car and gave my mum a hug. "How was the journey? Was the flight ok? Have you been waiting here for long? El can't wait to meet you!" It had been months since I'd last seen my mum, despite the long journey she looked cheerful and wide awake. Each of her blonde hairs fell perfectly in their usual way, no doubt straightened the day before. Menna was excited and ready to go, I could see the sparkle in her earthly green-grey eyes. I picked up her suitcase and placed it into the back of the car,

"Jeez mum! What on Earth did you bring?!" It was no surprise her bag was full to the brim; it always was whenever we'd go anywhere. I can tell you without a shadow of a doubt there was hair straighteners and a hair dryer in that suitcase, they seemed to travel everywhere with my mum. Even if we were going on a short holiday, my mum would pack what seemed like every item of clothing she owned.

"Hey! Most of the stuff in there is for you!" she retorted without missing a beat. As we got into the car, mum reached for her seatbelt.

"Trust me, you'll be far comfier without that on. It's a bumpy ride back to the orphanage." I said with a smile as I rolled the windows down. Welcome back to Africa mum. As I drove through the African bush with my mum in the passenger seat, I couldn't wipe the smile from my face. I drove slowly and kept my eyes peeled for wildlife that I could point out to her along the way as I told her stories of Ellie and the rhinos. I couldn't wait to introduce her to the family. I told her about Thando, who had arrived just a couple of hours earlier and before we knew it I was driving the steep incline towards the orphanage and pulling into the gate.

After parking the truck, I picked up mum's suitcase and showed her to the room she would be sharing with me, it was nothing special. To be honest, it was just my room except now we had moved a second single bed into it. The room was only just big enough to fit the two beds in; they were pushed up against the back and side walls with a very narrow walkway of not even half an arm's length between them. Despite the squeeze, the room was everything we needed; we had some shelves, a mirror and a wardrobe.

Besides, it's not like we'd be spending much time in there anyway. The room was very similar to where we had been staying when we were working together at another rhino orphanage, in fact, this room was a bit more pleasant so I was sure mum wouldn't mind… A downgrade from day-to-day life but an upgrade on previous experiences! Once in the room, I pointed to Menna's bed and told her there was space in the wardrobe for her clothes. After a brief catch up, we decided the rest of the tour could wait as the top of the list of things to do was to meet Ellie.

As we walked out of the accommodation block, Ellie was busy exploring the grassy area outside.

"Come and meet Ellie." I said with a grin. Menna didn't even hesitate as she walked out on the grass to introduce herself to the baby elephant I'd told her so much about.

"El, this is my mum!! She is going to help us take care of you." I said as Menna stepped forward and began stroking Ellie's forehead, he had his trunk in the air saying hello. He was so interested in Menna, his trunk wandered all over the place taking in her smell. He was excited, his eyes were bright and the two of them were so captivated by one another. The reaction Ellie had to my mum was very different from the reaction he had to the volunteers he'd met. Ellie was cold with volunteers; it took him around a week to warm to them being around and until then he was uninterested. He'd tolerate volunteers when we were all standing together but he never wanted to be with them one-on-one and would usually stand pressed against my legs, unsure of the new people. When Ellie met Menna he was friendlier, more welcoming and his attitude was one of sweetness. He walked away from me to say hello to her and was immediately at ease. I wondered if Ellie knew that Menna was my mum, if there was a familiarity in her smell or something he picked up on that indicated to him she was already part of the herd. Whatever it was, it was magical. Ellie had accepted my mum and seemed to be genuinely excited to meet her. I was ecstatic that the first meeting went so well and I knew the relationship would only grow from there. I was so grateful Menna had arrived to help us out, the timing of her arrival was impeccable and for her to dive right in to being part of the newly formed Ellie Team provided the boost we all needed.

It was such a relief that Ellie had taken to Menna straight away. However, it wasn't just the young elephant who was eager to meet her, while Ellie and I walked around the garden, Menna went to meet the rest of the family. Having heard so much about Aly and Axel it was as though she already knew them. We had a wonderful team and to now be sharing this crazy-cool experience with my mum was incredibly exciting. Menna would be staying with us for the next two months and she hit the ground running by getting stuck in with helping with cleaning, washing El's used blankets and learning the milk mixtures for the orphans. From now on, Menna and I would share the Ellie care during the day and the night shift was split into three manageable chunks.

After the introductions were out of the way, Ellie, Menna and I headed out for a walk in the bush. Before going for a walk, we made ourselves a cup of tea and packed an 'Ellie bag' with blankets, milk, a flask of hot water and electrolytes. We walked out of the orphanage gate and along a wildlife path down the hill, Ellie strolled enthusiastically by my side, his trunk swinging to-and-fro with the strut of his walk. A few minutes into the walk, Menna pulled a bar of vegan chocolate out of her bag and handed it to me.

"I brought you a gift." She smiled as she handed it to me. I grinned as I took the bar of chocolate,

"Chocolate!! Thank you!! Let's have some now!" I said as I eagerly unwrapped the bar. It had been a while since I'd had a sweet treat that wasn't dried mango, so this was a very exciting moment. As I walked alongside iconic umbrella thorns within a South African wildlife reserve with a cup of tea and a bar of vegan chocolate in hand and the company of my mum and a baby elephant, it's safe to say I was feeling very content. It had been a really challenging few weeks but now stopping to inhale the scents of the wild African bush and let Ellie play with broken branches that lay on the path, my spirit felt revitalised. We walked with no destination in mind, just enjoying the journey and catching up with each other.

The impact of the drought was evident, the sun continued to bake the land and further shrivel the already leafless branches. The dry, dusty ground was barely disturbed by our steps.

"I hope you are wearing sun cream!" Menna said as we walked under the cloudless sky.

"Of course I am. Always." I said, catching her eye as I smirked.

"Meg!! You need to wear sun cream! How many times have I told you?" It was one of the standard 'mum questions' that always came up… Are you eating properly, are you getting enough sleep, are you wearing sun cream…? We had had this conversation countless times but even I was surprised that with all that was going on, sun cream came up just a couple of hours after my mum had arrived. With that said, Menna's skin is much fairer than mine and wasn't used to the African sun so I knew she'd be applying sun cream diligently.

"Relax mum, just enjoy the walk!" I smiled as I held my arms out to gesture towards the breath-taking views. As we explored, I filled Menna in on the care routine and the past few weeks with our baby elephant.

After 40 minutes, Ellie began to get hungry and he expressed this to me by raising his trunk up to my side and pushing his weight into me, mouth open and eyes looking intently at mine. We stopped to mix some milk using the flask of boiled water we carried, ensuring the milk was at just the right temperature for feeding. Once the milk was mixed and warm, I found a sturdy spot against a tree to use as support while feeding the small but pushy elephant. Ellie lifted his trunk up to my face and began to push against me while drinking the freshly made milk. I explained to Menna how strong Ellie was and how harsh his pushing could be. Although he wasn't anywhere near as bad as he used to be, I always steadied myself against something such as a tree during the feeds just in case… it would take a lot of strength to hold your position against Ellie's pushes. The baby elephant didn't seem to quite know the limits of human strength just yet.

Ellie drank the milk in big slurps, touching my face with his trunk during the feed. He had started to make a habit of touching my face when it came to feeding time. It started with him hovering his trunk in front of my face, as if he was trying to catch my breath as I exhaled. This is something baby elephants sometimes do for comfort. I started to give Ellie kisses as a bit of a game and a distraction, he would be so focussed on his trunk that he would drink the feeds with much less pushing. Now, almost every feed he held his trunk up to my face and touched my nose and mouth while he drank. He was doing this for comfort, and it was a bit of a win for me too because he wouldn't push as much. However, when El had been playing in the mud it meant he was smudging mud across my face while he drank his milk. Ellie would happily slurp his milk and if I tried to move my face away from his trunk or move so his trunk was resting on my cheek rather than on my lips or nose, El would stop drinking, look up at me and move his trunk back to where he wanted it then carry on drinking. Once all the milk was finished, Ellie would drop his trunk down and toddle off to carry on exploring and I'd have mud smeared all over my face from the elephant kisses I had received.

After over an hour of walking, Menna, Ellie and I made our way back to the orphanage for a snack and a nap. Ellie would always be ready for a sleep after a good walk, he'd shuffle to his room and plonk down onto the mattress, enjoying the warmth and comfort of the heat lamp. It had only been a few days since El switched rooms but he was enjoying his new room and it was far better suited to him than the ICU. We could play more games, we had a wardrobe for all his blankets (this was formerly a volunteer's room after all) and we had a shelf positioned high enough to keep all our equipment out of Ellie's reach. Whenever El came to help me make milk in the preparation room, he'd always see what he could reach and play with while I would whisk the milk. To be able to have his blankets as well as various equipment such as aqueous cream, wipes and disposable gloves available on hand in El's room without needing to constantly argue with him to leave them alone was a huge bonus.

In light of the increased workload, our team was growing and we had spoken to the local chief to get members of the local community to come and work with us. We had three new team members, a lovely lady named Goodness who helped us to keep the house and volunteer accommodation tidy and organised and two men named Senzo and Sihle who helped us with the maintenance and animal husbandry. Each morning while Ellie was out walking and exploring, his room would be cleaned and straightened out so he could run in from a walk and dive into a bed of fresh blankets. Fortunately, Ellie's new room was far quicker and easier to clean than the rhino rooms as El's room did not have any floor mats to lug around. Having more people on the team made such a huge difference and working with the community is a critically important part of conservation work.

Thanks to our new team members, Axel, Aly and I now had the time we needed to focus solely on the animals. Seeing the excitement on Goodness, Sihle and Senzo's faces when they saw the orphans for the first time was divine. Even though they had all grown up in a village close to the wildlife reserve, they hadn't had the opportunity to see wild animals close up before. Their eyes lit up as they saw the orphans and although they were keeping their distance as they were worried the animals would hurt them, they soon warmed up to them and realised the orphans were all young and just needed gentle love and care. Seeing how our new team members warmed to the animals and how they grew to truly care for them was beautiful. Each morning, they would greet Ellie with enthusiasm and while stroking him and giving him attention, they would ask me how he was. This became a staple of our morning routine on weekdays and Ellie loved it just as much as Sihle and Senzo did.

16: Ever Playful Elephant

When El was feeling mischievous you could see in his eyes he was out to cause trouble. Those smiling, cheeky eyes told you when he was up to something naughty, usually he'd pull things off shelves with his trunk, play with the ball, tyre or cardboard in his room or demand attention from me. Sometimes he would even harass me for my glasses! I did not wear glasses every day but there were many times when I would be sat in El's room on one of the mattresses with my glasses on and the cheeky elephant would stand in front of me, reach his trunk out to tap my cheek or my nose and then shuffle his trunk towards my glasses. He would gently grip the centre of the glasses with the tip of his trunk (all that practice with sticks was paying off) and once he had a firm hold of the glasses he'd pull them down in a swift arcing motion that led directly to his mouth. It showed how good Ellie was getting with using his trunk, but it was a race against time for me to grab the glasses before the naughty elephant put them into his mouth. There was more than one occasion when I had to stick my hand into his mouth and retrieve the – slobbery and slightly bent – glasses. He loved this game and would play it at every opportunity he got, I didn't mind because he was like a naughty child looking up at me with smiling eyes and a big grin.

Ellie's room had multiple toys and enrichment around the place. We'd change the items often to keep his interest but on this day he had an egg carton hanging from the top of the wardrobe, a large yogurt pot attached to a rope, a tyre and a cardboard box full of sticks to keep him entertained. Ellie really enjoyed playing with the ropes. He particularly loved the one that was hanging from the wardrobe as he'd lift his trunk up and wrap it around the rope before walking and pulling it along with him. Then as he'd let go, the attached carton would swing away from him and he'd chase and charge it. He also enjoyed the rope on the floor as he could pick it up easily and drag it around with him. He'd kick the rope around with his front legs and he'd put his trunk into the pot to see if there was anything hiding in there. We were always looking for new things to keep Ellie busy and keep him on his toes. He loved to play with the football when he was outside too, he'd kick it and chase after it. Sometimes he'd even kick it gently with one foot, spin around and kick it with another – it was quite a skilful move for a six-week-old elephant.

Ellie loved to play games and create mischief. Everyone on the team had experiences of Ellie's mischievous ways. After a week of Menna working with Ellie, I noticed that he would become increasingly mischievous when Menna was coming to take over for an hour or two. It was kind of like Ellie saw Menna as the fun relative that he knew he could play around with and mess about around because no matter how naughty he was, she'd give him all the love in the world. El would be full of beans so when Menna would come and spend time with him he'd always be ready to play.

Since Impy arrived, I had been spending a lot of time with Ellie but because he was always by my side and could never be left alone, I wouldn't be able to go into the house unless someone else was around to watch over him. With everyone else being so busy with our new arrivals, there was hardly ever an opportunity for someone to watch over Ellie for me. This was fine most of the day but if I needed to use the bathroom or needed some food, it was certainly not ideal. If by a stroke of luck there was someone in the kitchen as Ellie and I walked past, I'd knock on the window or poke my head in to ask someone to put some toast on for me.

With Menna part of the team and Ellie happy to be with her it made a huge difference. When Menna was watching Ellie, it would free me up completely so I could go into the house, cook, make tea, go down to see the rhinos and catch up with the team! It was great. I'd go back to the room with a big smile on my face and there would be a lot of laughter when I'd open the door to see Ellie and Menna playing around,

"He's been so naughty!" Menna would laugh while Ellie pushed his forehead into her legs.

"I've had to sit on the chair because if I sit on the floor he wants to climb on me…!" There were several pieces of enrichment in Ellie's room but his favourite game to play was two player. We'd play it a lot, not everyone would be as enthusiastic to play, but that didn't stop El. As I walked into the room, Ellie dramatically turned his shoulders to face me, his trunk swaying behind, I saw the glimmer in his eyes as he ran towards me grumbling. If he was greeting me he'd lift his trunk up but he wasn't saying hello, he was saying "LET'S PLAY!!". He held his head up with his trunk pulled down ready to nudge my legs, his steps were fast and he was closing the distance between us…The game was on.

The aim of the game is simple. You need to throw your front legs (or arms, if you're not an elephant) over the other players back. Once you've got your front legs (or arms) over the other player, you win the game as you have effectively overpowered your competitor. The main rule of the game is, well, there are no rules. You can push, shove, take a charging run up, head-butt, tackle… and those are just the tactics Ellie uses! Oftentimes, I would let Ellie win but mostly because he's a sore loser. He'd push into me, spin around, wrap his trunk around me and he would be determined to win the game, as soon as he managed to throw his legs over me he would strut around with some swagger in his steps. At one point, I decided he was getting a little bit too big for his boots so I threw my arms over his back and pushed my weight onto him, which meant quite simply, he had lost. He had lost the round and he couldn't believe it. He looked at me with utter betrayal and dragged his heavy feet to the corner of his room where he stood, facing away from me, and sulked. The mere loss of one round after countless wins and he hated it.

"El, come on. Don't be in a stress!" I think the laughter in my voice maybe worsened the situation but I knew there was one thing he would not be able to resist, a REMATCH.

"Come on grump, let's have a rematch!" I exclaimed as I pushed Ellie's bum and started to get my arms over his back so he could see we were playing again. As I did, he spun around to stop me from "winning" and put his trunk onto my shoulder, trying to put his legs over me. "Not so fast." I thought.

"If you want to beat me you're going to have to put some effort in." I chirped to him as I scattered to the other side of the room. Ellie ran after me, pushing his forehead into my side as he caught up. As we nudged each other, I made a beeline to the other side of the room, using the tyre as a barrier between us. After another scuffle, I let El win. Instantly, he was as cheerful as Ithuba at feeding time. We would play these games first thing in the morning as Ellie would be excited and full of energy after a good night's sleep and all he'd want to do is run around and play. Ellie was feeling better, he was becoming increasingly playful and energetic and he was gaining weight and strength. Some mornings we'd have a full-on play war in his room, he'd run at me with force and chase me with speed. To see his energy levels rise and for it to be so abundantly clear how settled he had become made my heart flood with joy. Almost one month ago we took this little elephant in and he was on his last legs, he was desperate and alone… Now look at him. He had a love for life, a will to live. You could see it every single day just by looking into his bright, twinkling eyes.

17: Petrichor, The Earthy Smell After Rainfall

I ran to Ellie's room as the heavy raindrops pummelled the sun-baked ground. Rainy days were rare and Ellie had yet to learn to love the water droplets that danced onto the dust. As I swung open the door and let myself in, Ellie came to greet me from his cosy pile of blankets and infrared lamp. His quick steps indicated his excitement and before I knew it his trunk was in my face and a deep rumble was erupting from him. Straight away he was nuzzling into me, demanding kisses and cuddles. There's truly no better way to start a day than this, the love this little elephant radiated was something words will never do justice.

"Good morning El, brrr, it's a bit chilly out there today boy!" I said as I moved my fingertips along his cheek and gave him a kiss good morning. I left the door open so he could see how miserable the weather was looking, but he already knew. He didn't go to investigate the weather, instead, he stood beside me tickling my legs with his trunk. My raincoat was dripping with water so I unzipped it to hang it up. As the zip jolted apart, water dripped from the jacket onto El, like when the wind blows a tree branch full of droplets just as you are walking beneath it. Immediately, Ellie's eyes darted up to meet with mine. The big grin on my face was not mirrored by El but I knew he wouldn't be able to remain annoyed if I made a big fuss of rubbing the raindrops away. El thrived on attention; he wanted to feel safe, secure and loved at all times and if, even for a second, he wasn't sure he would just reach out his trunk and get the reassurance he needed. The anticipation alone of receiving a kiss was enough to make his eyes light up.

I created a game out of giving Ellie kisses, if I was sitting down somewhere El would often stand next to me and lean on me. I would always give him kisses so now I started to make a humming noise that would 'build up' as the kiss was getting closer. Ellie absolutely loved it; his eyes would be screaming with anticipation as I'd hum. Then the kiss would land on his face and he'd put his trunk up to touch where the kiss had been placed. He'd look at me, waiting for the humming to start again. If I didn't begin to hum, he'd reach his trunk up and gently touch my face as if to say 'Again! Again!'. I'd start humming and he'd watch with anticipation, if he couldn't take it anymore, he would put his trunk onto his face as he waited for the kiss. We had a lot of fun with this little interaction. Sometimes, I'd begin to make that same humming noise at a random time just to watch Ellie's eyes light up as they'd dart across the room to meet mine as if to say, 'A KISS IS COMING?!?'

As Ellie and I were staying in the room for a little while, until the sun broke through the clouds and warmed the day up at least a little bit, I decided to take off my wellington boots. I began to pull the first one off but Ellie was slowing the process by putting his trunk in between the edge of the boot and my shin, exploring the gap, looking for anything exciting. Once that boot was off I gave it to Ellie as a gift to play with and while he was distracted I took the other boot off. Ellie's interest very quickly shifted from the shoes to my feet. Ellie seemed to be intrigued by my feet. In fact, he was fascinated. Slowly and with great care, Ellie guided his trunk over my foot, feeling it with the tip of his trunk. Seeing his fascination, I took off my socks so he could see the feet better. Intrigued, he moved his trunk down from the top of my foot to my toes. He was touching my skin ever so gently, as if unsure of the strength of the foot that was under investigation. Then, not satisfied with the light prodding of my skin and eager to put some of his new trunk skills into practice, Ellie began to pinch my foot using the tip of his trunk. First, he pinched the top of my foot but that wasn't the area that most interested the young elephant. It was the toes that really caught his eye.

"Hey! That tickles!" I exclaimed with a laugh, causing Ellie to retract his trunk at speed. I think I surprised him as he was in such deep thought regarding the toes. After a couple of seconds, Ellie moved even closer to me and continued with his investigations. I wiggled my toes under his trunk to see if he'd react. He was captivated. He continued to use his trunk but this time, as he reached my toes, he slowly picked up his front right foot. He moved it over my toes and very, very slowly, he lowered his foot onto mine pressing ever so carefully before lifting his foot away again. He did this many times as if to investigate what the toes felt like. He made sure he did not put any pressure onto my foot, he was just so intrigued. As he put his foot over mine and pinched my toes with his trunk, I realized that this is the first time I wasn't wearing shoes around him. I took a seat and held my feet up in the air so we could look at them together.

"These." I said proudly, "…are my feet and these… are my toes!" I exclaimed as I pinched my toes, Ellie was enthralled. He was looking at my feet, touching them and studying them with such a purpose of understanding. Feeling satisfied that he could now answer anyone's questions related to a human foot, he turned his attention to the human they belong to. For the first time since taking my boots off, Ellie's eyes return to me. He smiled with his eyes then came over to push his face into me and dose up on kisses.

Despite the early downpour, the clouds began to disperse allowing the sun to break through. Seeing the weather clearing; I pulled on my socks, shoes and coat and chose a nice warm blanket to wrap around El. Ellie's pile of blankets was not dissimilar to a wardrobe of clothes you or I may have. Each time we'd go out, the little elephant would get wrapped up nice and warm in one of his blankets. Once Ellie was suitably wrapped up in his patchwork blanket we went outside. The ground was spongey and full of water underfoot, puddles had formed, and we had a stream of rainwater passing the front of the house and flowing eagerly down the hill. The earthy smell we all know and love after rain has fallen filled the air and the most beautiful, vibrant rainbow had formed overhead. This breath-taking moment of fragrant life rejuvenating in the rare rainstorm was completely overlooked by Ellie, who remained in the doorway of his room looking at me with a

"No. Not a chance, have you seen those puddles?" kind of expression. I could see the cogs turning in his mind… he wanted to return to the heat lamp.

After some coaxing, Ellie finally came out from his cosy, warm room and hesitantly walked across the mud to me. His utter displeasure was indicated by his moody strut and his tense, rigid tail. He greeted me with his trunk raised and rubbed his head against my legs. Then he stood beside me, waiting to see what we would do next. On a warm day, Ellie would've trotted past me almost falling over himself to reach one of his favourite spots to play (the sand pile that had been delivered by a building company a few days earlier was the current favourite place and the 'rhino café' food storage area was also high on the list) but today he stood beside me, clearly hoping that I would decide a "pyjama day" was in order.

Inhaling the fresh air, we began to walk across the grass and into the surrounding trees. Ellie walked beside me - evidently hating the cold wet grass brushing against his feet and legs - he picked up each foot a little higher than necessary and tried to make each step count. I wouldn't tell him this, but he looked very silly walking like that. Once we reached the trees the ground was firmer and Ellie didn't seem to mind it so much. The rainbow was still proudly smiling above us, although I would classify Ellie's feelings on that as categorically uninterested. I tried to stop to show him but as I admired the beauty of the vivid rainbow, Ellie bumbled around behind me muttering about the wet ground underfoot. I could only laugh,

"It's not all heat lamps and blankets kid! You are an elephant after all." I knew he would soon learn to love the water; he just didn't understand how important it is yet.

The older rhino orphans always seemed to enjoy the rain when they were outside. It didn't fall often but when it did the rhinos would run around their enclosures, full of life and enthusiasm. As I stood with Ellie outside his room I could hear Ithuba trotting around loving the rain and mud, although he had shelters he would opt to stay out in the open during the rainfall.

Apparently, Thando and Impy were less convinced by the rainy weather, but in fairness it was their first rainfall since being with us so they were still settling in and regaining health and, like Ellie, they were particularly fond of the heat lamp and warm cuddles.

El and I made our way out into the bush, walking down the hill, passing some impala and giraffe as we journeyed through the veld. We often encountered giraffe during our walks, they seemed to enjoy eating from the trees around the orphanage and they would often stare at us with great interest before deciding they did not want to get too close. They'd calmly make the decision to move along and disappear majestically (and in what appeared to be slow motion) into the bush. Ellie never seemed too fussed by the other animals, he'd only be interested in something that was close to him and the animals in the bush made sure to always keep their distance.

One creature that did not keep their distance from El was butterflies. No, butterflies had yet to learn about Ellie and they would often fly close to his face. The colourful wings would catch El's attention, and he'd be so drawn to them that he'd lift his trunk and try to touch the butterfly. Fortunately, the first few times he tried to do this he'd miss the butterfly and the butterfly could continue its journey unharmed. However, once El had become accustomed to the speed and movement of a butterfly, he had more success. When a butterfly would flutter around his face he would swat at it with the tip of his trunk. Sometimes he'd only get them lightly and they'd fly into his cheek and then graciously flutter away as Ellie would lift his front foot as if he was trying to kick them. Unfortunately, not all the butterflies that encountered Ellie were so lucky, he managed to swat a couple of them with a bit too much enthusiasm. Thankfully, this game he had developed soon became boring as he learnt that the butterflies were fragile and could not withstand the enthusiastic strike of a baby elephant's trunk. Ellie learned to be gentler and his eyes still lit up when the butterflies would flutter around his face but he no longer tried to swat them away.

As we walked, the clouds were darkening as they moved across the sky above us. There was no doubt another rainstorm was about to hit. In an attempt to beat the incoming storm, we decided to walk a little faster as we began the incline back to the orphanage. This was something Ellie was incredibly enthusiastic about. In fact, he was trotting on ahead of me with the spirit of a homing pigeon. I can imagine he was thinking about the cosy blankets and warm milk that awaited him at home. The raindrops began to fall, sporadically at first and then, all at once. Fortunately, thanks to the enthusiasm of the little elephant we were almost home when the rain started to fall. We were in the rain for just enough time to enjoy it without getting cold. Despite his eagerness to get home, I was sure Ellie had begun to enjoy that walk, and dare I say he had even started to forget how damp the ground was.

18: Making Friends

With Ellie ever playful but remaining susceptible to illness, we decided it was time for him to spend more time around water. We decided to fill a children's paddling pool with fresh water for El to investigate and play in. I placed the hose into the pool and waited as the water level slowly rose. Ellie and I stood next to the bright blue lip of the children's pool looking at the crystal clean water glistening before us.

"Look at this El! This is going to be so much fun!!!" I shook my hand under the water to create bubbles, ripples and splashes. This caught Ellie's attention and he was soon dipping his trunk into the refreshing water. After feeling the water with his trunk, El realized the potential of the pool. He slowly lifted his foot over the pool edge and took a hesitant step into the water. As I had no intention on missing out on any of the fun, I too, stepped into the pool beside El. The water gushed up my legs, gluing the fabric of my trousers to my skin. Ellie, now standing in the middle of the pool, lent into my leg before turning his bum to me and pushing backwards against me. He wanted to play. As he backed into me, his feet were sloshing in the cold water causing fast moving ripples to surround us.

If we were going to play, we had to make it a fair game. As my hands hit the water and my knees became soaked in the pool, I was more than ready for the latest rematch. It was incredible to see how Ellie was reacting to the water, it had taken some time but he was finally starting to enjoy it. The fact he had just been introduced to the pool and he already wanted to play in it made my day.

Ellie swung his head around, pulling his trunk through the water at speed, he allowed his trunk to breach the surface slightly before returning it into the pool with great force. Spinning towards me, his movement left a crown of water rising from the surface where his trunk had entered moments ago. I could finally see it shining through the happy glisten in his eyes, it was clear as day, Ellie loved the water. This was a surprise considering each rainy day we had experienced up until now had been met with grumpy rumbles and tiptoeing around trying to avoid the puddles. Even the large bowls of fresh water in his room would yield little to no interest from him.

Now, Ellie was determined to play but I was not willing to let him win the games straight away. Before the sloshing water had a chance to slow down I further aggravated the soup of swirls by turning and moving away from Ellie. It was a move he had not expected and he was a little slow to follow me. The splashes were rising from each of our movements, the ripples were crashing together and we were both already soaking wet. I felt so refreshed, like nothing else mattered than this afternoon having a water fight in the African sun with a baby elephant. The games continued and Ellie kicked a tidal wave of water into my face as he tried to throw his front legs over me. Temporarily blinded by the sudden, unexpected splash, Ellie managed to win the first game. This was surely not the same elephant who begrudgingly walked beside me through the puddles on rare, rainy afternoons. His enthusiasm was infectious and his energy levels were through the roof.

With the first round being awarded to El, he moved to the edge of the pool, climbed out and began to wander off, dripping a trail of water as he walked.

"Oh. Giving up already hey?" I called to him from the other side of the pool, dripping wet as my clothes heavily stuck to my skin. At that, the baby elephant stopped in his tracks, turned around and took a run up into the water. His goofy run, floundering trunk and excited eyes were quite a sight. Ellie's first foot pressed down the edge of the pool and the water began pouring out towards him. He continued through the wave and into the pool, surrounding himself in a huge splash of water. He emerged the other side triumphant and proud. Ellie threw his trunk against the water in excited celebration, then he went onto his knees putting his face into the water. This is how a baby elephant would drink water in the wild. Unable to use their trunks to suck up water as the adults do (a skill that needs to be learned) the very young babies will go onto their knees, put their mouth to the water and drink like that. After a few slurps, Ellie was back onto his feet and ready to play. He decided it was fun to leave the pool and enthusiastically run up and dive back into it. With half the water now on the ground outside the pool (thanks to Ellie's run-ups and dives) the water that remained was dark with mud. We played another round, before deciding to find a quiet spot in the sun to dry off. I followed Ellie as we headed for the room, there was no hesitation as we passed the house but as soon as we approached the sand pile the young elephant decided that it was the place to be. He practically ran the final few steps to reach it and enthusiastically rolled around in the sand. I took a seat on the warm, sun-baked sand, closing my eyes and feeling the rays of sunshine on my face as Ellie frolicked beside me until he too grew tired and lay down to sleep.

Each day Ellie seemed to become livelier, more adventurous and more himself. There would have been nothing more ideal than our baby elephant having other elephants to interact with, it was a situation I dreamt of frequently but one that wouldn't materialise. While Ellie was set to remain alone for the time being, until he was well enough at least, we decided he may find Duma to be a loyal friend. Duma, a German Shepherd Dog, who was a fly-chasing, toy-carrying ball of enthusiasm had arrived to stay with us for some time and seemed to be a suitable play pal for El. Duma and Ellie were similar in size and had a shared enthusiasm for playing. Upon introducing the two, Duma was ready to play but Ellie was much more cautious, unsure of the intentions of the dog.

After a few times of meeting, Ellie realized Duma was a harmless if not slightly overenthusiastic friend. Ellie was full of life, he enjoyed chasing Duma and playing with him in the sand. The pair would tease and test each other like siblings. Ellie loved to charge his new friend whenever Duma was not expecting it. In fact, the young elephant would wait patiently for the right moment before pulling his trunk back, slightly flaring his ears up (he hadn't quite mastered it yet) and running towards Duma. Of course, Duma would always notice and simply dodge out of the way causing a game of cat and mouse to begin. Ellie and Duma could keep each other entertained for hours. They would dig and roll around in the sand, sleep in the shade of the trees together and would race to wherever they'd be going. Ellie had found a friend in Duma, and it was wonderful. Now, even on the wet days, Ellie wanted to go outside to play. He was learning more and more, and all the playing was helping Ellie's development too.

Duma would often lay in front of Ellie and fall asleep. I'd sit under the trees with them and everyone would be quiet, tired from running around. One sleepy afternoon following a lot of playing, Duma was sleeping and Ellie stood with his trunk over Duma, watching carefully. Ellie glanced over at me then, looking back down at the German Shepherd laying in front of him, Ellie slowly pulled back his trunk as if springs were tightening ready to be released. El held his trunk close to Duma before letting go and flicking his trunk straight into Dumas side. Ellie was out to cause trouble and wind Duma up! The sibling-style relationship the pair held was evidently clear. Obviously, Ellie did not feel like taking a nap and instead wanted to carry on playing. You could see the mischief written all over his face, he was plotting how he could wind Duma up and ultimately wake him up to play...

To watch Ellie bound around and play was brilliant. To ensure Ellie had time to catch his breath and relax, Duma would stay at the orphanage when we'd go for walks and he wouldn't be allowed into Ellie's room but if El had energy to burn then the pair would play outside. Duma and Ellie were starting to understand each other, they began responding to each other's body language and respecting each other's limits. They played and enjoyed each other's company and this brought a new, exciting aspect into Ellie's life at the orphanage.

19: Rhino Introductions

Ellie wasn't the only one making friends. The day had come to introduce Impy and Thando. Aly and Axel had been caring for them around the clock for the past two weeks, treating their wounds and getting them settled in Impy and Thando were now both on the same feeding routine and they'd met each other at the barrier several times in the lead up to the introduction. We'd been looking forward to this day so after my usual morning walk with Ellie I gave him a kiss and left him with Menna so I could help with the rhinos.

I met with Aly and Axel in the preparation room and we decided I'd close Ithuba into the back enclosure leaving the two front enclosures that are linked to the intensive care unit and high care unit open to give Impy and Thando plenty of space to move around while they became properly acquainted with one another. I walked through the enclosures with an armful of lucerne and called Ithuba, who willingly followed me. Once Ithuba and I were in the back enclosure, I pulled the gate along its rails, closing it behind us before securing it with the padlock and placing the extra lucerne down with his dry food. As Ithuba bumbled over to the food, I gave him a scratch admiring how big he'd grown. I shouted across to Aly and Axel to let them know the gate was closed and Ithuba and I were in position.

Aly walked Impy out of the ICU and to the open gate of the enclosure connected to Thando's room. I kept Ithuba busy, enjoying some rare time with him – it was amazing how far he had come and to see what a beautiful big rhino he was growing into. While with 'Thubes, I was also on hand to help shuffle the rhinos around and open or close gates as needed depending on the success of the introduction. We were sure the introduction between Impy and Thando would go well but we wanted to have the three of us there in case we needed to separate them for whatever reason. We hoped the pair would become friends as this would be fantastic for their rehabilitation journey and would also result in the rhino care routine being simplified. With Impy and Thando together it would mean one person caring for the two of them together rather than two people caring for them separately. The two becoming friends was a win-win situation that would work in everyone's favour.

Impy and Thando had met each other at the barrier a few times in the run up to this day so they could get used to one another before the introduction. Meeting with the barrier between them allows the orphans to become familiar with each other so that when they finally meet without the barriers it won't be as daunting. Impy and Thando seemed interested in one another and we felt quietly confident about them meeting. Aly stood with Impy just inside the enclosure where Thando was waiting by Axel's side. It was now up to the rhinos whether they wanted to approach each other or keep their distance as they sussed each other out. I watched the introduction from the gate of the back enclosure and Ithuba stood next to me eating the pile of dry food that I'd mixed some extra lucerne into as a special treat.

Impy approached Thando slowly and, with Aly by his side, he seemed to be confident. Introducing the younger rhino calves is usually easier, especially when the rhinos being introduced are around the same size. It is easier to comfort the younger ones and have some control of the situation, generally each calf will have a carer by their side as they slowly build up the courage to say hello to one another. Then, if things become scary or overwhelming the calf will simply move away and seek comfort from their carer. It tends to take a few approaches for them to figure out that the other rhino means no harm and then both rhinos become more confident. It can be difficult when the calves are older, stronger and more boisterous. Try controlling a rhino who weighs three or four times your weight, it can be a little intimidating! Fortunately, the rhino orphans tend to be friendly towards each other and will quickly sort things out between themselves without too much fuss. As Impy and Thando were still small and were both very gentle souls it was unlikely that the situation would become rowdy or out of hand.

Slowly the two calves approached each other, taking apprehensive steps across the sandy ground until finally, they met, in the open space of the outdoor enclosure. As expected, both initially felt unsure, not wanting to get too close to one another. They remained close to their carers but after some cautious smelling and a couple of retreats away from one another, Impy and Thando began to interact. Supported by Axel and Aly who stayed close by, the two orphans were soon captivated by one another. A nudge here and a nudge there, gentle smelling and pushing. Impy and Thando quickly realized that neither of them wanted to chase or charge the other. They both started to relax and were now figuring each other out. They began to walk around side by side, smelling the same things and exploring together. They walked with centimetres separating them, and quickly became a lot less concerned about the proximity of Aly and Axel - who were now standing at the side-lines providing words of encouragement when they were needed. The two rhino orphans were quickly gaining each other's confidence.

While Impy and Thando spent some time getting to know each other I heard the unmistakable scream of Ellie coming from the direction of the preparation room. This was the noise he made when he wasn't getting his own way and judging by the proximity of the scream to our rhino introduction I was pretty sure that what he wanted was to come into the enclosures and see what we were all doing. At that moment, El wasn't the centre of attention and he wanted to know exactly why. He must've heard us talking and had made his way to the preparation room where he presumably thought we were. Once he was in the preparation room and discovered he couldn't progress any further, he screamed. Fortunately, the rhinos were unfazed by Ellie's nearby tantrum and continued to explore the enclosure together. With Ellie moaning and groaning, I slipped out of the gate leaving Ithuba to enjoy his dry food.

"Alright, this seems to be going great so I'll go check on El and make sure he's not causing too much chaos." I checked the time, "Do you want me to make the milk feeds for these two?" I asked as I clunked the padlock closed on the gate between Ithuba and I.

"That would be great. I'm thinking we do the feeds separately, so they don't fight about milk. If you could help us move them apart with the milk that'll be a huge help." Aly said, keeping a close eye on the new friends.

"Sure, no problem at all. I'll be back in a minute!" I smiled.

I quietly walked around the edge of the enclosure, through the ICU and into the prep room. As I reached the door of the preparation room I was met with a trunk hanging over the top of the half door.

"Hey you cheeky monster. I told you I'd be busy for 20 minutes! What are you shouting about?" I said as I squeezed myself through the gap of the door. El grumbled into life, putting his trunk onto me and staring up at me as if to say, "What you doinggg?!".

"He ran down here so quickly and when I tried to get him out of the preparation room he started screaming at me. I think he could hear you and wanted to join in." Menna said with a laugh as she stroked Ellie's side.

"Oh Ellie!! He likes to scream at us when he's not getting his own way. He can be quite demanding, can't he?" I laughed before looking at El, "I'm not quite finished yet my boy. I just need to mix up some milk for the rhinos then I'll be five or ten minutes and we can go for a walk, okay?" I said to El who was pushed up against my side with his trunk wrapped around my leg.

"You can stay here while I mix the milk if you would like El? I can show you what we feed the rhinos, it's not the same as what you eat! You just need to be quiet, okay boy?"
El's eyes were already mischievous, but he stayed in the preparation room while I mixed the milk for Impy and Thando. I told Menna how the

introduction had gone so far as she tried to catch a glimpse of the rhinos through the preparation room window.

"Can you still see 'Thubes? He's in the back enclosure I left him near the gate eating dry food." I asked as I whisked away the lumps of milk powder.

"Ah look at him! He's looking so big compared to Impy and Thando. Doesn't he want to join the crash too?" Menna asked as she watched Ithuba eating his lucerne.

"We wish he could, he's just so much bigger than the babies at the moment. We want to give them a bit more time to settle in and build their friendship and then we will introduce Ithuba to them too if no rhinos of Ithuba's size have been brought in in the meantime. Impy and Thando are going to grow a lot over the next couple of months so they will soon be catching up with Ithuba and we'll carefully introduce them all. That'll be another day you'll have to keep yourself entertained for a bit El!". I pulled the teats onto the bottles of milk ready for the rhinos.

"Right Ellie, the milk is ready so how about you go outside and I'll be out in a few minutes?" I said as I gently guided Ellie out of the preparation room. I told Menna that I was almost done and I'd be out to give her a hand with El as soon as the rhinos were fed. I closed the preparation room door and went back outside into the enclosure.

Impy and Thando had barely even realized when it was time for milk as they were so distracted by the new friendship that was blossoming between them. We did the first few feeds separately to ensure there wouldn't be any concern or fighting over the milk, even when you've been feeding two calves side by side for a while there can still be disagreements and cheekiness at feeding time. Particularly when the milk is finished... We decided not to add this pressure to Impy and Thando's new and fragile friendship. We would only start feeding them side by side when they were used to being together and knew there was enough milk for them both.

There was no doubt that the pair were slowly but surely building a friendship. Of course, nothing quite solidifies a friendship more than having a mud bath together. So that's what they did. The two orphans were so gentle and were the perfect match for one another. We only wished we could introduce Ithuba into the group too. Unfortunately, Ithuba was much larger than Impy and Thando but we knew he so desperately craved the companionship another rhino could provide. When Impy and Thando were a bit bigger and had more confidence, then they could build a friendship with Ithuba but for now, the three of them settled for regular conversations and interactions at the enclosure fence.

After a few of these successful play dates as well as lots of milk feeds and mud baths together, we decided it was time to leave Impy and Thando together permanently. We left them to do their own thing and began bringing them into the same room at night. Our hearts filled with joy when on the first night together, the pair snuggled under the heat lamp side by side. Impy rested his head against Thando and they slept soundly in each other's company. The two orphans now supported, reassured and encouraged each other. With Impy and Thando making fast friends and needing a lot less human involvement and interaction, the rhino team were able to free up some of their time.

Ellie remained an intensive case and required 24/7 individual care but now Menna was on the team that also allowed me some time to myself. After all the chaos, it seemed as though we were coming out of the other side largely intact. A little worn out maybe but still in one piece. With the routine, for the moment, stable I joined Aly to do the food shop in our closest town. It was now early November and it had been months since I had left the confines of the reserve so this trip, although seemingly mundane, was actually very exciting. After a feed, I said bye to Menna and Ellie (I gave El specific instructions to behave himself for Menna while I was in town). We would only be gone for a few hours so I knew he wouldn't be able to cause too much chaos. After getting the various shopping requests from Axel, Menna, our local staff and our volunteers (chocolate, airtime, milkshakes… the standard orders that were repeated every single time someone left the reserve to go to the shops), Aly and I climbed into the truck.

As we drove out of the reserve gate and onto the dirt road we opened the windows, turned up the radio and let the music lift our energies with its loud and lively tempo. To be away from the orphanage gave us some much-needed respite where, for a moment, we could switch off our brains and relax. Our minds had been in overdrive since the day Ellie arrived but for that moment in time, we could dance, talk and enjoy the fresh air and views of rural South Africa. We drove through the local village, weaving around the goats and cows who stood, entirely unconcerned, on the road. We smiled to the children who enthusiastically waved and shouted 'HELLO' as we drove by.

"Oh man. I needed this. Just to be out, getting some fresh air." I commented to Aly as we rattled along the uneven, pothole filled road.

"Me too. It's been so stressful, we haven't had any time for us…" Aly was right. We hadn't and it was less than ideal. We knew burn out was all too real and it was something we'd been bordering on.

"… I've been keeping an eye on job openings to see what's around." Aly continued. Although it saddened me to think of our team without Aly I knew that our situation was tough and, ultimately, unsustainable. I completely understood why she was keeping a look out for other work. This job meant we couldn't have a life outside of the orphanage and, unlike Axel and I, Aly had a long-term relationship to consider too. We lived in rural South Africa, had a job that was so intense we hardly slept, and our team was so small that a trip to the supermarket was essentially considered a "day out". There was no home life: work life balance and we knew it.

"Oh Aly. I'd be gutted if you left but jeez, I completely understand. Have you seen anything that has caught your eye?"

"Not yet but I think I will leave before the end of the year." Aly replied, we ended up having a heart to heart on our drive to town. It was needed, being able to be away from the orphanage and talk openly was therapeutic. We'd been struggling under the strain of the intensive cases but agreed things were levelling out.

With the white rhinos spending time together it took the pressure off the rhino team and in a couple of days a new long-term volunteer, Angie, would be arriving to spend a couple of months working with us. Everything was becoming more manageable, less urgent, less life-or-death and it was a huge relief. After 45 minutes, we reached the town. It was teeming with people, cars everywhere, crowds of people crossing the roads at their leisure with no reaction to the hooting of horns or oncoming traffic. I was quite taken aback by the sudden activity after the very quiet drive that led us there.

"Welcome to town." Aly said as she laughed, she was used to this and navigated the pedestrians and stationary taxis with ease. We reached a quieter part of town and pulled up in the supermarket car park. We grabbed a trolley and headed into the store with our shopping list in hand, we began to fill the trolley with the essentials; fruit and vegetables, rice, pasta and tinned foods. In a separate part of the trolley we stacked the treats that we would pay for with our own money, that was the chocolates, the milkshake powder, the crisps. Walking around the supermarket turned into this nostalgic trip of seeing our favourite food, pointing at it and saying "Ohhh remember this? This is SO delicious." Followed by an in-depth description of the best way to eat that specific food before finally proceeding to walk straight past it because we knew there was no way we could afford it. We had a card to buy the food shop but the directors who controlled our funds were not willing to increase the amount on the card, even though we now had twice as many people to feed as well as additional basics to buy for the animals. It was an ongoing struggle, but we added up the rands as we put items into the trolley in an attempt to keep below the budget. That's why we bought the snacks and more 'luxurious' items with our own money, but snacks weren't the only thing I was buying on this trip… As we turned down another aisle, it was filled with children's toys and a green dinosaur soft toy caught my eye. I picked it up and turned to show Aly,

"I NEED to buy this for El!!!" I said with a huge grin. Aly laughed and agreed that El would love the dinosaur. Let's face it, there was no way I'd be away from El for the first time in months and not return with a gift for him. I laughed at the absurdity, not sure whether I was laughing at myself or just at the situation. Either way, undeterred, I carried that dinosaur teddy for the rest of the wander around the supermarket and put it onto the counter to pay with a rather satisfied smirk. Clearly feeling like I had not spent enough money, I then found out there was a health food shop in the same block of stores and proceeded to spend the little I had left on dried mango, a couple of different types of tea, seed and nut mixes and chai latte powder. Feeling quite animated about my purchases, we went back to the truck and loaded up the goods on the back seats. Although it had crossed my mind to place the dinosaur on the seat nicely and plug the seatbelt in, I resisted, knowing I looked crazy enough as it was. Instead, I sat him on top of the shopping (looking out of the window, obviously…) so he could watch the world go by as we drove.

We reversed out of the parking space, Aly gave a couple of rand to the car guard and we continued our journey. In South Africa, carparks and shopping centres have guys who point you to open spaces, watch your car while you shop and (very) enthusiastically direct you when you reverse out of the space – all for your spare change. Car guards often have a big smile and are super friendly, they'll help you with your trolley and carrying your shopping too if you'd like. So, after giving the car guard some loose change, we went to a pharmacy to stock up on some of the over-the-counter medicines we used for the animals. After about an hour and a half in town, we had finished the shopping. My senses had been overwhelmed by the trip, after living in the middle of the bush, the hustle and bustle of the town was quite something.

"Is there anything else we need before we head back?" Aly asked as we climbed back into the car.

"I don't think so." I said as I opened the dried mango and offered the bag to Aly. We checked the list of stuff the team had requested and had everything ticked off.

"Alright! Time to head home!" Aly said as she pulled her seatbelt on and turned the key in the ignition. The trip to town was short but sweet. We'd needed the time away from the orphanage and it had given us the chance to properly catch up. Now driving alongside sugarcane fields on route back to the orphanage, we listened to our favourite music and danced all the way home.

After we'd offloaded the shopping and put the food away in the kitchen, I took the dinosaur and went in search of El. The triceratops toy was adorable; it was green, fluffy and had a white horn on the end of its nose and two white horns on the top of its head. It was great, I loved it and I couldn't wait to show Ellie. I went into his room and he had just finished a bottle of milk.

"Hello little love… I'm home!!" I said as Ellie ran towards me grumbling a hearty greeting. After saying hello, I stepped back and revealed the triceratops toy from behind my back.

"Look what I found for you in the shop El!" I held the dinosaur out to Ellie, who put his trunk up to touch the fluffy Triceratops. He felt the fur of the dinosaur and then slowly wrapped his trunk around the teddy. With El's trunk now wrapped around the dinosaur, I let it go and Ellie gently lowered it to the floor. Placing the dinosaur onto the floor, Ellie began touching it and lightly kicking it with his front foot. After determining the sturdiness of his new toy, the inquisitive elephant pulled his trunk along the soft fur and lightly wrapped his trunk around the body of the dinosaur, lifting it up again. I put my hand out and El placed the triceratops onto my palm keeping his trunk firmly holding on. I began making a humming noise as I moved the dinosaur towards El's face to give him a kiss on the cheek. Upon hearing the humming, he let go of the toy and his trunk flew up to his cheek before then returning to the dinosaur. After receiving a few kisses from the new toy, El spent a good few minutes rubbing his trunk into its fur, lifting it up and lightly kicking it around. Once the games were over, I picked the triceratops teddy up and placed it onto El's bed. He spent another few minutes moving it around before he decided it was time to go outside to play. I think he liked the triceratops, I placed into onto his bed so he could snuggle up with it in the evenings (which he did!).

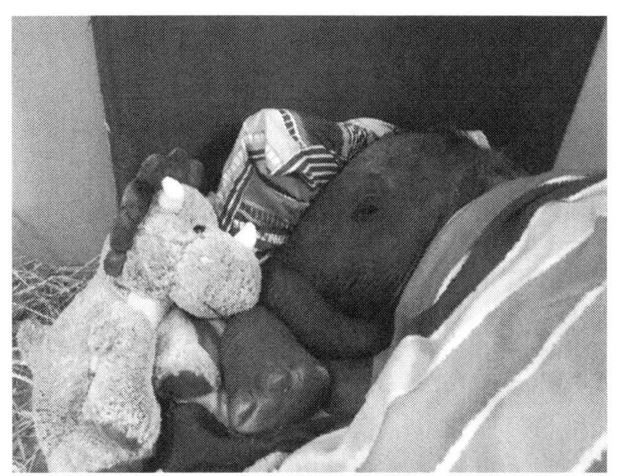

20: Growing Team

Although we continued to work around the clock, life at the orphanage had become more relaxed. It was nowhere near as laid-back as it had been when we were only caring for Ithuba but more relaxed than it had been since August, three months earlier. All the animals at the orphanage were now stable and in good health. Impy and Thando were together 24/7, Ellie was gaining weight and was keeping me on my toes and Ithuba was slowly beginning to be weaned. Things were going really well.

As the rhino team had more free time Aly and Axel would sit and spend time with Ellie every so often and would join us to play in the garden too. This was a lot of fun, Ellie always loved it when members of our dysfunctional herd would come and spend time with him. El loved to be the centre of attention, he'd be really cheeky and playful and we'd all laugh so much our cheeks would hurt. Ellie would often try to climb on top of people when they sat down and would creep up behind you before enthusiastically throwing his front legs onto your shoulders before you had a chance to react. We had finally got a grasp on the situation and we were very excited to soon have another long-term volunteer arriving to join the team. Although I rarely had time to spend with the volunteers - particularly with the short-term volunteers who I didn't have the opportunity to get to know properly - it was always great to have some new energy and enthusiasm around the orphanage.

Ellie and I were in his room resting after a long walk when our new long-term volunteer, Angie, arrived so it was not until some hours later that we were able to meet. Menna came to watch our little elephant for a while which gave me some free time. As I walked up to the house, I was met by a blonde lady with a big grin and an infectious laugh sitting and chatting with Aly. Although from the UK, Angie already looked settled in the African bush, she was wearing shorts and a t-shirt and had several rhino tattoos on her arms that were absolutely beautiful. Something told me this wasn't Angie's first time working with rhinos in the African bush!

"Hey, how's it going? I'm Ang, nice to meet you." Angie said with a grin as I approached them.

"Hey! Good to meet you too, my name's Meg. I'm one of the carers for Ellie, the baby elephant. You'll meet him a little later today!" I responded, it turned out that through my tiredness and the (what felt like) constant stream of changing volunteers I'd spoken to in the past couple of months that I had become quite matter of fact when it came to these interactions. Angie, immediately determined to break through the walls I'd put up, said,

"Amazing, can't wait! I've heard a lot about him and the rhinos… Oh, I love your hoodie!!" This comment was in reference to an ocean conservation jumper I was wearing, and it struck up a conversation about our mutual love for the ocean and our previous experiences relating to ocean protection and conservation. It was refreshing to speak about something new and Angie was so passionate and down to earth.

As we began to connect, the conversation went on as we talked about Angie's tattoos and she told me about her experiences volunteering with wildlife vets to help Thandi, a rhino who survived a poaching attack and was receiving treatment for her facial wound. There was no doubt that Angie was going to be an asset to the team and it was a relief to know she would be staying with us for a while, it was giving us stability that we needed. I suppose for me Angie's arrival was an important and necessary breath of fresh air as, although I was happy with my hands-on around the clock work with El, I had become distanced from the team.

Since we had split into two teams, I was almost exclusively with El from six a.m. – eleven p.m. every day with a couple of short breaks in between which meant by the time I had finished my shift everyone was sleeping or on their night shifts and I was going straight to bed too. Then I'd wake up first thing in the morning before the rest of the orphanage had begun to stir to start the day with Ellie. This didn't leave me much time to participate in the team interactions and although everyone loved to spend time with Ellie during the day it was always short and sweet. Once there were different people each week I started to shut myself off from it all but when Angie arrived, she helped to pull me out of this rut with her friendliness, energy and interest. Angie slotted into the team straight away, her sense of humour had us all laughing and her no nonsense, get up and go attitude was perfect.

A couple of days after Angie arrived we received a call about a Jackal pup that had been found in a cage by a maintenance man who was working in someone's garden. The man was going to bring the Jackal to us as we were the closest animal rescue centre. Although very different from our usual arrivals, we would provide the pup with short-term care before transporting the Jackal to a wildlife rehabilitation centre a few hours away once he was stable. Jackals are small canines; they are sometimes described as looking like a cross between a fox and a German shepherd.

The Black Backed Jackal pup arrived scared and dehydrated, he had a small face with large, pointed ears and deep dark eyes that looked as though they could've been lined with a black eyeliner. He was gorgeous but he was very afraid. Fortunately, we suspected he wasn't held in the cage for longer than a couple of days. Angie took the Jackal pup under her wing and made sure he was always warm, secure and well fed. Our plan was to move the Jackal to another wildlife centre as soon as we could so he could be raised with other Jackals.

With the unexpected arrival of the little Jackal and the constant need for new equipment, after the first white rhino milk feed of the day, Aly and Ang headed into town as Ang had offered to buy the orphanage some much needed equipment as a donation from her non-profit organisation. This was incredibly generous and very exciting for our team. To see the pickup truck pull up with Aly and Ang's beaming faces surrounded by new stuff for the orphanage was quite a sight. The inside of the car was chock-a-block with equipment, it was so full that Angie had items stacked on her lap the entire car ride home. When they parked outside the house all you could see was their two grinning faces in amongst a heap of milk mixing equipment, buckets, fencing material, troughs and even a new hide for the jackal. It was a huge list of goodies for the rhinos, jackal and even for us!

Helping to unload the truck was great fun, it was impressive how much stuff they'd managed to put into the vehicle in a Tetris-style manner. The atmosphere was light-hearted and full of laughter as we replaced old, worn and damaged equipment with brand new items. Everyone was so excited to have shiny new equipment, we could finally say goodbye to items like the broken, taped-up rakes. After unloading all the goodies, Angie and Aly got to work setting up a secure area for the jackal to enjoy while he was under our care. The young Jackal stayed with us under Angie's diligent care for several weeks before being transported to a wildlife rehabilitation centre that dealt with smaller animals and had other jackal pups already in their care.

Our team felt like a family, it was such a privilege to be part of this group of ordinary people living life with passion and purpose. Whenever anyone had free time, they'd join Ellie, Menna and I at his new favourite hangout spot – the veranda that wrapped around half of the house. Ellie absolutely loved spending time on the veranda, I think he felt closer to everyone when we were there. We had been spending time around the rhino café, but Ellie soon realised that since the introduction of Impy and Thando there weren't many people working down at the rhino rooms, upon noticing that the house was a more active spot, we had started to spend time on the veranda.

After the daily sunrise walk in the bush, Ellie and I spent countless afternoons in the garden and the veranda gave such a great vantage point (as well as shade from the blazing sun). I would sit on the wall of the veranda while Ellie would play on the grass in front of the house, rub himself against the walls or lean against me and watch the world go by.

Sitting out on the veranda was great, Menna would usually sit out there with us and whoever was in the house would come and join us too meaning we always had people joining in and chatting. It was lovely spending time at this new favoured spot because it really was keeping us close to the team. We had a lot of fun, laughter and long conversations sitting there looking out at the incredible rolling views of the wildlife reserve while Ellie minded his own business, playing on the grass with Duma.

It was also very handy when El would be on the veranda for feeding time because I could make use of the small veranda wall. If I stood on the ground on the other side of the veranda wall and Ellie stood on the veranda it put El at a great height for feeding and it meant he wouldn't be able to push me because of the sturdy brick wall between us. The wall came up to the top of El's legs which was perfect, he'd stand still with his trunk touching my face and he'd drink all his milk with ease.

Of course, sitting on the veranda meant Ellie would often see people disappearing through the door going into the house and seeing that the house was one of the consistently busy spots on the property Ellie had decided, rather adamantly, that that was where he wanted to be. I was in complete disagreement; I was more than happy for us to spend time on the veranda but I had told El many times that he's an elephant and elephants shouldn't be spending time in the house. This didn't stop him from trying to push his way through the door whenever he saw the opportunity.

While he couldn't go inside without a fight, Ellie loved looking in through the windows and he'd push his face up against the glass (much to Goodness' dismay as she would be frequently cleaning the muddy smudges away). While peeking over the windowsill, Ellie would put his trunk through the gaps of the open windows. With his trunk now inside the house, El would see if there was anything he could reach and grab. He'd be side glancing at me the whole time with this mixed look of pride, amusement and cheekiness. One day when Ellie had his trunk outstretched trying to find something within grabbing distance, Aly walked by on her way to the office. She looked towards the window to be greeted by the fuzzy forehead of a young elephant, his trunk reaching into the room and his cheeky gaze as he peeked over the window ledge.

"Oh! Hello Ellie!" Aly said with a smile, approaching him as he watched with delight in his eyes. I'd be sitting on the floor leaning against the wall a few feet away, smirking at him as if to say, 'See, I told you they'd catch you'.

"What are you looking for in here Ellie?" Aly asked as El gave her trunk kisses through the window,

"Hmmm" Aly said as she glanced around, "It looks like there's nothing here for an elephant I'm afraid." Of course, El didn't believe this for a second and it certainly wouldn't stop him from trying his luck whenever he saw the windows were open. As Aly walked away, El pulled his trunk out from the window and trotted over to me. He pushed his head into my lap and put his trunk onto my cheek. I think he wanted to know if I'd seen him get caught so I laughed as I put my arms over him and said,

"Yes El, I saw. I warned you didn't I!" I was sat with the clipboard of El's records in my lap, I continued adding in comments from the last couple of hours of feeds and observations as El stood next to me, leaning his chin against my shoulder. Ellie looked down at the records and at the pen in my hand and then gently wrapped his trunk around the pen.

"Oh, you want to help me write the records? What shall we write? Shall we write about how cheeky you are?!" I asked as El held the pen with me, he held the pen with such a gentle grasp that I could continue writing without much interference. Once I'd finished the sentence in slightly messier handwriting than usual, it was Ellie's turn to direct the pen. We drew a few squiggles before El released the pen from his trunk and nudged his head against me. Ellie leant against me as he began to drift to sleep; his eyes heavy, the tip of his trunk now resting on the floor and his legs locked in place. It looked like it was time for a little power nap while on his feet, being mischievous is tiring after all.

If all was quiet and El had recently had a feed, I'd be able to leave Ellie with Menna and use the time before the next feed to say hello to the rhino orphans and spend some time with them. On a relaxed afternoon, I went to see how Impy and Thando were, I went into the preparation room and looked over the half door to see Angie laying on the floor with Impy lying next to her with his head resting softly on her back and Thando laying as close as he could next to Impy. It was so sweet. Angie was besotted with the boys and you could see they felt exactly the same. They were completely unconcerned when Ang and I started chatting, the rhino calves were so cosy and content that they barely even opened their eyes. The boys were still young so needed someone close by keeping an eye on them. It wasn't unusual to find one of the orphans resting their head on someone's lap or being spoilt with belly rubs. More often than not it was Impy, who was slightly younger than Thando.

One morning I had some free time as Ellie and Menna were exploring in the garden so I went down to the rhino rooms to help give Impy and Thando's room a full clean. With a bucket of disinfectant, a pair of disposable gloves on and a brush in hand I was knelt on the floor scrubbing the barrier rails clean (they often became muddy and clogged up with bedding and dry food). As I cleaned the muck from the rails, Impy walked over to me and gently rested his head on my shoulder.

"Hey boy. I've missed you. How are you doing?" I asked as I looked up and his eyes met mine. His eyes were bright, his look tender, genuine and expressive. Impy was always gentle, his heart open, he would give love freely to those who showed him kindness. With his chin resting on my shoulder as I was knelt down cleaning the floor, the young rhino let out a contented sigh. The mere action of ever-so-slightly leaning on me and it was all he wanted. The gentlest of souls, soft in touch but strong in spirit - Impy was a very special character.

After seeing Impy and Thando I went to see how 'Thubes was doing. Ithuba would mostly keep himself entertained in the larger of the enclosures but it was clear he wanted to be with Impy and Thando.

Ithuba and Thando were particularly fond of each other and would often meet at the fence to have lengthy discussions. Sometimes Ithuba, Thando and Impy would all sleep side by side at the enclosure poles. We knew that soon Ithuba needed to be integrated in with Impy and Thando to form the white rhino crash. We rarely went into the enclosure with Ithuba anymore, only a couple of times a day to clean and sort his feeds. Although Ithuba was big now he remained gentle. At times, he was a bit overly enthusiastic when we went into his enclosure. Particularly when he was feeling energetic and he wanted to play, he would demonstrate his desire to play by running directly at you – something that felt a little overwhelming considering his size, strength and speed. Although he'd never run into us it still felt like a test of nerve. Rather than standing in the open and hoping for the best, we would always make use of trees and poles as barriers. These were a small but significant protection that ensured Ithuba couldn't run full force into us.

'Thubes would sometimes play with open gates and barriers, causing them to become dislodged from the rails. Each day we would have to go around realigning any of the open gates. This was easy enough but there were times 'Thubes took whole steel gates that stood eight feet tall and five feet wide off their frames with minimal effort, causing them to tumble to the ground. As only Aly, Axel or myself would go in with Ithuba, Aly and I decided to go in and put the fallen gate back in place. It was a two-person job as the gates were heavy and putting them back into the frames and onto the rails was an awkward task.

When Ithuba saw us enter his enclosure he came bounding over very enthusiastically. We said hello and gave him some attention, commenting on how huge he now was. Ithuba's size was particularly noticeable when going to see him straight after spending time with Impy and Thando.

After we'd made a fuss of 'Thubes, we carried on walking across the enclosure and Ithuba started to bounce around telling us that he wanted to play. Despite us trying to tell him that we needed to fix the gate 'Thubes was adamant about playing. He began to sprint around the two open enclosures so while he was running Aly and I took the opportunity to try to reposition the gate. The gate was heavy and awkward so getting it back into position within the 30 second window Ithuba had given us before he was bounding full speed towards us again was not going to happen. As Ithuba emerged from the trees and sprinted towards us, we had to put the gate down. Aly ran one way to seek protection behind a tree and I ran the other to use a thorny bush as a barrier.

After a bit of cat and mouse, Ithuba once again went sprinting around both enclosures. This time, we decided it was best to pick the gate up and take it out of the enclosure entirely so that it would be out of the way until Ithuba's next feed when we would be able to put it back in its place properly while he was distracted. We lifted the gate and began shuffling across the enclosure, hearing Ithuba's footsteps gaining on us we looked at each other, looked over our shoulders and looked at each other again. Seeing very little choice, we agreed to put the gate down and move to the trees before Ithuba reached us. Ithuba was throwing his weight around and having an absolute whale of a time. We knew that on his next sprint around we could get the gate out so as soon as Ithuba started running, we grabbed the gate and continued across the enclosure. As we reached the sliding enclosure gate that we needed to go through to get out, we stopped so I could open it just enough for us to slip out. There was still no sign of Ithuba.

"Okay. Ready? Lift on three. One. Two. Three." I counted as we lifted the steel gate again, then we heard Menna's voice coming from near the volunteer rooms where she was standing with Ellie, looking across the grass at what we were doing,

"Ithuba is coming!!! QUICK, QUICK!!!" she shouted as she watched us racing Ithuba to try to get out and close the gate before he reached us. We could hear the panic in her voice and the thudding of 'Thubes running towards us so we knew we were cutting it close but we'd already committed ourselves to the decision so we carried on. Thankfully, we had a second or so to spare as we made it out and pulled the gate closed behind us. Ithuba, unfazed, ran to the gate before making a swift turn and continuing his sprint.

With the gate Ithuba had removed now safely out of the way, I went back into the enclosure to build up the log pile so he could have some fun charging at it and hitting the logs around. He clearly had lots of energy to use up and although I wasn't fast enough to run with him anymore it didn't mean we couldn't play. I threw the worn tyre bowl towards him to try to distract him while I moved the logs. As soon as I picked up a log or started dragging the larger logs Ithuba began to throw his head around and mock charge the log from just a couple of steps away.

"Hey! No boy! I'm holding the log, don't do that. Just wait a minute." I said firmly to the 300kg white rhino, trying to dissuade him from attacking the logs while they were in my hands. Catching Ithuba in these playful moods was a lot of fun. Sometimes he'd just want to lay in a mud bath or would be more than happy eating his dry food when we'd go in to do maintenance, clean or check in with him but every now and then he would be in this cheeky, mischievous, playful mood and the only thing on his mind was playing and having fun. After I'd stacked most of the logs, I gave Ithuba a scratch and told him I'd see him later. I left him to use his energy playing with the stack of logs and for well over an hour afterwards, I could hear him enthusiastically knocking and throwing the logs around from the other side of the orphanage. He was loving it.

21: Wild Encounters

Being at the orphanage, each day would merge into the next. We had our daily routines; the cleaning, the feeds, the time spent with the orphans playing, walking and wallowing. As we were all getting on with things, there'd be the occasional moment that would stand out and make our day.

One such moment was when we saw the elephant herd casually walking next to the orphanage fence. Whenever we saw the wild elephants or rhinos close by, whoever spotted them would tell the whole team so whoever wasn't on shift could find a quiet place to sit and watch the wild animals as they'd go about their day. After seeing the elephants nearby, Angie, Axel and I called Goodness, Senzo and Sihle so they could come and watch the herd with us. The elephants were very relaxed and were browsing from the trees that stood on the other side of our fence. Although nervous at first, our local team members joined us as we quietly walked across the grass and found a place close to the fence to stand and watch the herd of 25 elephants as they walked by the orphanage. What a moment – getting an up-close and personal glimpse into the wild from the comfort of our own home!

Right in front of us, the elephants wrapped their trunks around branches and effortlessly pulled them from the trees into their mouths. The branches produced almighty cracks as they were snapped away from the trees under the pressure of the elephant's trunks.

"Aren't they amazing?" I whispered to Goodness.

"Wow, wow, wow. They are so big. They are not dangerous? What if they come here to us?" She looked over at me with a concerned look on her face but Goodness couldn't contain her excited grin for long.

"Don't worry. They shouldn't come over here, they are really relaxed. We just need to be quiet, stay on this side of the fence and keep our distance." I smiled, easing her nerves.

"So, Ellie will grow big like this?" Senzo turned to ask, then he laughed saying, "he will not fit inside that room anymore if he gets this big!!"

"Aww! Look at that little one over there!!" Ang exclaimed as she crouched down, looking at a baby elephant through gaps in the bushes. The calf was dwarfed by the rest of the herd, he was slightly larger than Ellie but looked to be only around a year old. It was beautiful to see this healthy youngster at the side of his mother and surrounded by a loving, protective herd. I imagined Ellie being there, eating the twigs and leaves surrounded by a herd. I imagined him growing up to be big and strong like these elephants that were so close I could almost touch them. A herd of gentle giants.

Being able to watch the elephants like this was exceptional. The herd communicated with each other through occasional deep rumbles as we watched on in an awe-inspired silence. My heart felt full as we admired them. Being so close to the elephants on foot allowed us to truly appreciate their size and strength. An adult human is barely the size of a fully-grown elephant's leg! Then, with measured, purposeful steps the herd began to move off down the hill. Beaming from ear to ear, we returned to the house to carry on with our work. It was such a wonderful moment. To be able to share the wildlife encounter with members of our team who had never had an opportunity like that before made it even more special.

We'd try to keep Ellie inside if the elephant herd were really close to the fence, just in case. Fortunately, the elephants generally came to the orphanage at night, when El was safely snuggled up in a pile of blankets under his heat lamp. One afternoon, Menna and I were sitting on the veranda with Ellie when we spotted the herd making their way up to the orphanage.

We decided to take Ellie into the house to avoid any difficult to handle situations. As we didn't really have any control of Ellie when he wanted to do something we knew if he decided to go down to the fence to see the herd or if they decided they wanted to break through the fence and come up to us, we would have no hope of controlling the situation. We would rather avoid that from happening altogether so a quick shuffle into the house seemed like a good option. As we usually kept Ellie out of the house, and made quite a point of keeping him outside, he thought going into the house was very exciting. As soon as we opened the door he barged his way in and began exploring. First, he was met by the sofas in the communal living area. He immediately started head-butting the first sofa in his path and began pushing it around the room.

"No El, hey, hey, hey. Don't do that. Don't fight with the furniture." I said, trying to dissuade him. It wasn't the best start to him being in the house. Once he got bored of the sofa – he'd pushed it against a wall so it wasn't moving anymore meaning he quickly lost interest - Ellie then turned his attention to the rest of the house. Ellie shuffled his way to the hallway where he found a large ornamental pot that caught his eye. He moved a bit quicker as he closed the distance between himself and the pot. I knew exactly what he was going to do as he bee-lined towards it. First, he put his trunk straight into it to see if there was anything inside. He peered inside too but as the pot was empty (other than a bit of dust that had settled inside) it soon lost the inquisitive elephant's interest. When El was taking his trunk out of the empty pot he realised that he could pull the pot over onto its side, potentially creating a whole new game to play. As I saw the pot about to tumble I ran over to catch it, not wanting Ellie and I to be responsible for breaking anything in the house. Ellie knew I was putting a stop to that game and I tried to gently persuade him back towards the door we had come in through, slightly regretting the decision to bring him inside. He gave me a look that could've easily been accompanied by a scoff and the words,

"No way!!! Not when we haven't even looked in the kitchen yet." Ellie strode ahead of me and went into the kitchen; his sudden and unexpected presence gave Goodness a fright. Goodness and Ellie then stood in the middle of the kitchen having a chat and every time Ellie would put his trunk up onto the worktop to see what he could reach Goodness would gently tap the end of his trunk and say,

"No Ellie… There is nothing here for you!" Naturally, Ellie wanted to make sure of that himself. After a thorough look around the kitchen, we made our way back to the communal living room. I looked out of the window to see if I could still see the elephant herd. I couldn't see them and when we saw them walking towards the orphanage, it seemed as though they were on their way to one of the dams with their long strides and purposeful walk so I was sure they would be long gone. I figured I'd give Ellie a few more minutes inside so I sat on the sofa that he'd had pushed against the wall and watched as he looked around to see how else he could cause trouble. I was surprised when he decided to pick a fight with the fire extinguisher that hung on the wall. It was possibly the only thing I didn't expect.

"Okay, okay, okay. You hooligan, you win. Let's go back outside!" I said, getting up from the sofa and trying to nudge El towards the door. It was a bit of a scuffle as El wanted to stick around and fight with the fire extinguisher but eventually we made it back outside.

Thanks to Angie's arrival and the introduction of Impy and Thando, the workload had eased and there would now be only one person on night shift with the rhinos. This meant the rest of the rhino team could have the evening off and get a good night's rest. One of the people not on night shift would make dinner for the team. We would generally keep our dinners basic, but it would really depend on the mood and enthusiasm of the person cooking. We all had very different meal ideas and cooking methods… Axel loved to make pizzas or tarts with homemade bases – they'd always taste delicious but when he was done the kitchen would be in a state with piles of dishes stacked in the sink and flour absolutely everywhere, Ang on the other hand would make very tasty roast dinners that reminded me of home. Aly and I would often opt for simple pasta dishes or a stir fry. Everyone gravitated to the kitchen, we would all hang out there whenever we had free time in the evening, sitting on the floor chatting and drinking tea or chopping vegetables and cooking dinner together.

After dinner, whoever was not on shift would usually spend an hour or so chatting and then everyone would go to bed early, savouring every hour available to sleep. While Menna was on the Ellie team with me I had an hour between five p.m. – six p.m. each evening to spend time in the house with everyone and then I'd be back on shift until eleven p.m. This shift pattern worked surprisingly well as it gave me the chance to spend time with the team in the early evening as well as giving Menna time to spend with everyone after shift change. During these times of stability and routine, the evenings were the part of the day our team was able to relax. Having the opportunity to hang out together in more of a social situation was good for us, you'd think we would be fed up with each other considering we lived, worked and socialised in this rarely changing group but, on the contrary, these evenings allowed our friendships the opportunity to bloom and for us all to de-stress. The evenings were filled with laughter and jokes, and this kept us connected on more than just a work level.

Some evenings Aly and Ang would come and spend time with Ellie which was nice because then he'd use up all his energy playing with his "crazy aunties" before bedtime. When Aly, Ang and Ellie were in a room together there was hysterical laughter that you'd be able to hear across the orphanage. Ellie would be the centre of attention and he absolutely loved it. He'd climb over Aly and Ang, chase them around and start a play war that I don't think any of them could ever actually win. I'd leave them to it and I'd come back to Aly and Angie crying with laughter and Ellie with the most mischievous look in his eyes.

Getting El to use up his energy before nightfall was always a worthwhile endeavour, the nights went by a lot faster when you didn't have to stay awake to keep a very energetic elephant entertained. Most of the time El would sleep until eleven p.m. and then Menna would come on shift where there would be a 50/50 chance of him sleeping or him causing havoc for a few hours. Sometimes he would sleep for an hour and then after the next feed he would insist on wondering around the orphanage. He'd walk to the preparation room, shuffle around outside his room. One thing that I'd hear him do most nights at around 11pm when we switched shifts would be shuffling around outside my room and window. I'd hear him dragging his feet around on the small section of concrete underneath the window and it would make me smile every time. If I'd only just finished my shift I'd say goodnight to him again through the window, which he always loved.

Ellie could be quite naughty at night and you'd be trying so hard to keep him quiet so he didn't wake everyone else up. Menna would finish her shift at three a.m. and one of our long-term volunteers would do the final three hours until six a.m. when I'd be back on shift. By the time Menna was finished at three a.m. I would be fast asleep but most nights as she would quietly come into the room I'd sit bolt upright and I'd usually be alarmed thinking that I'd fallen asleep next to Ellie and hadn't woken up in time for his next feed. There was one night when I put my arm out to stroke Ellie's head and I was met with Menna saying,

"Meg!! I am NOT an elephant." Turns out, I wasn't on shift and it was just after three in the morning and I had accidentally stroked my mums face. Like I said, our beds weren't even an arm's length apart, so this was easily done.

I woke up at around half past three one morning to the sound of El screaming. I jumped out of bed and pulled my shoes on so I could go and find out what the problem was. I slowly opened the door to El's room and peeked inside,

"Hey, is everything alright? I heard Ellie screaming…" I asked.

"He's fine… He just doesn't want to sleep, and I won't let him go outside so now he's screaming at me." Replied the tired volunteer who was clearly not in the mood for Ellie's nighttime shenanigans.

"Want me to come and sit with you guys for a bit?" I asked as I walked into the room. Ellie came over to me, grumbling with bright eyes and welcoming me with an enthusiasm level that was much too high for half past three.

"Hey my boy. Listen, I was just sleeping and I'm going to be honest with you… I'm still feeling pretty tired so what I'm going to do is go and lay down on your bed and then you can just come over and tell me what your problem is over there okay?" I said as I slowly walked across his room and laid on the mattress on the floor.

"I've tried that. He just wants to go outside to play." The volunteer said as I laid on El's bed. I closed my eyes and before I knew it I felt Ellie lightly kick my leg with his front leg. After nudging me, he carefully stepped over my legs, trying to squeeze himself in between me and the wall. I rolled over to make space for him and he laid down in the gap.

"Alright boy, go to sleep. It'll be a couple of hours until sun rise so just get some rest and we'll play in the morning, okay?" I said softly as the little elephant began to drift to sleep. I laid there for five minutes while El fell into a deeper and deeper sleep.

"Alright, I'm going to slowly move away so as I move you sit in my place, okay? He should stay sleeping but I'll be as quiet as possible. Hopefully the rest of the shift will be quieter now. Sweet dreams El, I'll see you at 6." I began to edge away from El so I could stand up and leave them to it. I snuck back to my room.

"What's wrong?" Menna said into the darkness as the bedroom door clicked closed.

"It's okay, I just went to make sure Ellie was okay because I heard him screaming." I whispered back, "He's fine, he was just being cheeky. I think he's overtired but he's sleeping now."

"Oh, okay… Goodnight." Menna responded before rolling over and going back to sleep. I climbed into my bed and got comfy again.

The months that Menna worked with us went by like a whirlwind and before I knew it, it was time for her to leave. It felt like I had only picked her up a week ago, but it had already been over two months. I knew she was sad to be leaving and the whole team were going to miss having her around, especially Ellie and me. It had been an amazing experience to share with my mum and I was so grateful for all her help. Angie had offered to drive Menna to the airport, so Ellie and I waved them off and then, just like that, all was quiet. We stood there for a while, just the two of us.

22: Princess Nandi

On the 26th [of] November, vultures were spotted soaring high above the veld, circling together before disappearing to the ground to feast. It was a sure sign of death. The anti-poaching patrol began to close in on the location, knowing that the vultures could well be feeding on an animal that was killed at the hand of man. The scavengers were guiding rangers to a gruesome sight. It's always the smell that hits first, like a wall of fog that makes you want to retch. A smell that is so familiar to each of the rangers they barely waste time acknowledging it, instead silent glances are exchanged as they pick up the pace, knowing they are close. As they get closer, they see the silhouette of what was once a majestic, prehistoric and peaceful mammal. Now, on her side with her legs stiff and high in the air, she hardly looks real. If nothing else, she is unrecognizable. This, this that the rangers are faced with resembles nothing of the confident, careful and critically endangered black rhino they had seen alive and well just days before. The sighting no more than a week ago had brought the team such joy. Not only had they spotted the endangered black rhinoceros in good condition, but they had finally caught a welcome glimpse of her calf. The next generation of black rhino, a little girl. A little happy, bouncy girl who stayed close to her mother's side as the rangers watched on, their hearts full of joy and pride.

On the careful approach to the lifeless body of the black rhino, the rangers spotted that same little calf. The young rhino nervously clung to her mother's side; she was frightened but she was too young to leave her mother. As the anti-poaching rangers approached, the calf was, as she had been since the day she was born, at her mother's side. They silently gave thanks for the fact the young calf was still alive and seemed to be physically unharmed by the poachers. She was still so small, dwarfed by the size of her mother. She nuzzled into her mum's body attempting to awaken her, she cried loudly with her ears standing up as she listened to the sound of the approaching footsteps. The thought of the dreadful humans who traversed this same landscape during the night of the full moon no more than 24 hours earlier surely haunted the baby rhino's mind as the rangers closed in on the scene. This two-and-a-half-month-old black rhino would later be known as Nandi. With arrangements being made for young orphan, Nandi, to be rescued and cared for, the crime scene was secured and the investigations began.

As with most poaching scenes, there is only so much evidence that can be collected and the sad reality is that often very little can or will be done with even the most damning evidence found. Sometimes it seemed as though the rangers could find evidence and proof of poaching, catch the guys and take them to the police but then in a few short days (or less) the poachers just simply pay bail and carry on like they were never caught. Of course, there are a lot of factors that impact the result of such a scenario, one of them being the country the crime has taken place in. Right now, we are talking about South Africa. Home to a large percentage of the world's remaining rhino population and unfortunately, also home to a large percentage of corruption and greed. It is a disappointing realisation that the current system does not help to save rhino but even with such odds stacked against them, wildlife warriors continue to do everything in their power to prevent, stop and catch poachers. Even if the system isn't in the favour of the ones trying to save life on Earth, that has never stopped those driven by passion. The sad reality is that if we relied on authority figures, there'd be nothing left worth fighting for.

As the anti-poaching unit gathered information from the tracks, the vet and wildlife capture team arrived. The young calf was captured by the veterinary team and the nearest rhino orphanage were on the way to pick the calf up. The nearest rhino orphanage just so happened to be us. After receiving the call, the whole vibe of the orphanage changed.

When we got the call informing us of orphaned black rhino calf Nandi, our whole mind-set shifted. It was like the rough seas suddenly became calm. We knew we had a job to do. For the best results and to give this calf the best chance at life, we needed to be clearheaded and working efficiently, so that's what we did. As soon as the responsibility of another's life falls upon your shoulders your mind does magical things to ensure you are at your best. In an instant, your focus shifts and you forget all those things that were holding you down. Now, the only thing that mattered was the traumatised and dehydrated rhino calf that was on the way to the orphanage.

After we received the call, we gathered everyone in our standard meeting place (the garden) to make a plan. We were running out of space and the neonatal unit was still in the process of being built. This, combined with the cold nights, led us to decide to keep young Nandi in the rhino ambulance for her first few nights with us. This meant we could keep her temperature stable and get her drinking and used to us as quickly as possible. It also gave us the opportunity to get the new neonatal ready so we would be able to move Nandi in in a couple of days.

Back in 2013, I had the privilege of working with my very first black rhino orphan and I experienced one of the most incredible bonds with him. I learnt for the first time how inquisitive, gentle and clever these creatures are. Spending time with that young black rhino gave me an entirely new perspective on the beings we walk this Earth with and at that moment of hearing of this orphaned calf on her way to us, I felt so grateful that we were able to give her love, comfort, warmth and a chance at life.

The first few nights with Nandi were challenging. Keeping her in the ambulance was good for her but it wasn't ideal for the team. The ambulance was split into two sections; one larger area where the rhino was held and one much smaller section where you could sit or stand for monitoring purposes. This meant there was no room for you to be comfortable in the ambulance, so you'd have to sit on one of the kit boxes to monitor her. During the day, this was fine but at night it was extremely uncomfortable.

As expected, Nandi's first few nights were full of confusion, crying and searching for a mum she would never see again. The first few days with a newly orphaned rhino calf are the worst because it is at that time you feel most helpless. You are there with the traumatised rhino but they don't see you as a source of comfort yet. You can talk to them and be there with them, but they want their mum and you aren't even of the same species. As the nights wear on and you continue to offer your voice, warmth and touch, things change. You offer milk and electrolytes which the desperate young rhino cautiously begins to accept. You offer to sit in the corner while they cry and finally, they decide to sit with you, resting on you for comfort and warmth. Nandi began to find comfort in our presence and she began to realize the danger was no longer imminent, that she could go back to being a baby, go back to recognizing the feeling of hunger, the desire to wallow and so on. Once you break those barriers the calf is taking those first, vital steps on the long road of rehabilitation.

Fortunately, Nandi settled in quickly and in no time at all earned herself the nickname "Princess Nandi". Nandi was very cute and she utilized this to get what she wanted, all the time. The two-month-old, knee-high black rhino needn't do much more than flutter her eyelashes and point her (ridiculously adorable) triangular prehensile lip at us and we'd melt and give her whatever she wanted. Everybody fell in love with Nandi and she truly took everything in her stride.

With Nandi now drinking well and getting used to us, we moved her into the Neonatal. The Neonatal was a much larger circular room with a hip high barrier separating the rhino's area from an area for us to sleep and carry out the milk and medicine preparations. This was perfect for caring for the smaller rhinos as it meant we never had to leave them alone and we could do everything we needed to do from within that room. The neonatal also had an air conditioning unit with heating and cooling settings so we could keep the room accurately temperature controlled. The neonatal unit was positioned just off the main house, so it was away from the other rhino rooms allowing us to deal with the very young rhinos separately and giving us more space for the older orphans. It was lucky that Angie had bought us all that new equipment because with a whole new unit requiring stocking up, we certainly needed it. We were so happy when we moved Nandi into the neonatal facility. It was perfect for her and we knew the little, energetic black rhino would love the small outside enclosure that was attached to the unit too.

23: Changes

With Nandi getting settled in the Neonatal, it meant that the rhino team (Aly, Axel and Angie) had to split their time between Ithuba, Thando, Impy and Nandi. The white rhinos were becoming less hands-on, Impy and Thando were content keeping each other company and they now only needed the team for their milk feeds and to put out their dry food a couple of times a day. While the white rhinos required less intensive care, new arrival Nandi needed someone with her around the clock. To try to make nightshifts with Nandi more comfortable, we moved the bed that Menna had been using from my room and into the neonatal.

A few weeks after Menna returned to the UK, the time had come for Aly to leave too. Having found a job at a veterinary centre closer to civilisation, Aly handed in her resignation to the orphanage. It was a very sad time as Aly had been an important part of the team since orphanage opened. Her caring nature, skills as a veterinary nurse and love for the animals made her an absolute pleasure to work alongside and I knew the team was going to be a lot poorer without Aly as part of it. There was something about Aly, Axel and I at the orphanage together that just worked and in the time we'd spent together with Ithuba, Ellie, Impy, Thando and Nandi we had created lifelong memories. With Aly leaving, we needed to find new people to join the orphanage team – something that we discovered was easier said than done. Fortunately, we still had Angie working with us for another couple of weeks and we had some volunteers organised for December to help us over the festive period too.

We still did not have an elephant friend to introduce to Ellie but he was growing into quite the elephant nonetheless. He was now flapping his ears when he felt warm and he'd flare his ears out when he'd play with Duma or when he was being very naughty and chasing the anti-poaching unit's land rover that would rumble far louder than a vehicle should. Ellie had also begun trying to throw sand over himself on warm days but he was only picking up a small pinch of sand each time and he'd drop it almost immediately onto his front legs as he'd try to flick his trunk up to throw the sand onto his back. His trunk would wriggle in the air as he'd try to throw the sand up onto himself. Ellie would use his front feet to kick the sand backwards while attempting to pick up as much sand as he could using his trunk. It was a new skill that he would master one day. Eventually, Ellie would lay down in the sand and cool down that way instead. I loved to sit and watch El when he'd start learning something new. He was determined, he'd know exactly what he was trying to do and he'd get a little bit closer with each attempt.

One of El's favourite spots to sit when the house was quiet was the "rhino café", the simple food storage area provided Ellie with lots of "toys" (feeding and cleaning equipment) to play with as well as an excellent vantage point looking over the orphanage. I'd sit on the step of the Rhino Café, often joined by Axel, Angie or the volunteers and we would chat while El kept himself busy playing with buckets, rakes and whatever else he could find. El would also walk around to the fence of the rhino enclosures, he'd push his face against the poles and watch as the rhinos walked around or bathed in the mud. Ellie would walk along the fence until he found the biggest gap between the enclosure poles, then he'd hold his trunk through the gap to see if there was anything he could touch or take hold of.

El would always be the first one investigating an area where a new calf has been. He took no time at all to hoover up the smells that surrounded the ambulance upon Nandi's arrival. Despite the ambulance being closed, he knew there was another animal in there. He inhaled all the new scents and patiently stood outside, waiting to meet whoever was inside. When he realized his new friend wasn't coming out to play anytime soon, he and Duma made their way to the sand pile to play there instead. Although Ellie would be sure to check back later in case his new friend would be ready to say hello.

As the neonatal was still not fully complete, every so often we'd have odd jobs to do to make it a bit better for Nandi. Gradually working our way to it being fully up and running.

I went to the house to make breakfast first thing in the morning when I saw the light was on in the neonatal so I made two cups of coffee and went to see Ang who was just finishing the night shift with Nandi. She mentioned we needed to put shade cloth onto the door so in our pre-six a.m. enthusiasm we decided to do it there and then. At that time of the morning there was no way we were going to bother getting the keys for the storeroom so we could dig the ladder out. Instead, we decided I'd hold the shade cloth and Ang would hold me up while I attached it to the top of the door. Nandi was snoozing under her heat lamp and she had just gulped down a few litres of milk so we readied for our D.I.Y. knowing she wouldn't need anything for a while. Ang took hold of my legs around my knees and then said,

"Okay Meg. You ready? On three. One. Two. Three." As planned, Ang picked me up energetically. Unfortunately, we hadn't fully thought our plan through. As I rose into the air, I was abruptly stopped as the top of my head hit the concrete doorway. We were just a little bit too enthusiastic and we very nearly knocked me out.

"I'm so sorry Meg!!! Are you okay??" Ang said as she lowered me back down to the floor. With my mind dizzy but my feet firmly on the ground, we looked at each other and burst out laughing. We laughed so much we had tears rolling down our cheeks. We looked up at the doorway to see that there was a 30cm rectangle of lower concrete that was flanked on one side by a far higher ceiling and on the other side by nothing at all. As we were thinking about the door rather than the doorway, we inadvertently positioned ourselves directly under the lower section of concrete which abruptly put a stop to our D.I.Y. We decided putting the shade cloth up could wait until later and that we would use the ladder after all. We sat in the neonatal for a while laughing and joking and then, with a lump on my head and a smile on my face, I went to start the day with Ellie.

24: Rescuing Storm

Nandi had now been with us for eleven days. She was comfortably living in the newly built, but not quite finished, neonatal unit and she was adapting well to life at the orphanage. As I stood with Ellie in the garden we looked out towards the horizon, the usual beauty of the sunset was blocked by dark, angry clouds rolling in. There was no doubt that these clouds brought with them a promise of rain, and it was about time. The ground was dusty, the dams were all but dry and the animals on the reserves were struggling to survive. Rain brings with it life, water is essential and unless you've been in a situation where you've been without it, the chances are you under-appreciate the lifesaving droplets. We were so thankful for the coming rains, our water source -like the animals- had also begun to run dry.

With the daylight fading, the team did the final night shift preparations; the animals were locked in; the milk powder was topped up and those taking on the feeds for the night were getting themselves as comfortable as possible on the preparation room floors. Every night the thin, well-worn camping mattresses would reappear from the storeroom and were carried to the necessary spots to add at least a little bit of comfort for the night ahead.

You'd see those destined for night shift carrying blankets, books and laptops from their rooms before the darkness descended, we'd always try to take everything we could want or need during nightshift with us at the beginning of the shift so that we wouldn't need to venture out later on. On the more intensive nursing cases those not on shift would take dinner to the preparation rooms so the team members on nightshift wouldn't need to leave, enabling them to continue monitoring the sick, newly arrived or very young calf.

Once settled in for the night ahead, an alarm would be set ready for the next feed. I would always set an alarm, even for the earlier feeds, just in case my eyelids became too heavy to stay awake. The more night shifts you do the easier it is to fall asleep at the drop of a hat… and stay asleep for that matter. When you're fresh from a week of proper sleep you'll be more aware of what's going on, you'll wake up straight away if a rhino cries or kicks their leg out. Being this well rested is rare so you'll more likely wake only once a rhino has knocked their small horn against the steel barrier a couple of times or your alarm has rung out more than once.

Suddenly waking up in fear of having missed a feed was common too, this would always bring a lot of confusion. You'd wake up asking yourself so many questions: "What time is it? Have I missed the feed? When was the last feed? Wait, what time is it again?". Working with the rhinos, you could expect to wake up every three hours in order to prepare milk, feed the hungry calves and wash up. This was for the stable calves, for the sick or new arrivals you'd be lucky to get any sleep at all. Over on the elephant team hourly feeds remained standard.

There were many times I startled awake to darkness and silence, thinking that maybe I had slept through my alarm. My hair would be pushed in all directions from sleeping awkwardly, my dry eyes half closed as I'd be trying to figure out the situation. I'd be squinting at the screen of my phone to see the time and then using the phone to light up the record sheet to see when the last feed was because, for the life of me, I couldn't remember. Even though you'd worry about it, you never missed a feed, mainly because the rhino wouldn't let you. If the orphans were hungry before you were awake, they'd make a fuss until you picked your tired body off the floor, switched on the light and told them,

"OK, OK, the milk is coming!". Only then would they ease up on the tantrum and give you 45 seconds of peace before they'd grow impatient again. If I was asleep while on shift with Ellie and he wanted to wake me up, he'd walk over to me and stand a few centimetres from my face. Then, he'd slowly tap my arm with his trunk and if that wasn't enough to wake me, he'd nudge me a bit harder or tap my face and grumble. It was one of the best ways to wake up, with a baby elephant standing in front of me, grumbling and looking at me with love in his eyes.

Ellie and I had just gone into his room to settle down for the evening when a flash of lightning forked its way through the darkening clouds, flexing its power for all to see. This impressive display was very closely followed by a sudden, sharp crack of thunder that developed into a deep, formidable rumble that rolled its way across the sky. The thunder was introducing the heavy drops of rain to the parched, dusty ground. In a split second, there was a curtain of oversized, enthusiastic raindrops pummelling the earth. The noise alone was musical, it was loud, domineering but welcome. The repetitive drumming, the dancing of the drops as they bounced against the ground. I watched out of the window as the Earth was blessed with rain. I looked at El who stood by my side, wondering why I was staring out the window and not giving him my undivided attention. I sat down on the mattress and smiled as this was the perfect opportunity for me to snuggle under the heat lamp with Ellie - who, on cold evenings, appeared more like a pile of blankets with a trunk than an elephant.

Within the world of animal rescue the unexpected ceases to exist, you can go from calm to crazy in the blink of an eye and it pays to be ready. The storm was powerful but everyone was settled, dinner was cooking and spirits were high. Over the noise of the heavy storm, the phone began to ring. It was one of the vets from a nearby reserve and we all knew that a vet would only call at this time and in this weather for something urgent. The phone call was quick and to the point, we were needed. While we cooked dinner and the sky opened its floodgates on the drought-ridden land somewhere out there was a tiny black rhino who needed the food, warmth and love that we provided.

The team was informed of the orphaned calf who, without rescue, would likely not survive the night. Everyone bolted into action, with teamwork and precision we would be organised and on route in ten minutes flat. We decided that Angie and I would head up the rescue, Angie had been a significant part of the team for several weeks now. I was thrilled to be going on the rescue with Ang. We'd already seen that Ang handled emergency situations with practical, careful thinking and her skill and experience when it came to driving with a trailer would be hugely beneficial given the weather conditions we were up against too. Angie was one of those people you'd get the work done with but you'd be doing it with a smile the whole time. We had a long drive ahead of us, but I knew the journey would be filled with interesting conversation, light-hearted jokes and cheesy music.

The team got the rescue trailer prepped with bedding and emergency kits while I did a shift handover for Ellie, I gave him a kiss goodnight and went to my room to get changed into warm, waterproof clothes. As I pulled on my fleece and grabbed my jacket the dim light in my room was overpowered by another flash of lightning. I put an additional jumper, a notebook and a pen into my bag while the sound of the heavy rain hitting the roof filled my ears. Satisfied I had what I needed I put my phone into my pocket, pulled on my boots and headed back out into the storm. As I approached the sheltered parking Angie and the team were busy hooking up the trailer to the car. I carried on past and ran through the rain into the preparation room, I filled a flask with boiled water and checked we had all the necessary equipment packed. I closed the plastic carry box and carried it up to the car, rushing across the open grass in the downpour.

Everything was loaded and in full working order, we double checked we had our phones and the two-way radios and said goodbye to the team. It was dark, cold and the rain was relentless. It was the heaviest rainfall we'd seen all year. Everyone had worked as quickly as possible to get us on the road but it was not time for the team to rest yet, while we drove into the night Axel and the volunteers could not relax as they prepared for the weak, traumatised calf we would be returning with.

Angie and I were on our way, the reserves roads were already washing away with the rains and with the reduced visibility we knew it was going to be a very long night. We did not have time for dinner before we left, Angie was just finishing making a small roast dinner before the call came in. Realising the food would be long gone by the time we returned and not being able to resist, we took a bowl of roast potatoes for the journey. Sitting in the car; we slowly pulled the rescue trailer along the dirt road in the torrential rain, listening to pop music on the radio and devouring some of the best roast potatoes I'd ever eaten. That was it, our evening had been transformed and we were now on our way to rescue a critically endangered black rhino calf.

We finally reached the tarred road but thanks to the weather we were still crawling along, we could barely see the bonnet of the car let alone anything else. We were under no illusions about the danger of the roads in these conditions, so we continued cautiously. Fortunately, the vet agreed to meet us along the way in order to reduce our journey time and get the rhino calf back to safety quicker. In good weather, we would've been there by now but we'd only just reached the slip road to join the highway. We were two hours into the journey and the rain was relentless, as a fan of lightning I was rather enjoying the electrical show the evening had presented to us.

"What is that? Up ahead..." Angie asked as I squinted my eyes and tried to make out the shape hidden within a blanket of rain. All I could see was a large, vague shape ahead of us on the unlit highway, As we got closer, we realised it was a huge truck driving in the storm with no lights on. We couldn't believe it, by now it was coming up to eleven p.m., the rain was still hammering down and we could only just see in front of our car with the help of our headlights and extremely slow driving, surely this truck driver could see nothing at all. We could not believe our eyes; in that kind of weather we could've easily ploughed into the back of the almost invisible truck. This just reassured us that taking it slow was the right choice. After around four hours on the road and a relatively short distance covered, we pulled into the meeting place.

As we approached, we saw the vet's vehicle parked under the shelter, we positioned the ambulance next to their open vehicle. We could see two men standing on the back of the vehicle monitoring the three-month-old black rhino calf that laid between them: one observing the rhino's respiration rate and the other holding the drip bag in place. There was a third man sitting in the driver's seat of the vehicle, facing outside the open door, resting his elbows on his knees and typing on his phone. We were glad to see there were going to be five of us altogether as even though the calf was just a few months old, rhino are heavy animals that are difficult to carry and move.

We introduced ourselves, discussed the details of the calf and opened the rescue trailer. This was the first time we had opened the trailer since we left the orphanage four hours earlier. It was immediately clear that during the journey the torrential rain had leaked through the seals of the trailer and had caused everything on the inside to become soaked through. The bedding we had put down for the rhino was saturated and now unusable and the pillows we'd left at the front of the trailer (where I would be sitting on the way back to the orphanage) were now pooling with water. We couldn't believe it.

As the vet and his assistants checked the vitals of the young rhino, I dug through the kits in the trailer to find dry blankets to use for the calf in place of the wet bedding. With the blankets in place, the rhino calf was lifted onto a stretcher and moved from the back of the vet's vehicle into our trailer. As we lifted the rhino orphan into the trailer, his small size became more apparent. This rhino was so small there would've been ample space for him on the backseat of a car, it was astounding to think how big he would one day become. We placed the rhino down onto the blankets, fortunately we could also control the temperature inside of the trailer allowing us to do more to avoid the calf from becoming cold on the journey back to the orphanage. The rhino was sedated but the jerking movement of switching vehicles caused him to suddenly kick his legs and try to stand up. This brief movement, although generally insignificant, caused the catheter that was allowing the drip fluid therapy to flow into a vein in the rhino calf's ear to become dislodged.

The vet evaluated the situation and after some thought, decided it was not necessary to put a new catheter into the rhino's ear as the first bag of rehydration fluid had already been administered while they were waiting for us to arrive. Once back at the orphanage we would offer electrolytes and if the calf wasn't cooperating and we were concerned about dehydration we could put him on I.V. fluids again.

We took a bandage from the emergency kit in the trailer and used it to make a blindfold for the orphan - covering the eyes reduces stress and makes working with the rhino easier during rescue and transport. After confirming we had everything, we closed the back of the trailer. Angie handed me one of the two-way radios and I climbed into the front section of the trailer so the door could be locked behind me. The small, waterlogged space did not present the most comfortable of journeys home but fortunately I could sit on top of one of the plastic storage boxes and keep dry as I watched over the sedated black rhino calf.

We set off on route back to the orphanage, it must have been around midnight and I was feeling a cloud of tiredness over me. I sighed as I looked down at the water pooling at my feet, the leak coming from the roof seals hadn't gone unnoticed either. At least the rain had calmed down quite substantially compared to when we left the orphanage. The two-way radios were essential for communication between Angie and I, they certainly helped with keeping both of us alert throughout the journey too. According to Ang, the visibility was much better when we were driving back (there were no windows in the back of the ambulance so I couldn't see out) but we still weren't travelling fast. I sat and watched over the black rhino calf, taking in his vulnerability and the immense sadness of the situation. The reality is dark and the poaching battle is far from being won, this little calf was a symbol of all that has been lost and all that can be saved.

It didn't take long before the blanket we'd laid down under the rhino orphan had become damp too. I took the jumper from my bag, folded it up and wedged it under the calf. Not feeling satisfied that the black rhino calf would be warm enough I took off the fleece I was wearing and laid it over the rhinos back as if it were a blanket. The extra layer wasn't much but would hopefully help. The leaks in the trailer were not making the journey any easier but at least the air conditioner was working and could provide us with warmth.

The gentle hum of the air conditioning had become the steady background noise inside the trailer, I sat on the storage box, my elbows resting on my thighs and my chin lazily leaning on my hand, the sudden bang of the calf kicking his leg out brought my focus back from a daydream. The sedation had begun to wear off and the black rhino started to twitch and kick, preparing to stand up. I spoke to Angie on the radio and we assessed the situation. The blindfold was still securely over his eyes, he gently cried although it was clear he was drowsy and understandably confused. I spoke to him softly, calmly telling him the stories of the storm, what was happening and reassuring him that he was safe now.

As the black rhino calf stood up, I climbed over the barrier and made the area as comfortable as I could for him while talking continuously so he would always know where I was. I moved the wet bedding out of the way and tried to create a comfortable bed for him with what little dry material we had. The rhino, who when standing only stood slightly taller than the height of my knees, lent his exhausted body against my legs, craving the comfort and warmth he would normally get from his mum. I waited to see if he would go back to sleep but he was becoming more alert and calling more frequently. I tied a new blindfold over his eyes as the first had become damp from the floor.

These were the first moments I was truly appreciating the small size of the black rhino calf. As I lifted his head to tie the blindfold, I admired his little pointed lip and the love I already felt for this calf bubbled up inside me. I stepped back over the barrier with the old blindfold. The rhino began kicking his back feet and his tail curled up. This was a good sign and something I was actually excited to see. Anyone working with animals will know that their toilet habits are of great importance, they have the potential to become quite the fixation and talking point. As soon as the rhino was finished passing faeces, I climbed back over the barrier with my head torch to take a look… As we had feared it appeared the rhino had been eating sand and mud while he was trying to survive. His faeces were dark and dry, there was no doubt that he was desperately trying to survive and was doing whatever he could to suppress his dehydration and hunger. I climbed back onto my side of the trailer to dispose of the gloves I was wearing and to write down the observations.

The tiny black rhino slowly wobbled around the confined area, he stopped to rest his face against the barrier that separated us and then out of nowhere a wave of fear came over him. He began to buck his head and his little stump of a horn against the barrier poles as if to protect himself and show he had fight left in him. I continued to talk to him, my heart pulling knowing it would be at least a few days until he would feel reassured. After a while, the young rhino was becoming more alert and showing no signs of laying back down. We still had a couple of hours to drive so we decided to stop and administer the remaining sedation, as the wildlife vet had advised during the handover.

It must have been close to two a.m. when we pulled over at side of the road to give the half dose of sedation. This would allow us to get back to the orphanage with minimal stress, there was just too much of the journey left and we were mindful that a large portion of the remaining drive was the uneven dirt road. We knew that the young rhino's stress levels would become unnecessarily elevated should we leave him awake for the remainder of the journey back to the orphanage. We gave the sedation, and we were on the move again within minutes. It did not take long for the rhino to lay back down and fall back into a deep sleep; we were confident this would last until we reached the orphanage.

I sat leaning against the wall of the ambulance, my eyes feeling increasingly heavy as the tiredness ran through my whole body. The drive then became very bumpy, the tyres were no longer connected with a tarmac surface. We had turned onto the dirt road; in the trailer we could feel every bump and uneven surface we drove over so I knew the dirt road was going to be uncomfortable. I pushed myself away from the wall of the ambulance that was now rattling my brain rather than allowing me to rest. I couldn't stop yawning but I also couldn't sleep. It was during this last stretch of the journey Angie and I had the most frequent radio contact, the baby rhino was being jolted up and down with the bumps of the road and I was worried he was going to wake up in a panic.

"Hey Ang, can you slow it down a little please." I spoke into the radio.

"Sure, how's it going back there? We are crawling along." Ang responded instantly.

"Thanks, it's a little bumpy. It feels like we're driving over boulders. The little rhino is still asleep"

"Alright, we are on the last section now. We're on the dirt road, not long left." Ang reassured. I sat watching as the whole ambulance shook. It wasn't that we were driving fast at all, it was the state of the road we were driving on. The rain had washed away any evenness the dirt road ever had and replaced it with holes and ridges.

"Woah woah woah, a bit slower." I urgently radioed Angie.

"What's up? Is everything ok?"

"Yeah sorry, we hit a bad bump and the rhino basically lifted off the ground for a second. I was sure he was going to stand up, he's starting to get fidgety… I don't think we've got long left of this sedation especially with this rough ride." I explained.

"Hang in there, we are passing the road that leads to the post office now." Ang said in a moment that felt very much like déjà vu. The "road to the post office" would've been a great reference and very reassuring if I hadn't heard it 20 minutes earlier...

"You told me that ages ago." I laughed.

"Ahh but this time we are there, it's so dark and I thought that's where we were earlier but it turned out we weren't anywhere near there. I was confused but I know where we are now. Don't worry we are almost there." I could hear the smile in Ang's voice and couldn't help but laugh. There weren't many reference points between turning onto the dirt road and the reserve but the road to the post office was ten – fifteen minutes away from our access gate into the reserve so it was a great relief to be so close to home after such an eventful night.

Less than ten minutes went by and this time it was Angie who broke the silence.

"Hey Meg, we are approaching the bridge. We are close to the gate now, but the bridge is flooded. The water is flowing over it pretty fast. I'm not sure if it's a good idea to try to drive over it, I'm going to stop so you can take a look too."

I pulled my phone out of my bag, it was 3:30 a.m. We were cold, tired and a little damp… A flooded bridge was the last thing we needed. We came to a standstill and Ang opened the ambulance for me. I stepped out of the trailer into the darkness of the night.

Although the night was cold, it felt good to get some fresh air and stretch my legs, I walked to the front of the car where the headlights shone onto the bridge. The river had swelled causing something of a flash flood which now blocked our path. We stood and watched the fast-flowing water, every now and then we'd see debris and logs float by. We tried to see how deep the water was and slowly waded onto the bridge in our boots. The water very quickly threatened to climb over the tops of our boots, so we turned back after only a few steps. The rain had stopped for now but we decided to wait it out, by sunrise at the latest the level of the river should've dropped and we would be able to cross without any risk.

We contacted the team at the orphanage and explained the situation. I took my waterproof off and laid it on the wet floor in the smaller section of the trailer, if we were sticking it out for a few hours I figured I might as well try to sleep- the black rhino calf was still out for the count and as we had stopped I knew he wouldn't be waking up in the next couple of hours either. Angie locked me into the trailer and then locked herself in the car. We had agreed trying to get a few hours of sleep would be the best thing to do.

Around 30 minutes had passed when Angie radioed me,

"Meg, one of the reserve vehicles is approaching behind us. I'm going to open up the trailer again." We were astounded to see the reserve manager and three of his team had come to our aid. It was 3:45 a.m. and as soon as they heard we were stuck at the bridge they made some fresh coffee, grabbed some snacks and drove through the reserve to help us. As we sipped the hot coffee, they evaluated the water up ahead. They decided to try to drive their large game viewer through, that way we could see how high the water was and whether we could make it through safely, without any water coming into the ambulance. If they made it across and it all looked good, we would follow their exact path and try to cross too. Before we set off, the team who had come to assist us had a quick peek at the sleeping black rhino and, like us, they were enamoured by him. They couldn't believe his size and were as eager as us to get the rhino back to the orphanage safely. Angie closed me into the trailer and we followed at a crawl as the game viewer drove slowly ahead of us.

My radio burst into enthusiastic life,

"Meg, we are across! We are going to follow them up to the orphanage. We should be back at the orphanage in ten minutes, we'll take it slow because of the state of the roads." We were almost home. It was the best news. Around ten minutes later Angie radioed again,

"Ok Meg, we are hitting the steep incline now so hold on tight, it's going to be bumpy." I knew exactly where we were, another couple of minutes and we'd be back at the orphanage. We idled for a minute, and I knew we were at the gate waiting for the night guard to let us in. We continued forwards and then the car engine cut off. We had made it. After an arduous eight and a half hours we were back, safe and sound.

It was past four a.m. when we pulled the ambulance under the cover of the orphanage parking. After a quick debriefing with the two team members who were awake, we knew the young rhino would be fine until the morning. It was decided the team member on the Ellie shift would regularly check on the rhino for the next couple of hours as they'd be up and about for Ellie's hourly feeds anyway. By seven a.m. everyone would be awake and the black rhino orphan's sedation should have started to wear off.

Satisfied, relieved and exhausted. Angie and I said goodnight to the three-month-old male black rhino who could have no name more aptly suited to him than 'Storm'.

I showered, set my alarm and fell into bed... My alarm was set to go off in an eye watering one hour and forty-five minutes. I wasn't going to waste a single second of that time and I am pretty sure I was asleep before my head even hit the pillow…

25: Critically Endangered Black Rhinos

Before I knew it, the buzzing of the alarm broke the silence in my room, as I opened my eyes and stretched out to grab my phone my bed suddenly felt like the comfiest place in the world. It was warmer, softer even, the blankets were cuddling me, caressing me, holding me down. My eyes felt dry and heavy, my body felt weighted. I closed my eyes allowing myself a final few blissful moments in bed, as I felt myself begin to drift back to sleep I knew I had to stop myself or else it would be mid-afternoon before I would awaken again.

With a grumble, I pulled myself out of bed, pausing for a moment in front of the wardrobe to decide which outfit to wear, or more accurately, which t-shirt was the cleanest. My body felt sluggish, I knew a quick, cold shower would wake me up, so with my clothes draped over my arm and a towel over my shoulder I shuffled to the bathroom to get myself ready for the day. The cold water on my skin felt shocking at first, like tiny pins transforming into steam as they danced along my body. As stunned as I felt under the icy water, I forced myself to stay there for just a few seconds more, holding my face up into the waterfall and exhaling a deep sigh before turning the taps off. Now that the tiredness had disappeared down the drain I dried off, got dressed and brushed my teeth.

It was just coming up to six a.m., I pulled on a jumper and a coat and went out to get some food and check on Storm before taking over on the elephant shift. The ground was soddened and mud had been tracked all over the place from the busy night before. I sighed as I took my clogged up boots off at the door of the house and went to make some breakfast. With no one around yet, I tried to navigate the kitchen quietly, wondering what time everyone managed to sleep, if at all. I decided a cup of coffee was in order and I made some toast. No longer bothering with the luxury of plates I held the toast in my mouth as I pulled my mud-caked boots back on and went to see Storm. I crept slowly towards the ambulance, not wanting to wake Storm or give him a fright. I sighed as I saw the pile of wet blankets piled up outside from the night before. I couldn't believe the extent of the leaks we had experienced inside the ambulance. Upon arrival back at the orphanage we switched out the soaking wet blankets for clean, dry ones so Storm was nice and cosy. I spoke softly as I stepped into the ambulance. The tiny black rhino, who was smaller than Duma, our German Shepherd, was still sleeping and was at least warm and dry now. I lightly touched his skin to make sure he was warm enough and checked on his notes to see if anything had happened over the past couple of hours. As expected, it was noted that he'd been checked on several times but remained sleeping.

The rain had brought with it new life for the plants and wildlife in the bush and it had brought us this tiny black rhino calf. Despite the terrible weather and the late-night call, we had managed to get the young rhino to warmth and safety. He now had a chance of survival.

We estimated Storm to be only three months old, the same age as Nandi. It was less than two weeks prior that Nandi had arrived; her mother was poached in the light of the full moon. With more rhinos than rooms and more care needed than caregivers, we needed to be resourceful. The new neonatal provided a perfect place for Nandi, the unit allowed the caregiver on shift to mix milk, measure medicines and rest at night while still watching, comforting and listening to the rhino calf. With Nandi settling into her new room, Ellie enjoying the volunteer room he had been given, Impy and Thando continuing to build their friendship and Ithuba minding his own business in the largest of the enclosures, we decided to give Storm a day or two in the ambulance to let the sedation wear off. Then we would introduce him to fellow black rhino Nandi.

It had only been about eleven hours since I last spent time with El but so much had happened it felt like I hadn't seen him in days. It had been no more than fifteen minutes since the initial buzzing of the alarm, and I was now going into Ellie's room. The mornings were my favourite time of day with El because no matter how the night went for either of us, we would always be so happy to see each other. It was as if each day was a fresh start as of the moment I opened the door into his room. With so much activity around the orphanage, he hadn't slept well but it didn't seem to matter… As I walked in El bounded to the door to say good morning to me. He grumbled deeply as he approached, the greeting was music to my ears, my favourite sound. He threw his trunk in the air to give me kisses and nudged enthusiastically at my hip. Despite the lack of sleep I'm sure he also experienced, he had a lot of energy this morning. I think part of him loved the busyness of it all. It got him excited and this morning he was very eager to play some games. I'd barely walked in the door and he was already playing.

"Good morning El!!!" I looked down at him as he put his trunk on my face, pushing into my side again. He was looking up at me with great anticipation.

"Don't you even want to say good morning to me El? You just want to play?" I grabbed his trunk playfully and then walked over to the other side of the room to sit down. He was half a step behind me pushing me along at the backs of my legs. Now sitting, I stroked him and steadied myself in case he decided to push into me or try to climb on me. He stood centimetres away, waiting to play his favourite games. As I did not quite mirror the energy he had, I decided I'd first shower him with kisses. Making a humming noise that built up as the kiss got "closer", Ellie stood excitedly with his eyes watching my every move. To my relief, El was no longer concerned about pushing and shoving, he just wanted the kisses. After the first kiss landed on his cheek, he threw his trunk up to touch it. With his trunk on his cheek and a smile in his eyes, he looked back at me, waiting.

"Oh! You want another kiss?" I laughed as he stared, I started making the humming noise once again. Ellie dropped the trunk away from his face and moved it towards mine. I dodged his trunk and landed a kiss on his forehead. He was getting more and more excited by the moment. I decided to get up and run to the other side of the room while he was distracted. He swung his trunk around, followed by his body and charged his weight towards me. I used the tyre as a barrier to slow him down. He clambered over it with absolutely no grace and used his trunk to take hold of my leg. Now, the games could begin.

Ellie pulled my leg towards him with his trunk and scrambled to bring me down. I broke free and ran to the other side of the room. He didn't follow, instead he pretended to be busy with the tyre. This was a tactic I hadn't seen before. Using his trunk, Ellie played with the tyre flippantly as his eyes watched my every move.

"Oh… I guess that's it then. I have nothing to worry about because you're playing with the tyre now." I said loudly as I crouched down next to the slightly deflated yoga ball, looked the other way and waited. Unable to resist the opportunity to launch the 'surprise attack' and win a round, Ellie charged over as fast as his legs would take him. He pushed and shoved and threw his legs over me, winning the first round of the game with glee. His eyes were smiling and he was full of boundless energy. In that moment of pure joy, all the tiredness, the grogginess, the worries, they all slipped away so silently that I merely blinked and they were gone. All the fatigue evaporated away because of Ellie's positive attitude and enthusiasm for life.

I decided he had way too much energy to continue playing this game inside and quickly ran out of the door and into the morning light. The sun was rising following last night's storm and it was a truly beautiful start to the day. Ellie followed me, hesitating as he felt how damp the ground was.

"Come on El, last one to the sand pile is a loser!" I jested as I skipped towards the sand. He followed me, unable to resist a race, picking up the pace as he went. He plunged himself into the sand headfirst - elegant. He was pushing the sand around and covering himself with it. After some more games Ellie finally began to slow down. Only to realise he had been so busy playing games he hadn't yet investigated the new arrival.

Before he even thought twice about it Ellie was trotting to the ambulance, on a mission of his own. El loved to go on these missions, he'd get an idea in his head and he'd be off. The fastest I'd seen Ellie run was when he'd decide he wanted to go somewhere, he'd often disappear down to the preparation room, rhino café or ambulance. He wouldn't even look back to see if you were coming too, he'd just go. There were times when rhino rooms were being cleaned or feeds were taking place and Ellie would just appear over the hill, sprinting down to see what was happening. The only warning to those minding their own business was the distant shout of

"ELLIE'S COMING". Everyone had become used to hearing this shouted across the orphanage at least twice a week and knew that it meant gates and doors needed to be closed quickly so Ellie couldn't start investigating or making a mess of the preparation rooms or letting himself into the rhino rooms. If there was a feed going on, El would want to be involved and would insist on sticking his trunk in the buckets or through the barriers. He just wanted to be a part of everything and he always wanted to know what was going on.

This time Ellie had sprinted down to the rhino ambulance. He walked around it, taking in the smells, investigating the sopping wet blankets and giving the whole place the once over. Of course, he couldn't see Storm but, just like when Nandi was in the ambulance, that didn't bother him much. Ellie slowly walked the perimeter of the ambulance before deciding the strongest and most interesting smells were at the back panel, where he proceeded to stand with his trunk pushed flat against the ambulance. I sat on a wooden pole that was laying on the ground as Ellie investigated, I told him about the late-night rescue and the rhino who was sleeping inside the ambulance. I told Ellie how small the rhino was and that he was a critically endangered black rhino. I was telling Ellie how a black rhino differs from a white rhino as the orphanage slowly came to life around us.

The white rhinos were out in their enclosures feasting on their dry food, Axel was scrubbing and refilling the water troughs and the night rooms were being cleaned. Angie was up and had gone to the neonatal for a morning shift with Nandi. Ellie decided he did not want to go for a walk in the bush this morning as there were such exciting things happening around the orphanage. Instead of our usual walk, El wanted to sit in on meetings in the garden, try to break into the house and, once again, attempt to meet Nandi at the fence of the neonatal unit.

Storms first few days with us were a bit up and down, he was drinking milk and electrolytes but he didn't seem to have much energy and when he finally passed faeces again we noticed that they contained worms. We called our wildlife vet to come and give Storm a thorough health check and help determine a suitable treatment plan for the young black rhino. We were concerned about Storm but were hopeful that with around the clock care and veterinary support he would recover from the internal parasites, emaciation and trauma of being orphaned. One thing we knew would cheer up Storm and bring a spring into his step was meeting Nandi so once he was treated for the parasites we introduced the pair in the neonatal unit.

Nandi was full of life as usual; she was standing near the heat lamp when we opened the gate and walked Storm into the room. As the two black rhinos of almost identical size walked towards each other we waited to see how they would react to meeting. They watched each other carefully and after a quick sniff of one another, they began to play… Both black rhinos began throwing their weight around and running around the room. Nandi started to charge the inflatable ball she'd often play with and she pushed it across the room while Storm followed enthusiastically. The pair jumped around, gently nudging each other. Nandi and Storm seemed so genuinely excited to spend time together… It was the best introduction I had ever been a part of, there wasn't any awkwardness or uncertainty. Nandi and Storm instantly accepted each other and seemed honestly excited about meeting. They played and played. It was as if they were both over the moon about seeing another black rhino, it was beautiful. Meeting Nandi brought Storm to life. After they'd been playing for around 20 minutes, Storm wanted to rest so found a comfortable spot under the heat lamp to lay down. Nandi still had plenty of energy so she insisted on playing with the inflatable ball for a while longer before settling down next to Storm. That was that. In less than half an hour, two black rhino calves became best friends.

It was nearing the festive season. After a couple of months working with us, Angie had gone back to the U.K. but, to our delight, would be returning at the beginning of February for a few more months. Not only had Ang gone, towards the end of December I had my first days off in well over six months as my family were visiting from the U.K. As we had known this was coming up for months, we had used the quieter period between Impy and Thando being introduced and Nandi arriving to organize volunteers for the next few months so there were plenty of people on hand to help with the orphans. We hoped a few of the volunteers would stay with us longer term too.

I was delighted when my family arrived at the orphanage. It meant I could finally give my dad and my brother, Tom, a glimpse into my life in Africa. The first thing to do was to meet Ellie, Ellie was playing in the sand when they arrived but was quick to run over to say hello. El hadn't seen mum in over a month and was eager to get a kiss and a cuddle from her. My dad was so excited to meet El, immediately crouching down to talk to him and to say hello. Tom held his hands out as Ellie lifted his trunk to smell them. It was so casual. Just my family meeting my baby elephant. El seemed to like them, he definitely liked the attention he was getting and once he had said hello to everyone he gave me a big kiss and smudged mud across my face with his trunk.

After introducing my family to Ellie, we walked down to see the white rhinos. Impy and Thando were in their room as they had just had a milk feed so dad and Tom said hello to them and gave them a gentle stroke across the barrier. Impy and Thando softly cried in an attempt to convince us they were hungry and had not yet been fed. Nice try boys! We then went into the preparation room to see if we could see Ithuba outside, when we caught a glimpse of him walking across the far enclosure my dad was surprised at how big he was and how much he had grown from the pictures he had seen of Ithuba standing next to me in the first few months of his rehabilitation. After seeing the white rhinos, I showed them the new neonatal unit and Storm and Nandi. We quietly crept into the Neonatal as the two black rhinos were snuggled up under the heat lamp having a snooze. I told dad and Tom about the pair as we watched them from a distance before we quietly snuck out again. It was so exciting to show my family where I lived and now we were going to spend a couple of days in a nearby national park, this was a much-needed break away from the intensity and isolation of the orphanage.

It was late evening when I returned to the orphanage after my time off, I saw Axel was up and about with the white rhinos so I went down to say hi.

"Hey stranger!" I said as I greeted Axel with a big hug. I couldn't wait to hear how things were going. Axel had just finished washing up after a feed so we sat on the step of the rhino café and looked out onto the quiet orphanage. While I was away, we received another white rhino calf and as Sihle and Senzo had been so incredibly helpful and hardworking since they joined the team it seemed fitting for them to help us name our new arrival – she was named Gugu, meaning precious one. This white rhino was a couple of months older than Impy and Thando and was wilder and more cautious of humans than our other orphans. She did not want to come too close to us so we were feeding her milk from a tray rather than a bottle. In a couple of days, we would be introducing Gugu to Impy and Thando. After catching up with Axel and hearing the latest on the orphans, I went to my room ready to get back into the routine in the morning. I was glad to have spent some time chatting with Axel as it was sometimes difficult to find time in the day to have proper, in-depth conversations so sitting under the stars on such a still and uneventful evening catching up was perfect. As we sat there, we saw a shooting star brightly streak its way across the sky before fading away, it was the perfect welcome back.

Bright and early in the morning, I went to Ellie's room. As we did the shift handover, I was told that El had been very, very naughty in the night and he probably knew I was home and wondered why I hadn't been to see him. It was exactly what I had tried to prevent by sneaking by El's room that night, I knew if I went in there he wouldn't have slept at all. It turns out, there's not much you can get past El and now he was in a mood with me.

The little elephant was giving me the cold shoulder so I covered him in kisses to try and melt the ice and convince him to forgive me for going away and not coming to say hello during the night. We went for a walk and then sat on the grass outside the house, enjoying the mid-morning sun. Then, something very funny happened. Since we had left the room that morning, Ellie was clinging to me and was more than happy to give me cuddles. As we sat on the grass, El had his chin resting on my shoulder and his trunk wrapped across my back. Then, one of the volunteers came over to chat and as they walked over, Ellie pushed himself away from me and turned his back to me as if to show he hadn't forgiven me yet. The whole time I was talking to the volunteer, El was saying hello to her and being very sweet and friendly but was completely blanking me. Then, as they walked away and turned the corner Ellie came right back to get more attention from me. I couldn't help but laugh, it was like he wanted people to think that he was standing his ground and showing that he was unhappy with me taking time off but in reality, he had long forgiven me and couldn't resist getting all those cuddles that he'd missed while I was away.

214

26: Growing Up is a Process

It was time to introduce Gugu to Impy and Thando. We felt that the boys could give Gugu the companionship and support she needed so we opened the enclosure gates and let them meet for the first time. As we watched the introduction unfold it became very apparent that Impy and Thando were going to need a bit of time to get used to the idea of Gugu being with them. They were not being aggressive, but they weren't being very welcoming either… Every time Gugu got close to Impy and Thando, they ran away. This was confusing for Gugu so she continued to approach the boys to try to say hello to them. At one point Impy and Thando were standing inside their room when Gugu nonchalantly walked in. As they saw Gugu both boys bolted in different directions to try to get away, Impy ran the wrong way and cornered himself in the room before quickly running back out of the door. It made me think of watching small children running around a playground saying things like "Ewww girls are smelly." And then running away every time a girl gets close to them.

Gugu soon grew tired of trying to talk to the boys when they weren't interested in making friends, so she decided to go and cool off in the mud. With the attention no longer on them, the boys sheepishly made their way to the wallow and the three rhinos finally started to interact. Thando joined Gugu rolling the mud and then Impy tried to squeeze in too. From that moment, they stopped running from each other and the friendship began to grow.

One of the changes of having the three of them together was organizing feeding time, we'd call them over as usual but Gugu would keep her distance. We needed her to start drinking at the same time as the boys otherwise they'd be finished before her and would tend to argue over the milk in Gugu's tray. We'd have to put the tray down over the barrier and then pour the milk in from a bucket through the poles of the barrier.

Sometimes the feeds went perfectly but sometimes Gugu wouldn't come for her milk until the boys had nearly finished or she'd drag the tray away from the barrier before you had a chance to pour all the milk in. Seeing that it was going to take some practice to master the feed, we started taking piles of grass and lucerne to offer Impy and Thando as a distraction after they had finished their milk to give Gugu a chance to finish hers.

The boys found it strange having Gugu around at first but adding this new dynamic to their crash was working well. It was wonderful to watch them when they'd play together and when they'd all pile up in the same room to sleep side by side. As Impy, Thando and Gugu were spending time together and were all in great health we only needed to be down with the white rhinos in the morning to clean their room, fill their water and wallows and then a few times each day for their milk feeds. Aside from that, they were keeping each other busy and no longer needed human contact as they used to.

The main focus was on the black rhinos. Nandi and Storm were younger than the white rhinos and they always needed someone with them. Nandi was strong, demanding and always full of energy. She would love playing games and running around the neonatal's outside enclosure. Whereas Storm was quieter and gentler. Storm was more than happy to snuggle under the heat lamp while Nandi wanted to be out and about.

Unfortunately, we were struggling to get Storm on the right track. He wasn't gaining weight, wasn't very enthusiastic when it came to feeds and his energy levels remained low. Despite the visits from the wildlife vet, we couldn't work out exactly what was wrong with Storm. We now split Ellie's pile of blankets into two, so Storm could use some too. Every day Storm would have a blanket draped over him to help keep him warm. We struggled to get him to drink enough milk and he would spend a lot of his time resting. Nandi was like a big, brash, naughty big sister. She would try to pull Storm's blanket off him and had even got into the habit of chewing on Storms horn while he was resting. We tried everything to deter her from doing this but nothing would stop her! The neonatal gave Storm and Nandi enough space to run and play, it was easy to temperature control and easy to keep clean making it a perfect space for them. Axel was feeling the pressure of trying to get Storm on track and although I'd try to help where I could, I was still spending most of my time caring for Ellie.

Ellie was beginning to show more interest in the leaves and the trees when we'd go for walks so I began to offer him small acacia branches. When he didn't eat them, I started to pull the leaves from around the thorns and offer Ellie the piles of leaves. I pinched the pile of leaves between my thumb and finger and held it against the branch. El would put his trunk up into the branches and then he pinched his trunk around the leaves, taking hold of them. He held the leaves tightly and put them straight into his mouth. I couldn't believe he'd taken the pile of leaves and I watched with anticipation to see if he would eat them. To my surprise, he did!

"El!!!! You ate them!! You ate the leaves, woohoo! Look who's becoming all grown up! Do you want some more?" I asked as I plucked more leaves from the branches to offer him. I wanted him to feel like he was picking them from the tree which is why I held them among the branches and was making him work for them. He took the next pile of leaves and put them straight into his mouth. This was a huge moment for us and I couldn't contain my excitement. This would also add a new factor to our daily walks. We could now spend our time learning to browse. This was a moment worth celebrating, I was so proud and couldn't wait to tell the team.

For the past few weeks I'd been offering Ellie a bite of whatever fruit I was eating, he'd normally put it into his mouth and taste it before spitting it onto the ground. Now he was eating from the branches of acacia trees, I wondered if he'd be more interested in fruit. I went into the house to get an orange, fed up of arguing with El I let him walk in the house with me. He stood at the shelf with me and knocked a few of the animal ornaments over so while I picked those up and put them back in place, El turned his attention to the fruit bowl. As I looked down, he had his trunk wrapped around the whole bowl and was pulling it towards his open mouth. I quickly stopped him and rather than letting him lick the whole bunch of grapes and the couple of oranges that were in the bowl I took hold of the bowl. El continued to pull and the bunch of grapes ended up on the floor, picking them up I took a few grapes from the bunch. I held half of a grape out and El took it with his trunk. Holding the grape, Ellie looked up at me and pretended to put the grape into his mouth but what he really did was dropped it onto the floor behind him, thinking I couldn't see what he was doing. He then held out his trunk for another one and I just laughed before telling him I knew he didn't eat the first one I'd given to him. I took an orange from the fruit bowl and went outside. El followed me without issue and as we went out onto the veranda, I closed the door behind us.

I sat on the veranda step and began to peel the orange, I took a segment for myself and offered Ellie a segment too. He chewed up the segment, as he has done many times before and then he spat it out. I think he liked the taste of the orange but hadn't mastered eating it. After he spat the chewed-up orange segment out, he held out his trunk as if to ask for another segment. I obliged, handing over another piece of the juicy orange. This time, he chewed it up and swallowed it!! Ellie ate his first piece of fruit!

With Ellie doing so well, we were spending more time out in the bush than ever. Most days were spent wandering around outside and we both loved it. If we were in the orphanage, we would be sitting near the neonatal watching Storm and Nandi in their enclosure (Ellie still hadn't won them over as friends but he was determined to keep trying) or we would sit in the rhino café and watch the world go by. We hardly ever spent time in El's room now and he had begun to play in mud too.

With the help of Duma, I dug Ellie a small wallow next to the house, El helped by trying to take the spade off me but when I said I was using it he got distracted by an empty watering can I'd put down next to the wall. After investigating the inside of the watering can with his trunk, El decided to pick it up by its handle and then very proudly walked away while holding on to it. When he reached the grass, he threw the watering can down in front of him, kicked it gently with his front foot and then picked it up again. The empty watering can was going to keep Ellie busy until I needed to use it to fill the wallow. Once the small wallow was dug, I went to ask El for the watering can back. He walked with me to the outside tap and as I filled the watering can up, he was exploring the tap - putting his trunk back and forth into the fast-flowing stream of water. I could see in his eyes he was excited and he was testing to see what he was allowed to touch and what he wasn't.

"You carry on El, I just need to turn the tap off so we don't waste water." I said as El looked up at me. He put his trunk on the tap and it looked like he was trying to turn the water back on but I quickly distracted him by running to the wallow, pouring the water in and calling his name. Ellie had already learned how to open doors; we definitely didn't need him running around the orphanage opening and closing taps. I called him again as I splashed my hand in the water and that did the trick, El came running over. To my delight, Ellie loved the wallow. He first splashed his trunk around in the water before stepping into the mud with his front legs. He kicked the mud around a bit and then took another step into the wallow. As the mud and water sloshed, El got down onto his knees before placing his head down into the mud and rolling onto his side. He got himself as covered in mud as he could and he was loving it. He was throwing his trunk around in the water and rolling in the cooling mud. Duma loved water too, so he was also quick to dig himself a little spot in the wallow to cool off as well. After El had caked himself in a layer of mud, he confidently walked over to the sand pile where he lay in the sunshine to dry off.

27: A Crash of Rhinos

It was time for something very exciting. Something we had all been waiting for. It was time to introduce Ithuba to the white rhino crash. I cannot tell you how exciting this moment was, not only because we were introducing Ithuba into the white rhino crash but also because it was a beautiful, reflective moment that allowed Axel and I to see how far we, and the rhino orphans in our care, had come. This was something that would give us the boost we needed as the situation with Storm was causing us some anxiety.

Impy and Thando were now much bigger and stronger than when they first arrived, their wounds had healed and they were much more confident. Not only that, but they also had Gugu who was helping to teach them some of her wild ways. This crash needed one more thing, Ithuba.

Introducing Ithuba to the crash was exciting but it was also a little bit nerve-wracking because if the rhinos began to disagree or decided they didn't like each other, there would've been very little Axel and I could do as we were dwarfed by the rhinos who stood at varied heights between our hips and our chests. We knew Impy and Thando wouldn't cause us harm and we trusted Ithuba not to get too rowdy around us, but this was a new situation and we couldn't be sure how they would react. Gugu was a bit of a wild card, she kept her distance from us and always had. Axel and I kept our distance and used trees as protection, hoping we wouldn't need to attempt to separate the large rhinos during the introduction. We opened the gate to allow Ithuba into the same enclosure as the three younger white rhinos, we called Ithuba over and then, we waited.

Ithuba was eager to enter and he slowly approached Thando and the others. They were all very well acquainted by this point as they'd had countless conversations through the wooden poles of the enclosures so they were not afraid when Ithuba strode towards them. Once Ithuba reached Thando, he dropped his head and nudged Thando gently. Impy stood behind

Thando and Gugu kept her distance while she waited to see how the others were reacting to Ithuba. After saying hello, Ithuba and Thando started to nudge each other in a playful way.

"Gently 'Thubes, remember Thando isn't as big as you." Axel said from the trees at the edge of the enclosure. We watched as Impy decided to join in, he nudged his head into Ithuba's side causing 'Thubes to turn around and tenderly nudge him back. Ithuba walked past Thando, rubbing against his side and it was clear to see there were going to be no disagreements in this crash. As Ithuba, Thando and Impy began to walk over to Gugu, she walked towards them and met Ithuba for the first time. Within 15 minutes of opening the gate that separated them, Ithuba was now walking with the crash and everyone seemed happy. Ithuba had such confidence, to think this was the same rhino that had run away in fear when he met a tiny four-week-old elephant through a barrier all those months earlier. Now, we watched these four large rhinos walking together through the enclosures, it was wonderful to see. Axel and I quietly left the white rhino crash alone and instead sat outside the enclosure watching in. We sat at the fence with huge grins on our faces, we were ecstatic… This was exactly what Ithuba needed.

While all was well with the white rhinos, Storm's health was not improving and even after receiving treatment for the parasitic infection, he was balancing on the edge. The young black rhino was erratic with his feeds, sometimes he would gulp them down and other times he wouldn't even want a sip. His energy levels remained considerably lower than Nandi's and he was not gaining weight. Being with Nandi was a help for him, she gave him comfort when they'd snuggle together at night and she'd encourage him to get up and move around during the day. We were unsure of the problem and even after multiple vet visits we were no closer to an answer. We had organized for Storm to get an ultrasound scan to see if this would help us identify any internal issues. Following the scan, the vets believed that Storm was suffering from aspiration pneumonia and treatment was started for this.

We were hopeful the treatment would help and did everything in our power to get Storm through this tough start to life.

Ellie continued to run around with healthy, chubby cheeks and an attitude to match. He had slowly started to become more interested in browse and he was in a great routine. Everyone loved him and after much of his adored sand pile was used for building improvements, we bought a brand-new sand pile exclusively for him. One of the biggest changes between Ellie's first couple of months with us and now was that he was absolutely loving water.

We had a huge plastic trough - it was almost like a small bath – and every day I'd fill it up with fresh clean water for El. He would love to splash his trunk around in the water and play. Ellie had even started trying to hold water in his trunk like the older elephants do but as soon as he lifted his trunk above the water's surface, the small amount of water he held in his trunk would spill out. It was still early days, but I could see that he was trying. Something else he had learnt to do was fully immersing his trunk under the water and blowing bubbles. Playing in water offered endless games and lessons to learn, Ellie would wiggle his trunk around the water as if it was an eel and took great pleasure in holding his trunk high above the water and dropping it with force to create big splashes and lots of noise.

We'd also created a new game we both loved to play, it started because Ellie would get in the way while I would clean the preparation room but it had developed into a much loved, almost daily, water fight. There was a hose in the preparation room so I would spray the floor with it before mopping. Ellie began to stand in the way of the hose so I'd spray his feet with it. He would splash his trunk into the water and kick his feet through the puddles and before I knew it we'd made the preparation room into a fun water park. Ellie enjoyed kicking the water around, splashing his trunk and standing in the way of the stream of water. I loved watching El play in the water, to watch how he was growing, learning and becoming himself.

As Ellie slept in his room in the late evening, the orphanage was quiet and I sat next to him reading a book. He'd wake up every so often, look up at me and touch my face with his trunk before falling back to sleep. This always made me smile,

"Hey my boy, everything's alright." I'd say to him softly as he'd look up at me with sleepy eyes. As I was reading this book, I had a sudden moment where the reality of these moments hit me. I looked up at Ellie and just thought "wow". I was filled with gratitude for these moments we were sharing. I looked over at Ellie as he slept so soundly under the heat lamp with his triceratops tucked under his front leg and I thought about how far we had come.

28: Sudden Deterioration

Things had been going so well with El, but he started to lose his appetite and in the latter half of January, things took an unexpected turn for the worse. I went to take over with the Ellie care one morning and heard that he had a really unsettled night, he had started having terrible diarrhoea and did not want to drink any of his feeds. I went over to say good morning to Ellie and he was not himself. He was holding his head high into the sky, a sign that he was suffering from nausea, and he did not seem at all well.

"Hey my boy, it's ok. It's ok, don't worry El. What's wrong my little love?" I asked him as I crouched down to his level. He looked at me but didn't grumble his usual greeting, instead he just leant into me. Something was wrong. Very wrong. We called the vet who said he could come to visit the following day and advised us on medication we could give El in his next feed to take away the nausea. As Ellie did not want his milk or electrolytes, I ended up giving him the medicine straight into his mouth using a syringe. He lay in his room resting. After around an hour he woke up, now hungry. The medicine must've done something to take away his nausea at least.

"Do you want some milk El? Do you want to come with me to the prep room and help me make it?" I said as he nudged against me. Opening the door and heading outside, El followed me but his steps were slower than usual. We walked slowly to the preparation room, when we were around ten steps away, Ellie ran the rest of the way.

"That's a good sign boy. Let's make you some milk." I made the milk and fed El in the preparation room, he drank it all without hesitation which was a relief. After this we had a little wander around the orphanage before returning to his room to get more sleep. This was the first day of Ellie's rapid decline.

When the vet visited the following day, Ellie had only managed to finish a handful of his feeds and was clearly feeling very under the weather.

Our vet thought Ellie was likely suffering from the infection that he had fought so hard against when he first arrived with us. He explained that because the infection originated in his open umbilical area that pockets of infection could sit in his joints and organs and it looked as though one of these pockets had burst, causing the infection to occur once again. Antibiotics were administered and we began intensive nursing to try to keep Ellie's strength up.

Ellie hardly wanted to drink, his appetite was diminished and his energy levels low. I had to regularly give him medication directly into his mouth with a syringe, the first few times were easy but the clever elephant was getting wise to my methods and he had begun to resist the syringe. It reminded me of when he first arrived and we had to come up with countless methods of feeding him, now I needed new ways of giving him medication. Fortunately, Ellie and I had a very good rapport so he couldn't resist lifting his trunk to greet me and, if I was quick enough, he would barely notice I'd given the medication until it was too late.

In the days following the visit from the vet, Ellie lost a lot of weight. Small black dots appeared on his ears, his temperature was erratic, and he had no interest in food. He was struggling and there was very little we could do. I gave him milk and electrolytes when he felt like drinking, took him outside when he wanted to go outside but mostly, I just kept him warm and comfortable wrapped in his blankets under the heat lamp. Ellie was not showing any signs of improvement. The wildlife vet visited again to offer advice on both Ellie and Storm. After a lot of talk, it was decided Ellie would be lightly sedated and a drip line would be attached so we could begin administering I.V. fluid and medication. After the vet had administered the sedation, he told me that Ellie should lay down in the next ten or so minutes. The vet also asked that I tried to get Ellie to lay down in a certain spot of the room to make it as easy as possible to work with El and put the drip in. Ellie was agitated about receiving another injection, so he paced around the room groggily. I paced with him, feeling so anxious I could throw up. I walked around the room with El, waiting for him to show signs of sleepiness so I could try my best to guide him to the area we wanted him to lay down. This continued for fifteen minutes, and Ellie showed no signs of wanting to go to sleep at all.

After a while, the vet decided to give the - very awake - elephant a bit more of the sedation. Again, I waited for Ellie to fall asleep. This time he was definitely looking tired, but I thought this could have easily been a result of the last twenty minutes of pacing rather than the sedative. He finally laid down. I sat with Ellie while a drip was attached to his ear. He may have been lightly sedated but he was still active. I spoke to him as he looked at me. Seeing the drip tray out of the corner of his eye, he reached his trunk up in an attempt to explore the tray of medical equipment that lay next to him. I took his trunk into my hands to try to distract him. Once the drip was secure and the fluids were making their way into Ellie's vein the next challenge was keeping the drip attached. While he was laying down this wasn't an issue but as soon as he would get back up, we would have to follow him around with a drip bag attached to a stick and do our best to keep the catheter attached to his ear – one awkward move or pull could easily tug the drip out of place. After a few hours, the drip came out of Ellie's ear but we were happy with the fluids he had received.

It didn't seem to matter what we did; Ellie's health was still declining. I couldn't believe it, I asked myself again and again "how is this happening?". I fell asleep late into the night feeling broken. Ellie was trying so hard to fight the infection, but it was winning. The next day Ellie stayed in his room, under his heat lamp. He woke up a few times and asked for milk, but he got tired quickly and soon returned to his bed. I lay with him, ensuring he never felt alone. He rested against me as he slept. That night I stayed with Ellie, I curled up next to him and if I fell asleep, the first thing I did when I woke up was check if Ellie was still breathing. I knew we were at the end. I knew that he couldn't fight the infection.

After Ellie made it through the night, he surprised me by getting up and asking for milk first thing in the morning. He had more energy and seemed enthusiastic as he walked with me to the preparation room. Everyone was surprised to see him up and about. This, unfortunately, did not last and before long Ellie was back under his heat lamp. The minutes went by slowly, Ellie had almost constant watery diarrhoea that had a terrible smell to it. The weak elephant was again put onto a drip, this was a specially sourced medicated drip that we hoped would help.

Ellie's skin was clammy, his breath shallow and his blood pressure was low. I sat with El and kept an eye on the drip as he slept. In the afternoon Ellie started to get severe cramps, I quickly administered medication that would stop this. I got him nice and cosy with clean blankets and his soft dinosaur and sat by his side. As the night drew in, I sat with El. Talking to him, telling him stories and making sure he knew I was there with him. I was afraid, his deterioration was happening so fast. I was watching it happen right in front of me and there was nothing I could do. I hoped the medication would do something, would give him what he needed to fight. As I sat there, listening to his breath become shallower... I knew it was time. At 11:20 p.m., our little elephant drifted away while he slept. As Ellie took his last breath, my whole world shattered.

I wrote this diary entry in the week of Ellie's passing:

"On Tuesday at 11:20 p.m. I lost my best friend, my partner in crime, my little love. Ubuntu 'Ellie' passed away peacefully in his sleep after an astonishing battle for survival. After the initial umbilical infection and poor health, he found a love for life but at almost six months old

his health took a rapid deterioration, and it seems nothing we did could help his body enough in the fight. Ellie knew we loved him, and we were fighting in his corner but that could only keep him going for so long, his body that is, his soul – full of love – is free and lives on.

I miss him and all his quirky little habits. His wandering trunk, gently waking you after a sleep – a light brush with his trunk and a deep rumble to welcome you back into consciousness. His hooligan antics in the house... Attacking the tumble drier, raiding the fruit that he never actually ate just put his trunk all over before crushing it onto the floor. There was one day he tried to fit a whole bowl of grapes into his mouth, a whole freaking bowl of them. I saw at the last second and tried to grab it, he had his trunk pushing it towards his open mouth as I was trying to pull it away... In the end, all the grapes fell to the floor and neither of us really won.

His apprehension of rain and stopping at the line between dry ground and wet ground, looking up at me like "nope, not happening... I'll be right here if you need me.". Of course, once he started walking he was fine but it was always that initial moment that was so hesitant.

Sleeping in the sand, rolling around and play fighting, playing in the pool, walking and trying to find new plants for him to try...

Every moment together is a treasured memory. The six months with Ellie will be a defining chapter in my life, I just know it.

*I love you El. I miss you every day and you have no idea
how deeply and truly I wish you were here with me."*

It is difficult to express the pain of this unexpected and sudden loss. In his short life, Ellie overflowed with love and each of us became enchanted by him. The last six months had been a whirlwind of experiences but when I think back on it, all I can think about is the gentle love and enthusiasm that Ellie approached life with. This tiny elephant brought a special kind of magic into our world and now, I see him in all elephants. I can't help but think about how different the world would be if we all loved and cared about wildlife as much as we love and care about El. Thousands of elephants are being killed for their ivory each year and, according to assessments, African Elephant populations have decreased by at least 60% in the last 50 years. When I think about how I feel about losing Ellie, I can only begin to imagine how we would mourn the loss of his species.

Getting to know these animals as the special individuals they are makes it easier to love them, to care about them. Having a deeper understanding and appreciation for them is part of the fuel that keeps you fighting for their future. There is immense power in realizing the animals within these pages are not the exception, all animals have these wonderful personalities that we could so easily fall in love with. Ellie has shown us how incredible elephants are, and how much they need our help. I'm sure if we all had more understanding of these wild animals then we would do more to help protect them. I know we all fell in love with Ellie over these past few months, and I hope this love extends beyond him as an individual to his species.

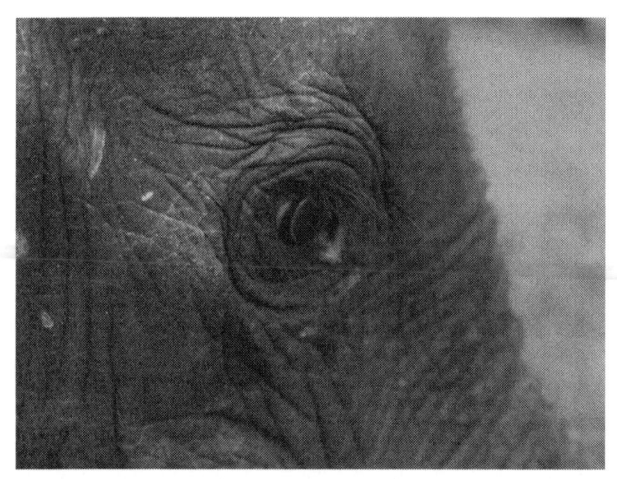

29: Crumbling

As the sun began to rise, I sat next to the baby elephant who had become my best friend over the course of almost six months. My heart was broken. We had spent so much time together and, although I was worried about his survival in the first months of his arrival, I thought we had pulled him through. I truly believed we had pulled him through. He had become so full of life; his cheeks had become chubby as he gained weight and he was growing into a healthy little elephant. And yet. Here we were.

As I sat there, I looked up to see Duma the German Shepherd laying down outside the door. I invited him in and he walked slowly over to me before resting his head in my lap and exhaling a deep sigh. Everyone knew what had unfolded through the course of the night, but no one knew what to do or what to say. We had all fought so hard to pull Ellie through and this was a difficult reality to face. I looked at Ellie, pleading him to lift his trunk or grumble at me.

With the help of eight local Zulu men who worked to maintain the wildlife reserve, we carried Ellie, wrapped in his favourite blanket, to the back of the pick-up truck. We then drove to a dry riverbed in the heart of the reserve. When we located the perfect spot to lay El to rest, the men began to dig. They listened to pop music through the tinny speaker on one of their phones and they made incredibly fast progress. The situation was bizarre, I found myself sitting on the bank of a dry riverbed in the middle of a wildlife reserve while a group of strong Zulu men dug to the tune of I Gotta Feeling by the Black Eyed Peas (a pop song I hadn't heard since school about five years prior to this moment). The men let me scoop a few shovels of dirt, wanting to ensure I felt like part of the process and knowing how much it meant to me. The hole was already chest high and the elder of the Zulu men swiftly lifted me up without even a hint of strain while another man took my hand as I stepped back onto higher ground. Soon, the hole was ready for the elephant I had loved with all my heart.

We walked up the riverbank to the pick-up truck, each of us grabbed the edges of the blanket and lifted. As we carried El, the deep voices of the Zulu men boomed a traditional song through the silence of the riverbed. Each of these men sang as we walked slowly. Their voices were powerful, their song roared like the ocean crashing into the shore during a storm. Although I could not understand the words of the Zulu song, I felt them. The song carried sorrowful waves throughout the riverbed and in that moment, I felt like I wasn't alone.

My tears flowed as we gently lowered El into the ground, he was wrapped in his blanket, and I placed his green dinosaur toy by his side. We stood in silence for a few moments before the men took a step back, giving me space. I spoke to Ellie, but I stuttered as I told him to roam free and reminded him of how loved he will always be. I sprinkled the first shovel full of dirt onto the blanket as the tears rolled down my face. I stood in a broken trance and watched as shovel after shovel of mud was tossed into the hole.

Before I knew it, we were done. The men took their tools and said they'd meet me at the car, leaving me to say my final goodbyes alone. Despite only knowing me and Ellie from the handful of interactions they'd had with us, the men knew how much this meant to me and they were so courteous, gracious and empathetic. I was deeply thankful to them for making this heart-wrenching day just that little bit better for me. Burying Ellie made his death more real, but it also gave me some closure to lay his body to rest and to return him to mother earth. I knew when I would return to the orphanage, nothing would be the same.

I tried to take my mind off the gaping hole in my heart by making the white rhino milk feeds with Axel. Everything felt off and awkward. To make matters worse, as I was talking, I automatically finished my sentence with "don't you think, El?" and the silence that followed was palpable. Nobody knew what to do or what to say. They just kind of, looked at me. It took me back a bit too I suppose, I wasn't expecting myself to say it either, it was just habit. I had spoken to El, all day every day for almost half a year and in an instant, he was gone. I knew that I needed to take a few days away to gather my thoughts.

I was invited on a game drive by the reserve rangers that afternoon, although I did not want to go, I also did not want to stay at the orphanage, so I sat at the back of the open game drive vehicle in a quiet, contemplative state. My one goal for the duration of the drive was to get through it without crying. An American lady named Kennedy approached me after the drive and invited me to join her table for dinner, I accepted and over dinner our conversation flowed as she told me about her trip, her work, her time spent in South Africa, and I told her all about the orphanage and about Ellie. I'd mentioned that I was hoping to take a couple of days away from the orphanage to clear my mind and Kennedy told me she would be driving back to the city the following morning and offered me a lift with her. Grateful for the lift, I went back to the orphanage to speak to the team and pack a bag for a few days off. Kennedy dropped me off at a friend's empty holiday home on her way back to the city.

For the first time in my life, I cried tears that would not stop. I fell asleep late into the night crying and woke in the morning crying. The loss of Ellie was a harsh reality that I was struggling to come to terms with. I called friends and family but all I could do was sob. I felt broken, entirely broken. On the third day away, I received a text from Axel saying that I needed to come back as he needed help with the black rhino nightshifts. It had been months since I was part of the rhino nightshift rota and now, just days after Ellie has passed away, I was being called back.

I began to make the arrangements to return, agreeing that I'd meet Angie at the airport the following day and we'd travel back together. I didn't know how to feel about going back, going back to an orphanage without El made me feel numb. That day, I was pulled out of my pits by a pod of dolphins. As I looked out of the window of the house I had been staying, I saw the fins of the dolphins as they breached the water's surface for breath. I pulled on my shoes and went down to the beach. I had been down to the beach once during my stay but all it did was make me feel worse because it was the one thing that I knew always made me happy but at that moment, It didn't. I didn't feel any more hope or any less broken. I just felt exactly as I felt except I was standing on a beach, it was not what I was hoping for. When the dolphins came, they focused my mind onto something other than the loss of Ellie and as I sat on the sand and watched them frolic in the waves, they awakened my sense of hope.

The following day I met Angie at the airport, she gave me the biggest hug as soon as she saw me,

"Oh Meg. I'm so sorry. How are you holding up?" In response, I forced a smile, but it was wearied at best.

"It's good to see you Ang, we've missed you so much at the orphanage. How was your time at home?" I asked, trying to avoid the topic while I figured out a way of handling the subject without crumbling. As we talked, the conversation made its way back to Ellie so I told Ang what had happened. It wasn't until months later Ang told me how exhausted and beaten I had looked on that day in the airport.

30: Routine

Back at the orphanage, everything felt out of place. Ellie's room was now back to a volunteer room and no one mentioned him. It was as though the last six months had never happened which was weird. I took the night shift with Nandi and Storm my first night back to give Axel a break. Storm was not in a good way; we were continuing the treatment for aspiration pneumonia as well as a gastrointestinal disorder and had added supplements into his milk to try to help him get the energy he needed.

On my first evening back, Angie came to join me for a while. We sat on the night shift bed, watching Storm and Nandi who were sleeping under the heat lamp while we chatted. It was great to have Angie back, she was such a determined, passionate and hardworking member of the team and she was the kind of person you could talk to about anything. When Angie left to give Axel a hand with the white rhino feed, I locked the neonatal door and settled in for the night ahead. It was quiet and I laid on the bed, looking up at the red glow of the heat lamp on the ceiling. I lay there and waited for the two critically endangered black rhinos to wake up for their next feed.

Nandi was very vocal when it came to feeding time, she wasn't shy in letting you know when she was hungry. Once Nandi was awake and calling, I began to mix the milk. I took the two jugs and scooped the milk powder into each under the light of the desk lamp on the worktop. Nandi and Storm received different food mixes because of Storms health issues so I put the necessary supplements into Storms and whisked both mixes until there were no lumps of milk powder. With the feeds ready, I opened the gate that separated us and I went inside. Nandi stood in front of me, her prehensile lip up in the air and her mouth open ready to drink.

"Wait a second Nandi, we need to wait for Stormy, don't we? Come on boy, there's some lovely milk here for you." I said as I closed the distance between us and Storm. Storm (who had tried to remain sleeping through Nandi's milk tantrum) got to his feet and opened his mouth.

"Here you go milk monsters, drink up." The pair started to drink; Nandi gulped her milk down a lot faster than Storm so once she'd finished her second bottle of milk, I had to try to keep her distracted while Storm finished his milk. Once Storm had sipped the last few mouthfuls, we walked around the room a bit. I rearranged the browse (fresh branches we'd cut for the black rhinos to eat) and offered some to them. Once they were both snacking on some freshly cut browse I went to the other side of the barrier to wash up the bottles.

As Storm and Nandi were black rhinos we needed to cut branches for them every day. We would normally do this first thing in the morning and last thing in the afternoon and sometimes again during the early part of nightshift if they were getting through it quickly. The neonatal was now always filled with bundles of fresh browse for the black rhinos to eat whenever they felt hungry. Storm and Nandi enjoyed eating browse, the noise of them munching and crunching through the branches often filled the otherwise quiet neonatal. We'd found that Nandi and Storm both had favourite tree species, so we tried each day to make sure there was at least a couple of branches from each of their favourite trees in among the browse collection. Sometimes Nandi would stay up long after Storm had fallen back asleep to eat browse.

Once I'd washed up the bottles, teats, jugs, whisk and funnel from the milk mixing, I sat back on the bed and watched the rhinos contentedly eating browse before they decided it was time to go back to sleep. Nandi and Storm snuggled up together under the heat lamp and I decided it was time for me to sleep too so I climbed under the covers in the bed next to the barrier that separated me from the black rhinos and I fell asleep. It would be just a few hours until the three of us would be awake again for another milk feed.

It felt good to be caring for the rhinos again; the rhinos gave me light, they gave me purpose. Caring for Nandi and Storm gave me something to focus on. If I wasn't on shift with them, I'd be collecting browse for them or feeding the white rhinos or cleaning and organizing the preparation rooms. There was always something to do. I was keeping myself busy and mostly keeping to myself, the dynamics of the orphanage team had changed dramatically in recent months – I think this was caused by a mixture of new team members, the pressure of caring for Storm and the passing of Ellie. Whatever the reason; I now much preferred keeping out of the way, if I had free time I loved sitting and watching the white rhino crash as they'd walk around the enclosures together, grazing and wallowing. The white rhinos were all in fantastic condition, they were eating well, getting on great and were no longer in need of human contact (aside from when it was milk feeding time). Gugu hadn't become any fonder of us but we didn't mind, as long as she drank her milk and ate enough dry food it wasn't a problem. In truth, we were happy she could show the boys how to be wilder. Ithuba was very content to be with the others now, he had waited for it for a long time. Ithuba and Thando were particularly close and it was beautiful to see them together.

The night feeds with the white rhinos required two people as you needed one person to feed Impy and Thando and someone else to convince Gugu to come over and drink her milk from the tray. As soon as they all finished their milk, we'd put a few more piles of mixed dry food into their room and enclosure so they'd have enough food for the night. They were getting older and were eating a lot of fresh grass and dry food which was brilliant as it meant they were becoming less dependent on milk. Ithuba had been fully weaned so we kept an eye on him to make sure he was eating lots of dry food and wasn't dropping weight or condition. The white rhinos were thriving together, it was such a pleasure to care for them and see their progress.

The night shift with the black rhinos was usually straight forward, you needed patience to get Storm to drink his milk but other than that the black rhinos loved to lay under the heat lamp sleeping meaning you could also get a good rest too. One of my nightshifts with the black rhinos was just not going to plan. Storm wasn't very enthusiastic when it came to drinking his milk so each feed took a long time. Even though it was taking a long time, Storm was finishing each feed and that's what mattered. It was now around two a.m. and Nandi started calling for milk. I pulled myself out of bed, feeling very groggy, and mixed both the feeds. As I went to put the teats onto the first bottle my hand slipped and I spilt both of their milk mixes across myself, the worktop and the floor. My half-asleep hand-eye coordination had let me down in spectacular fashion. I looked at the puddle of milk on the floor, at the pools of milk in my flip flops and at the milk that had spilled down my t-shirt. With a sigh, I began to make the milk again, knowing Nandi would not be willing to wait until I'd cleaned up. Once the milk was made, I very carefully put the teats onto the bottles before clambering over the milk puddle and going to feed Nandi and Storm. After the feed, I was faced with cleaning up the milky mess. It was about twenty past two in the morning. Under the dim light of the desk lamp I cleaned the side and mopped the floor in what felt like slow motion before I could finally fall back into bed and rest.

Storm would drink his milk slowly and it would often take a lot of time and effort to get him to drink. We were very worried about him and he needed to drink the milk if he was going to put on weight and grow as he should. Nandi was already outgrowing him even though they were the same age and Storm was underweight and frail. This was particularly evident when Storm would be standing side by side with Nandi, who was burly and strong. Nandi was like a miniature tank running around the place. She was brash and a bit of a bruiser. Storm, on the other hand, was smaller and skinnier, he was quiet, gentle and unassuming.

Storm would still walk around every day with a blanket over him and we'd try our best to get him to drink his milk. We hoped the medicine and treatment were working but the results were very slow to yield. We figured we just had to keep going, keep encouraging him to drink as much milk as we could and encourage him to spend time up and about in the hope that one day it would all fall into place. We were so glad that Storm enjoyed eating browse as this was a good sign and we'd always make sure there was more than enough browse for him. Fortunately, although he was not sprightly and energetic like Nandi was, Storm showed us that he wanted to spend time outside and wanted to play in small bursts. This was reassuring at least.

My favourite part of the day with the black rhinos was letting them out first thing in the morning. They would both be eager to get out and enjoy the sunrise, so I'd sit outside wrapped in a blanket while they'd walk around, eating browse and enjoying the stillness of the early morning. Nandi would often run around as fast as her little legs would take her and would chase and fight with the exercise balls. Spending time with the black rhinos was incredibly special, they were both characters and although Storm was not in the clear yet we were fighting for his survival and he was fighting too.

Over the next couple of months, several new people joined our team, so Axel and I trained them up and Storm continued to receive intensive nursing. Nandi continued to go from strength to strength, but Storm was still not thriving. Angie and I had lengthy conversations as we tried to find solutions to Storm's situation. There wasn't much we could do so we just kept on pushing. Then, over the course of about a week we saw incredible improvement in Storm's health. It had been a long road but Storm's appetite grew as he began drinking his milk with enthusiasm. At first, we thought maybe it was just a one off but he started to gulp down every feed.

For the first time since we rescued Storm three months earlier, he was enthusiastic to drink his milk and it was the first sign that he was feeling better. By the end of the week, Storm even started to join Nandi in asking for milk and suddenly the feeding that had been such a challenging, lengthy process had become a pleasure. Feeding time was transformed for the better and now Nandi and Storm stood side by side and drank their milk with mirrored eagerness. With Storm eating properly it also meant he had more energy. We started to see Storm's personality grow as he became more playful around Nandi. For months Nandi had run rings around Storm but now he was starting to join in, he was even starting to nudge her and instigate the games. We'd seen a beautiful transformation right before our eyes and it showed that all the hard work was paying off.

Storm was starting to gain weight and he was holding his temperature which meant he didn't have to wear a blanket all the time anymore. We were starting to tick off the milestones he was reaching and it was an incredibly exciting day when Storm had his first mud wallow. He rolled around, swishing his tail and flicking mud at everyone and he was pampered as mud was massaged onto his skin. It was like an afternoon at the spa, Storm loved the mud and was definitely going to be a regular at the wallow from now on. We did not doubt that Storm and Nandi would be spending many afternoons rolling around in the mud after seeing Storms reaction to the wallow. Storm had truly come to life; he had fought the illnesses and he had won. Despite everything that this tiny black rhino faced in the first few months of his life, Storm had pulled through and we were seeing him blossom in front of us.

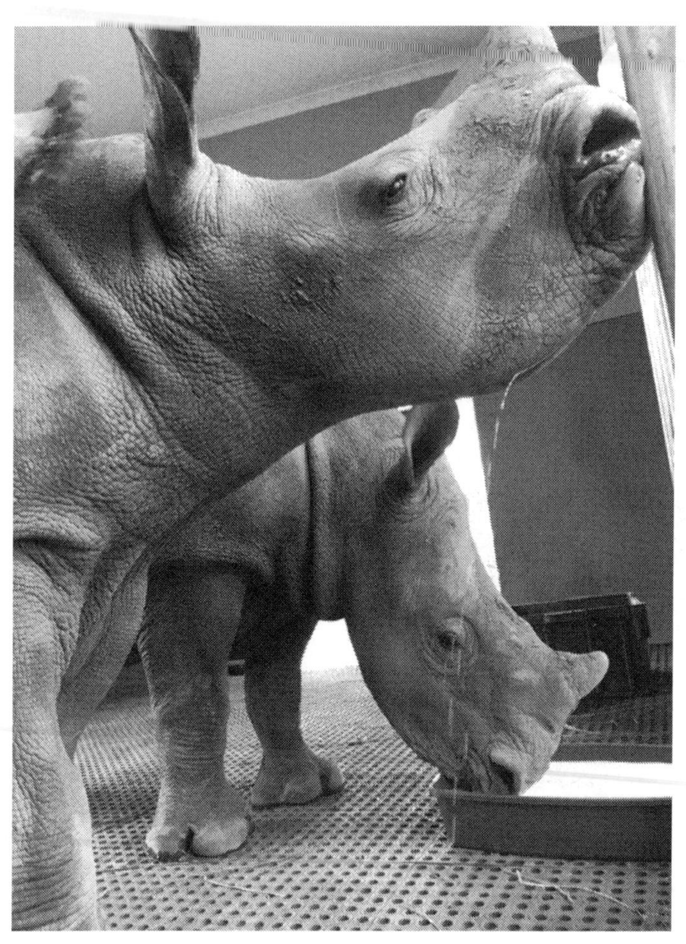

31: Time for a New Beginning

Seeing Storm's progress filled my heart, we had been working tirelessly to pull him through some dark days but now we were seeing the light. Storm had developed a healthy appetite; he was now actively asking for milk, and he was drinking it twice as fast as he used to. We could finally say with confidence that he was stable, and his progress was amazing.

Storm was building up strength, he was already starting to play and run with Nandi. We were sure in a couple of months Nandi would meet her match in Stormy. It felt like things had levelled out after a tough uphill struggle. Each day Storm and Nandi would spend most of their time outside, eating browse, playing and wallowing. We would spend the days sitting with them and watching over them as they still needed the reassurance and comfort of a carer but they were going from strength to strength. We would collect lots of browse for them to enjoy and the nightshifts became stress-free and straightforward. For the first time in a long time, we could relax.

Ithuba, Impy, Thando and Gugu were enjoying life as a crash and were doing great. It was amazing to see how far they had come; they were becoming increasingly independent and were spending their days as wild rhinos would. We'd watch them as they'd push each other around to try to get the prime spot in the wallow or lay together in the shade of the trees during the heat of the day. The white rhino crash didn't need much assistance from us anymore; each morning their room would be cleaned, we'd put out several big piles of dry food for them, fill up their water troughs and top up their wallow and after all of that was done, they'd only need us for their milk feeds.

With Storm stabilized, Nandi healthy, and Ithuba, Impy, Thando and Gugu all thriving in their crash, I felt like it was time for me to move on.

As Angie was leaving soon as well, we decided to plan a trip together. We'd reached a point where all the orphans were stable, we had a routine and a bigger team too so I knew if I left, I wouldn't be leaving Axel or the others in a struggle. I was proud of us and our efforts. We had given these rhinos another chance at life, and we had shown them that not all humans have lost their humanity.

It had been a challenging few months since Ellie's passing, not only with dealing with life at the orphanage without him and the pressure of pulling Storm through but also the changes in the team dynamics. We all deal with stressful, highly emotional situations differently and this had been a rollercoaster that put pressure on friendships, saw many people coming and going and put the team under immense strain. I knew I needed a break, time to rest and to heal, and now I could move on knowing all the rhinos were healthy and settled.

Working within wildlife rehabilitation and conservation can be exhausting at times, it can be draining, and it can be very emotional. We are driven by passion, and it always feels like there is so much to do, but it is important to take the time to care for yourself too. This is what I reminded myself as I prepared to leave the place I had called home. As much as part of me wanted to stay to continue looking after the orphans, I knew that they were being well cared for and I knew I needed to take time for myself.

As I packed my bags and looked back on this journey, there were parts of it that were going to hurt for a long time but there were also so many beautiful memories that had etched themselves into my heart. Our small, passionate team had worked so hard and had saved many lives. It is the nature of wildlife rehabilitation that not every animal you rescue will survive but that doesn't mean you shouldn't at least try. We had many success stories and it had been an honour to connect and work so intimately with some of the strongest, yet gentlest wildlife on earth. To have spent months of my life working so closely with a baby elephant was like living in a dream, it was something I will never forget. With a tear in my eye, I said goodbye to each of the rhinos I had come to know personally. They had all come so far and to be a part of their journey was a privilege.

Working with these incredible animals gives a unique insight into their personalities. Animals are so forgiving; their characters are ones we should be learning from and striving towards. It breaks my heart that rhinos and elephants continue to be exploited by mankind. It's hard to believe there is a demand for rhino horns, elephant tusks, and other animal products. To think there are people who place more value on the horns of a rhino and the tusks of an elephant than on the life of the animal is devastating. This demand is driving the decline of these species and if this continues, there will come a time when these animals no longer roam this Earth.

I hope everyone gets the opportunity to see these animals in the wild, to watch rhinos as they wallow on hot days, admire elephants as they cool off with trunkfuls of water, and enjoy the mischief of all the playful youngsters too. It's exciting to think that maybe one day you will see the rhinos that we raised living wild and free, maybe you will see their offspring too. I hope our children and our children's children can see these animals in the wild, but that will only happen if we work to protect them now.

Africa unlocks the wild glow of your spirit and spending time within nature is a special kind of healing. With this in mind, Angie and I drove away from the orphanage to embark on a trip across the beautiful country of South Africa. I knew this was what I needed; it was the healing my spirit craved. This trip was a time for reflection and self-care, it was necessary in order for me to continue working in conservation. The trip would also be an opportunity to admire wildlife in the wild, an experience that holds such power. I believe many conservation issues stem from a disconnect between humans and nature. Taking the time to reconnect with nature reminds us of what we are fighting to save and why it is so important. Following the adventure with Ang, I was going to start working at a rhino orphanage close to Kruger National Park, so this wasn't the end of the line for my conservation work, it was just the end of a chapter.

I hope this personal insight into what it's like to rescue and care for these orphans gives you a newfound love for them. A newfound will to help protect them. Establishing a connection with wildlife is vital. The more time we spend in wild spaces, the more we learn, the more we appreciate, and the more willing we are to make changes to conserve nature.

There is still hope. We each hold the power within us to change the world for the better. Together the difference we can make is beyond words.

Find your souls purpose and live it.

Find your passion and follow it.

Oh, and one more thing, be kind to animals, always.

Thank you for reading Eyelashes of an Elephant.

If you enjoyed this journey through wildlife rescue and conservation, please consider leaving a review. It would mean a lot to me and will also help others to find and read this book.

About the Author

Megan Richards is a conservationist and author from the United Kingdom.

Megan has worked within wildlife conservation and rehabilitation since 2013. Her work in Southern Africa has focussed on rescuing and rehabilitating orphaned rhinos with the goal of releasing them back into the wild. Megan can often be found spending time in nature, and she believes sharing her experiences with wildlife will help inspire a love and respect for the natural world.

Website: www.coexistwithmeg.com
Contact: coexistwithmeg@gmail.com
Social Media: @coexistwithmeg

Eyelashes of an Elephant
By Megan Richards

Printed in Great Britain
by Amazon

34213477R00142